S0-AKA-182

Last Page First

Last Page First

Allan Fotheringham
with Roy Peterson

KEY PORTER BOOKS

Copyright © 1999 by Allan Fotheringham

All rights reserved. No part of this work covered by the copyrights hereon may be reproduced or used in any form or by any means—graphic, electronic or mechanical, including photocopying, recording, taping or information storage and retrieval systems—without the prior written permission of the publisher, or in the case of photocopying or other reprographic copying, a license from the Canadian Copyright Licensing Agency.

Canadian Cataloguing in Publication Data

Fotheringham, Allan, 1932–
        Last page first

Includes index.
ISBN 1-55013-995-9

1. World politics – 1975-1985.   2. World politics – 1985-1995.   3. World politics – 1995-   . I. Peterson, Roy, 1936-   . II. Title.

D860.F673 1998   909.82'5   C98-931425-1

The publisher gratefully acknowledges the support of the Canada Council for the Arts and the Ontario Arts Council for its publishing program.

Canada

We acknowledge the financial support of the Government of Canada through the Book Publishing Industry Development Program (BPIDP) for our publishing activities.

Key Porter Books Limited
70 The Esplanade
Toronto, Ontario
Canada M5E 1R2

www.keyporter.com

Design: Peter Maher
Electronic formatting: Heidy Lawrance Associates

Printed and bound in Canada

99 00 01 02 03   6   5   4   3   2   1

For my two: Anne and Francesca

Contents

Around the World with Dr. Foth 137

The Scurrilous Scribe 201

Introduction

One day in the autumn of 1975, Peter C. Newman, who was about to morph stately old *Maclean's* into a newsmagazine, sent a letter across the mountains to me in Vancouver. In it he offered me "a job of your choice" on the exciting new project—preferably chief of his bureau in Ottawa.

I flew down to Toronto to have a chat. As a daily columnist at the *Vancouver Sun* for seven years, I had done occasional pieces for *Maclean's* (the first one, as it turns out, was the Beatles' initial performance on Canadian soil, at Vancouver's Empire Stadium).

I told him I couldn't move, for family reasons, to dreaded central Canada but would do a national column for him from Vancouver. He immediately called in his senior editors to sound them out on the idea.

Managing editor Walter Stewart, an old friend, said, "Foth, we love you. But no frigging way. You can't cover Canada from Lotusland." Newman went around the table, never saying a word himself. Three, four of them—all of whom I knew well—said the same, regretful thing: it would be impossible to write, from the Wet Coast, a column on national affairs.

Newman, puffing on his pipe as usual, listened in silence and then spoke. "You're all wrong," he said. "It may not be a national column, but it will be a Fotheringham column. Allan, please file your first column next week."

I flew back to Vancouver, sent off my first epic for the October 6, 1975, debut, and rushed out to the newsstand on Tuesday morning, when the mag arrived in Vancouver. A man of small ego, I instinctively turned to the opening pages, expecting my brilliant tome to be on page 2, if not 3. It wasn't there. I leafed through the mag with sinking heart; it wasn't in the first 20 pages. Nor the next 20.

Crushed in the realization that my first effort had been rejected, I finally—completely deflated—turned to the last page, there to find my orphaned piece. It turned out to be the most inspired positioning ever in Canadian journalism. There isn't a self-respecting journalist in Canada today who wouldn't give his left one for that spot.

Newman knew what he was doing. Two years later *Newsweek*, then *Time*, copied with a back-page column. Today there isn't a magazine in existence without a regular feature on that back page.

That was 1975. This is now 1999, some 1,115 columns later, and perhaps a time to contemplate. A few decades back, Jack Scott at the *Vancouver Sun* was the most beautiful writer in Canadian journalism, his words skipping across the page like a flat pebble across a lake. Before he died in 1980 at age 64, he wrote

a column musing over the fact that he had been doing that very same thing in newspapers for 40 years.

"I don't think that I would do it again if I had a choice, mind you," he wrote. "Even with columnists like Fotheringham, who seems born to do it, it may be created out of an anxiety."

I'd never thought of it that way, until I read that, but I guess he was right. Not about anxiety, but about being born to it. It's all I've ever done. I've never done anything else in my life. If I didn't do this, I'd have to get a job.

I wrote a column in the Chilliwack High School *Tatler*—in the Fraser Valley, an hour or so as the typewriter flies (flew?) east from Vancouver. The first one was a satire on the then-famous John L. Lewis, as head of the United Mine Workers' Union, a towering figure who annually brought the White House to its knees (hello there, Monica) with economy-breaking strikes. I made the analogy in my debut column, God save us, to Chilliwack High's student complaints about cafeteria food. I apparently liked understatement even in my callow youth.

There was also a column about a student experiment that involved feeding rats—in school corridor cages—Coke and junk food. We all know the resulting conclusions. A stiff-necked Coca-Cola lawyer threatened to sue for patent violation. (I was in *high school* for Crissake!)

At the same time, I was asked to write a column for the *Chilliwack Progress*, a weekly sheet owned by the best of all bosses—someone who is rich and eccentric. His name was Les Barber. He had noticed my manic rantings in the *Tatler* and invented a weekly pulpit for me: "High School Highlights."

He had on staff at the time one Stanley Burke, who had graduated, for some strange reason, from the University of British Columbia in agriculture and had started a turkey farm outside Chilliwack, featuring a large sign: COME TO BURKE'S FOR TENDER TURKS. His birds instantly expired from ailments hitherto unknown to the breed, and Stanley, to exist, had become the star reporter of the *Chilliwack Progress*.

Stanley moved on, as you will recall, to be CBC's star correspondent in Biafra and, eventually, the successor to Lorne Greene and Earl Cameron, as reader of the pre–Peter Mansbridge terribly respectable evening's news.

And I began my own move, inching carefully from Chilliwack to the wilds of Vancouver.

As a one-talent 18-year-old, on my first day on the campus of the University of British Columbia I went down to the Brock Hall basement quarters of the

Ubyssey, the most celebrated university paper in the country.

It was "the vile rag"—so described by a disgusted professor—that had produced Earle Birney, Lister Sinclair, Pierre Berton, Mr. Justice Nathan Nemetz, Ron Haggart, Val Sears, Jack Wasserman (John Turner was the sports editor), Joe Schlesinger, Helen Hutchinson, Peter Worthington, Alexander Ross and Eric Nicol, who won so many Stephen Leacock Medals for Humour that I understand he was asked to desist so someone else could have a go.

Les Bewley was Nicol's rival columnist on the *Ubyssey*. He was a quirky guy and one day, apropos of nothing, he put a classified ad in the *Vancouver Province*: "Man with Machiavellian intent in mind would like to meet at Birks' Clock at 5 p.m. Friday evening a female similarly-inclined."

Birks' Clock, then at the corner of Georgia and Granville, was Vancouver's favorite meeting spot. An alert *Province* news editor spotted the ad and sent a photog to the spot at the appointed time. Twenty-nine women showed up.

When Bewley realized, accurately, that he could never match Nicol, he opted for law school, and eventually a perch on the Bench. One day, a prostitute appearing before him in the witness box, he said, "This is undoubtedly an unusual request, but would you please stand up."

On that first day at the *Ubyssey*, I was sent out to do a news story—something completely foreign to me. On the second day, I was sent out to do a news story. Thinking this ridiculous, as well as boring, I sat down and wrote by hand, in pencil, a column mocking the alleged sexual prowess of the rollicking Engineering faculty on campus.

When I picked up the *Ubyssey* next morning, the column—"Campus Chaff" —was on the front page, where it remained for three years. The one-talent career remained in the rut.

As I approached my final year, the much-coveted editorship was held by Schlesinger, a mysterious, saturnine immigrant who had escaped from Czechoslovakia and arrived in Canada with a remarkable grasp of the language, working first as a waiter on the cruise ships up the B.C. coast to Alaska.

As a lowly sports editor at the time, I had barely spoken to the cerebral and more mature Schlesinger once during the year. He came into my office and asked if I was going to put my name in for editor. (The route to the editor's chair was democratic: a vote of the 14 members of the editorial board.) I told him everyone knew the next editor was going to be Edwin Parker, a son of the Manse, who had been waiting for the opportunity for years and, to cement his support, was currently sleeping with the news editor.

Joe, the world-weary European even then, just shrugged and suggested I think about it. He pursued the idea over the next few weeks and I finally gave in. The result of the vote? It was 12-2, Parker getting only his own vote and that of his *inamorata*. Schlesinger, the refugee from communism, who knew how to do such things, had stuffed the ballot box.

Over the years, as our paths went different ways, I have encountered him in Paris and Beijing and other journalistic haunts around the world and have told the story in front of our peers. He has never denied it, remarking sardonically only, "And yes, Fotheringham is still writing the same sports column he wrote then—only the names have been changed."

That's all true, of course, since sport is not much different from politics—there is the same spearing, the same blindsiding, tripping and tackling. The only difference is that in politics the stakes are slightly higher.

The long, stumbling path of one who has never done anything but write columns had some queer twists. The tradition for the final issue of the *Ubyssey* of its editor's term was a "Goon" edition. We decided on a satire of the three Vancouver dailies. We stole enough Gothic type from the composing rooms of the three to create our own mastheads. The *Vancouver Sun* became the *Vancouver Son*. The *Vancouver Province* became the *Vancouver Daily Providence*. Typical sophomoric stuff.

In our imitations, the Cromie brothers, Don and Sam, owners of the *Sun*, became the Crummy brothers. I had been working nights, for 25 cents a column-inch, writing university sports for the *Sun*. The sports editor was the fearsome Erwin S. Swangard, who had arrived in Canada as an immigrant from Germany, first sleeping in a boxcar in Saskatoon. He certainly frightened small university students.

Some wit on the Goon edition wrote a sports column "by Squirming S. Vanguard," highlighting the fact he insisted on prime coverage of the Little League baseball games featuring his son, who in truth was a very good young player.

Several days later, on a Saturday afternoon, I saw my life flash before my eyes. I was high in the press box at the UBC Stadium, covering the annual rugby classic between the UBC Thunderbirds and the University of California Golden Bears, the latter featuring the gargantuan Les Richter, who later went on to National Football League fame as a linebacker.

To my horror, I spotted the hulking figure of Swangard—who was menacing even while standing still—lumbering up the long concrete steps to the press box, from which there was no escape.

"Okay, kit," he said in his heavy accent that we always mocked behind his back. "I'm gonna sue you, I'm gonna sue da *Ubyssey*, da Alma Mater Society and da university." I was in the middle of final exams. I was three years in debt and now had no hope of future employment. I seriously considered suicide.

Two days later, things grew worse. A letter was received from "Office of the Publisher, *The Vancouver Sun*," addressed to "Editor, *The Ubyssey*." It read:

"Dear Sir:

"It has been drawn to my attention that a purported newspaper titled *The Vancouver Son*, imitating the type and head style and satirizing some of *The Sun*'s general styles and manners, has been published, allegedly by *The Ubyssey*. This satirical publication libels, ridicules and generally damages *The Sun* to a grievous degree, with malice aforethought. It also applies a lesser amount of its pages to similar malicious mimicry of two other local newspapers.

"After legal advice, it would be appreciated if the writer could be informed of the identity of author and editor of this work, and advised also whether said Perpetrator might be interested in a Salaried Position at *The Sun*. (see footnote)"

It was signed: "Don Cromie."

The footnote read: "We might refuse to break our editorial rule of starting newcomers above $1,000 a month, but despite our editorial condition of already being well staffed by highly skilled 'position foot-workers,' a person of the skill and ruthlessness of the above mentioned Perpetrator should have no misgivings about advancement once installed, as offered above, within knife's reach of the morocco-covered swivel chairs, previous frightening although temporary experiences notwithstanding."

Still not knowing if he was serious, I went to see him. The meeting took place in his palatial office at the *Sun*, where he confirmed his reputation as an eccentric genius by spending almost our whole time together flipping paper-clips to see if he could land them in the ceiling lamp.

As a further joke, he put me to work under Swangard, who did not speak to me for the first six months. Every Monday morning, at the sports department staff meeting, Swangard would turn to assistant sports editor Merv Peters and instruct: "Tell Fotheringham to cover the lacrosse game in New Westminster."

Peters would turn to me and say, "Fotheringham, cover the lacrosse game in New Westminster." It was an interesting first six months.

And so it was that I joined the *Vancouver Sun* in 1954 as a sportswriter. Sports-writing, as opposed to ordinary journalism, is a free-swinging, imaginative gig —all the circus acts you want to try, without a safety net.

The poor blokes who have to cover city hall have to write to a formula. Just the facts, ma'am, as Joe Friday used to say. Political reporting, cop-shop reporting—all of it to the strict, no-nonsense rules laid down by city desk. No opinions, no taking sides, above all no humor. There's a serious world out there.

No such strictures apply, of course, to the sports pages—the "children's department," as the serious, humorless scribes on the city desk used to describe us. If there's a disciplined sportswriter extant, there you will find a dull sportswriter, with even more dull copy.

It was the natural haunt for someone from Chilliwack High who wouldn't know a news story if he tripped over one, who needed a lot of elbow room and had lots of space to fill—miles away from the poor typist just yards away in the newsroom who would get eight paragraphs for the mayor's latest pronouncement.

It's no surprise that the two best sportswriters who ever lived, Red Smith of the *New York Herald–Tribune* and Jim Murray of the *Los Angeles Times*, won the Pulitzer Prize for the quality of their prose. No one covering a sewer bylaw ever won the Pulitzer Prize.

Red Smith grew tired of hearing, over the years in the press box, his companions telling how in their youth they, too, were great athletes, their careers cut short only because of some dreadful knee injury. "I, too," he wrote one day, "could have been a great athlete—except for several things. I was small, weak, uncoordinated, myopic and a coward."

My hero in life, a man I had never met, was Smith's sports editor at the *Herald–Tribune*, Stanley Woodward. A legendary figure in New York journalism, he was remembered at his death by one friend who recalled that he "was unfailingly kind to his underlings, barely tolerated his equals and was openly contemptuous of his superiors." I would like that on my tombstone.

Red Smith once observed that writing a daily column is easy: "You just sit down before the typewriter until little beads of blood appear on your forehead." As a 21-year-old acolyte, that wasn't then apparent and life appeared a joy, covering scarred lacrosse players who were going nowhere and sweaty monsters who drank a lot of beer and were far more fun than politicians.

Forever avoiding the newsroom that seemed the funeral home in my future, I sought further irresponsible escape hatches. Sandy Ross, the brilliant wordsmith who actually wrote the words of Keith Davey's royal commission report on the Canadian newspaper industry, had a memorable phrase.

He wrote that all newsrooms are "boneyards of broken dreams." It was my task to avoid that boneyard at all costs, since I had seen too many skeletons from the vantage point of the "children's department."

I wrote a travel column for the paper, jetting around the world on an expense account, proving—while all my friends justifiably hated my guts—the old adage that you will never be a millionaire as a newspaperman, but you can live like one.

I wrote editorials, the most irresponsible act of all since they are never (except in sensible places like Quebec) signed. Useless nostrums, always ending with either what the government "should" do or "only time will tell."

"Should" is the most useless word in the English language. You "should" wash behind your ears. Or you "should not" go out with that boy who rides a motorcycle. It is nonsense, which is why almost no one ever reads newspaper editorials.

I once bet Paul Manning, a Pierre Trudeau speechwriter, a case of Ballantine's scotch if he could ever detect the word "should" in one of my columns. He waited some years and—I must have been asleep that day—found one. He got the case, and has never stopped chortling about it since.

While wasting my time writing editorials, Erwin S. Swangard—who by that time was managing editor of the paper and finally speaking to me—muttered one day in his guttural way that I shouldn't be writing under someone else's name (i.e., the paper's official voice), but my own.

He was right, of course, and retribution swiftly came. A sportswriter—who else?—had been anointed as proprietor of the most prominent column in the paper. It was to troll the fleshpots and night clubs of Vancouver, to vacuum up all the failed marriages and dissolute corporate barons who were still loose at 3 a.m.

His Walter Winchell–like deadline was 7 a.m. and the newspaper would have his column on the streets by the 10 a.m. first edition. The perils of Demon Rum, alas, began to intrude on his very graceful writing, and I, from the fastness of the editorial pages, began to be called in to fill his gap while his liver took a rest.

One morning at 7:00, the copy boys who were to collect his column found a typewriter filled with words that turned into gibberish and eventually collapsed into pigeon-scratches. The managing editor called me in and offered me the job for which, as Chilliwack High could have told you, I was destined.

I had an idea. Most serious columnists, it seemed to me, came to the office, puffed on their pipes, looked out the window and then delivered Olympian overviews of the world's ills. A columnist, someone once said, is simply a good reporter who has strong views. I thought I should get out of the office.

It was only sometime later that I learned that, in New York, guys called Gay Talese and Jimmy Breslin and Tom Wolfe were doing the same thing at the *New York Herald–Tribune* and *Esquire* magazine. They called it the New

Journalism. In fact, I think it was Old Journalism, applying shoe leather rather than thumb-sucking.

Officially given the prime *Vancouver Sun* column and its precious space—as eye-catching as the *Maclean's* back page is today—I devoted my second column in October 1968 to a court trial in a way, I thought, court reporters would never be allowed to tread.

It was the sixth week of a trial in which seven young men of the Hell's Angels were charged with grabbing a young homosexual man, James Cannam, in Jerry's Cafe in Vancouver's West End and taking him out to their clubhouse to torture and humiliate him, thereby amusing themselves. Crown Counsel, before Mr. Justice Thomas Dohm, was T.G. Bowen-Colthurst, QC.

It seems I confused which of the seven accused made Cannam stand up (after they had submerged him in an ice-cold bath) and then beat his penis with a cane, before another one of them set fire to his plastic hat. What a bunch of party guys!

Next morning, when the paper carrying the column appeared, defence counsel demanded a mistrial before Mr. Justice Tom Dohm and that said columnist be cited for contempt of court. It was an interesting introduction to real-life column-writing.

We escaped that suit, but have kept the legal profession busy ever since. At last count, there were 26 threats of libel action over the years at the *Vancouver Sun* and *Maclean's*, the columnist winning 24 of them, which is a pretty fair batting average.

Stuart Keate, my publisher at the *Sun*, a man of great élan and brio, once made a claim for journalistic posterity after receiving three libel writs in one day, all of them, as I recall, for different columns of mine.

Most of them never made it all the way to the courthouse door. Mostly, politicians from the Social Credit government in British Columbia were simply using them to shut down debate, declaring their dispute with a columnist was *sub judice* during the legislative session. They would then drop the matter once the legislature's term was over.

The only losses, both at *Maclean's*, were most unusual. One was to England's eccentric Sir Ranulph Twisleton-Wykeham-Fiennes, who doesn't really have a job but bills himself as a modern explorer. He's attempted to walk to the North Pole or the South Pole, depending on what year we're talking about and which sponsors could be found.

The entire circulation of *Maclean's* in Britain is some 20 copies, found mainly in libraries and the reading room of Canada House on Trafalgar Square.

Nonetheless, he felt himself gravely wounded after my *Maclean's* column—based on knowledge of one of his farcical "explorations" down the Fraser River in B.C.—described him as a cheapskate, an innocent, a mooch who treated his British Army companions of lower rank horribly.

He did not sue on any of these obvious grounds, but on just one sentence, in which I suggested that none of his global adventures had ever revealed anything of value.

Not taking his complaint seriously, I had forgotten all about the suit until, passing by accident through London one day, I picked up the *Daily Mail* to find my mugshot on page 3 and the details of Sir Ranulph's first day in court.

Hustling down to the Law Courts on the Strand next morning, I arrived in the cramped public gallery over a courtroom just in time to hear the plummy-voiced lawyer for Sir Ranulph thunder to the jury, "And why is the editor of *Maclean's* not here in this court? Why is Mr. Fotheringham not in this court?"

At this point one member of the jury—most of them in T-shirts and looking not at all like characters from Masterpiece Theatre—strayed his eyes in boredom up to the public gallery, then down to his lap and the back page of *Maclean's*, which all the members of the jury had been studying. There the winsome countenance of the defendant adorned the top of the column. He whispered to his seatmate. The whisper went down the row, and all eyes determining my fate turned upward. I suddenly went hostage behind the pages of *The Times* of London. It was game over.

The most interesting aspect of my second loss was not the trial itself, but one of the participants. The litigants were two young men who had been executive assistants to John Turner in Ottawa. They did not appreciate my casual attempt at satire in reference to them, and went to court.

Peter Butler, one of Vancouver's most wily and clever defence lawyers, had defended me successfully in libel actions for 12 years, never losing a case. In doing so, he had become a friend. So much so that his wife and my wife became friends, and his kids and my kids became friends.

We used to spend weekends around his swimming pool at his retreat at Point Roberts, just across the border in Washington state. We holidayed together in California. He used to sit around in my kitchen.

It was therefore rather disconcerting, on the opening day of trial, to find Peter Butler rising across the courtroom, acting as lawyer for the two gentlemen suing me. Such is the legal profession.

In what is now regarded as almost a textbook case in journalism schools, a young reporter by name of Timothy Crouse had an interesting idea on the 1972 presidential campaign. Instead of covering the candidates, he would cover the press.

His book, *The Boys on the Bus*, revealed to the public all the unseemly truths that every reporter who has ever covered an election campaign knows only too well. The bad food, the numbing exhaustion, the furtive love affairs—the unspoken pact that anything that happened west of the Alleghenies was never discussed east of the Alleghenies.

Timothy Crouse's main discovery, riding on the bus with both the lowly grunts and the "bigfeet"—the code name for the star columnists and commentators—was that all journalists are "shy egomaniacs." So true; that's why we're in the trade.

Stuart Keate, my stylish publisher at the *Vancouver Sun*, used to tell the story that, when he was a teenager, he encountered a distinguished judge walking his dog on his well-bred street. The celebrated legal beagle enquired of his young neighbor what he planned to do with his life.

When the 16-year-old allowed that he wanted to be a newspaperman, the haughty Solon shook his head in dismay and suggested that his young friend should aim higher—doctor, lawyer, whatever. Keate, in later life, used to laugh at the memory: "He didn't know, and I couldn't tell him, that he was too late. … That afternoon my first byline on high school sport had appeared. I was hooked. Ball game over."

People always ask me how long it takes to write my column. My answer is always the same (and always accurate). Two hours for a good one, four hours for a bad one. It is in line with Churchill's apology to a friend that he didn't have time to write a short letter and so wrote a long one.

Some time ago I felt slightly guilty at not knowing, on sitting down before the typewriter—and now, at the computer—what I was going to say. I immediately relaxed on reading a profile of Alistair Cooke, the disgustingly erudite Manchester lad who, for a half-century now, has been writing his famous "Letter from America" to his adoring BBC listeners from his New York haunt.

He confessed that, each Sunday, he sat down before his Underwood two hours before his regular broadcast with, well, really, no idea what he was going to say. He explained that he found nothing wrong with this.

When you are driving with your wife to a Saturday-night dinner party, he pointed out, you do not rehearse your *bons mots* before you arrive. They come out, bruised by wine perhaps, as they happen.

Writing a column, if you must know—as only a columnist knows—is like squeezing the toothpaste out of the tube. Only a deadline squeezes out the best.

Scotty Reston of the *New York Times*, dean of the Washington press bureau and the most sensible columnist of his era, once found himself in a terrible swamp. His paper of record (now the best newspaper in the world) found itself silenced by a strike of its printers' union.

"How," Scotty moaned at the time, "can I know what I think until I have read what I wrote?"

All of us in the trade know his dilemma. We once had a nine-month strike at the *Vancouver Sun*. I was paid to stay away, so I wouldn't go work for someone else, and so had nothing to do but twiddle my thumbs while my mates marched in the picket line, in the rain.

My managing editor, the great Bill Galt, met me downtown every two weeks over a martini lunch and handed over the paycheque—under the table, if I recall.

My wife suggested, sensibly, that now was the time to pile up a number of fair-weather columns that could be stocked in the bottom drawer for the strike's end, so I wouldn't be holed up in the downstairs office with the usual midnight panic deadline.

And guess where, of course, I was at midnight the day the strike ended? Down in the basement, bashing away at Gutenberg's invention. It's the tooth-paste theory. Alistair Cooke is to blame.

There is an answer, as the husband of every columnist's wife knows, as to why the spare-column-in-the-bottom-drawer solution never works. After several weeks, you realize that if a column is any good, it should be printed instantly. The fact that a column can moulder in the drawer means it's no good. Forget it.

Where did "Dr. Foth" come from? I did not, as imagined, make it up myself.

It came about years back through the inventive mischief of Nick Auf der Maur, the legendary Montreal boulevardier who smoked himself to death, suc-cumbing in early 1998 at the ridiculous age of 56.

He qualified for the *Guinness Book of Records* since he was the only person on earth who both was thrown in jail (and never charged) under Trudeau's War Measures Act and later ran for mayor of Montreal—an adventure inter-rupted by being arrested for urinating in the alley behind his favorite pub, which did not help his campaign.

Through his column in the Montreal *Gazette* he absolutely owned Montreal. His quixotic role in politics as a meandering figure on the city council further enhanced his eccentric fame. He even ran once as a Conservative candidate for Brian Mulroney, who was a friend, as was Conrad Black. He was the first to predict the scandal of the Big Owe, Jean Drapeau's $1-billion folly, the Olympic Stadium, where the gravel trucks would roll into the construction site, collect their fee from the tollgate, drive through unloaded and go around the block to enter once again.

In my Ottawa days, he began to refer to me as "Dr. Foth" in his column. I never asked him why, but I presumed it was in reference to Dr. Hunter S. Thompson, the crazed American who invented "gonzo journalism" and once, when the press secretary for presidential candidate Hubert Horatio Humphrey lied to him—as all press secretaries are paid to do—went up to the man's hotel room and set fire to his door.

To this day, when I walk Montreal streets, total strangers yell out "Hi, Doctor Foth"—a testimony to the grip and reach Auf der Maur had on that great town that once used to be the most interesting stop in North America until the insane separatist dreamers ruined its economy and zip and importance.

The only embarrassing fallout is that there is really an authentic Dr. Foth, my younger brother, Jack, who worked for 14 years in the United States through night school and summer school to get his PhD in education. On his trips across the border, Dr. John Fotheringham, now a retired superintendent of schools in Washington state, is not amused by the fake degree conferred on this scribbler by the dear, departed Nick.

As a scribbler who occasionally gets into trouble at *Maclean's*, my strongest asset has been strong editors who stood behind their columnist. First Peter Newman, who as I recall never once questioned a column or any of its wilder language. Then quiet Kevin Doyle, who always addressed me as "Reverend."

He still does, to this day, when I run into him as Canadian boss of the Bloomberg financial wire. I have never once asked him what he means by the "Reverend" moniker (holier-than-thou?) and never will. I might not like the answer.

My current editor, Bob Lewis, is a good friend and a fine journalist. The friendship does not prevent occasional fights, as all editors inevitably have when dealing with tender-skinned columnists, but we get over them in time. Life would be dull without a little temper.

At the *Vancouver Sun* there was a young lady, a lively reporter, who apparently had a great party act that she displayed before fellow reporters at late-night gatherings when the grape flowed freely.

I never saw it, but it was described to me more than once. It involved said female imitating a certain columnist you might recognize who rushed into the newsroom in great agitation, shouting, cursing, on the edge of apoplexy, and finally throwing himself on the floor, kicking his heels in rage and screaming: "THEY CHANGED A COMMA!"

It was apparently a great show, highly applauded (and not too far from the truth). I jealously guard my copy, and am disliked by editors because of what they regard as an unreasonable attitude. At least two *Maclean's* senior editors (that I know of; there may have been more) have refused to handle the copy, because they regard me as too "difficult." Their actual words would frighten horses and children and won't be repeated here.

I plead guilty as charged. I am difficult, but it's my baby, it's my column and my name—no one else's—goes at the top of it. George Bain, who wrote the most brilliant column in Canada for the *Globe and Mail* from his Ottawa eagle's nest, said it all in his final effort.

"A regular column, more than anything else in a newspaper, depends on a relationship developing between the writer and reader. What a columnist depends on is the reader returning most days, at least to have a look, to see what is being said, and perhaps to stay on to have a read. There is something personal about it, like conversation, although the columnist does most of the talking."

It is very personal, and once a columnist develops a voice of his own, words that are not his own and are inserted by others ring a bell and stick out like signposts. One *Maclean's* editor, it may have been Lewis, once claimed that I would not allow anyone to change a single word in the column. That's not true—every writer needs an editor. It's just that I don't want any word appearing for my readers that I haven't agreed to.

I don't think I'm being unreasonable. I think I'm being faithful to the reader —to make sure said reader gets what the reader is paying for. The Full Monty, as it were.

Our Country, 'Tis of Thee

To write a national column for Canada's national newsmagazine requires, among other things, some luck.

The first bit of luck this scribbler inherited, through no fault of his own, was to be born in the navel of the nation, in downtown Hearne, Saskatchewan, a hamlet with one street, one general store, a blacksmith's shop, a church, two grain elevators and a railway.

People from Hearne are called Hearnias. The standard line is that the town was so small we couldn't afford a village idiot; everyone had to take a turn.

The town that no one has ever heard of—some 50 miles south of Regina —was named after Sir Samuel Hearne, an English explorer born in London in 1745. Sent to Canada by the Hudson's Bay Company, he became in 1771 the first European to make it to the Arctic Ocean overland in North America —travelling by canoe and sled, and following the Coppermine River north of Great Slave Lake.

He became chief of Prince of Wales's Fort, where he was captured by the baddies and taken to France in 1782. His release from jail was negotiated on the condition that he publish an account of his travels. This scribbler thinks that was propitious, some of those travellin' genes seeping down to the joint where I was born.

The second piece of luck, crucial to the development of a national colum- nist, was that my parents then moved to Sardis, British Columbia—some 65 miles east of Vancouver, in the Fraser Valley—and, being nine, I decided to go with them.

Growing up in British California through school, and then university in Vancouver (The Village on the Edge of the Rain Forest), added a further edu- cation in the strange country called Canada, which, as Mackenzie King said, has too much geography and not enough population.

A year's scholarship at the University of Toronto and then eventually graduation to the Ottawa Press Gallery—a spell on Fleet Street and five years in Washington somewhere along the way—helped to fill out the feel for the best country in the world. (A certifiable fact, since I've seen 69 of the other ones.)

The scribbler used to spend a lot of time in Montreal, back when it was the most interesting city in North America besides San Francisco. Sadly I haven't been there much lately, the zip and crackle having gone from the town with all its separatist angst. ("Going to tap the pulse of the Quebec public again, are you, Foth?" my press gallery buddies would banter as I set out for a Montreal weekend. "From the Maritime Bar at the Ritz-Carlton, we presume?") Who needs enemies, when you have friends like that?

The point—luck being better than talent or hard work—is that by osmosis the columnist who has never done anything but be a columnist has had a good grasp of most of the five regions that make up the country. The Atlantic Provinces, although I have travelled there a fair bit, is the only area I have really not been grounded in. (You've heard of the Newfie who sez he doesn't really care if Quebec separates—it would only mean it would take half the time to drive to Toronto.)

July 6, 1992

Stop whining, Canada, and celebrate

The young attractive blonde who is the seatmate on the trip home from Rome is on her way back to Vancouver. It had been her first time ever in Europe, visiting an Italian family. She was dazzled, of course, by the Eternal City, but she still couldn't get over the sense of not having her own space.

Her friendly, openhearted Italian hosts would charge into her bathroom to eagerly outline the day's plans. As someone who felt the bathroom was the last outpost of privacy, she found it hard to handle. When she wanted to retreat to her bedroom with a book for several hours, the family would be all over her, offering food, drink, companionship, talk—anything she wanted except the one thing she desired: being alone.

Twenty years ago this summer, this reporter travelled by steam train from what was then Peking, in the far north of China, to the border post outside

Hong Kong. It was roughly equivalent—chug-a-chug—to travelling by rail from Montreal to Vancouver.

Three things were memorable. The first was that, at each stop, wooden buckets of water would be hoisted aboard. In the buckets were live fish, to emerge at dinnertime from this rickety kitchen car, which, by the third day—waiters stained and rumpled and bedraggled—resembled something out of a Laurel and Hardy movie, as delicacies one would dream for.

The second memory was that the ancient coal train disgorged soot that would choke even Bill Vander Zalm. It being August, in fetid heat we had to open the windows or die. By the third day, one simply gave up trying to wash off the residue floating in the windows and so we all resembled the backup chorus to Al Jolson singing "Mammy."

The third, and most memorable, point is that throughout the long journey south, through the length of China, one never gazed out the window without seeing a human being. Day or night, there were always people in view—in rice paddies, on a road, on a platform. A China-watcher who now teaches at Harvard has written the most telling insight on the most heavily populated nation on earth—that you cannot understand it until you understand that practically every Chinese citizen, from birth to death, goes through life with someone else in eyesight.

Space. That's the operative message as a supposedly troubled Canada "celebrates" its 125th birthday. Nobody is in the mood for celebration (as witness the childish, picayune quibbling over the cost of shipping Betty Windsor over here on a Concorde and the expense of some statue on a horse. If the country won't grow up and still clings to the umbilical cord of a foreign queen in a foreign country, why bitch about the cost?).

The young lady from Vancouver would undoubtedly agree with the suggestion that the cure to our supposed problems would be to ship every single Canadian abroad (it surely would be only the price of the rear end of the horse) for two weeks to experience how the rest of the universe exists. Most of the whining and despair, the endemic Canadian belief in the worst, would disappear.

On St. Jean Baptiste Day, the Quebec government's man in Toronto—he has a staff of 40, by the way—threw a great party in a leafy grove on the edge of the city. There were no bombs in mailboxes, there were perhaps 300 people there, 300 people who lived outside Quebec eager to celebrate its great national day.

The dignitary from Australia (if that is not an oxymoron) thought—re our "troubles"—we are all nuts. The chap from Belgium, serious without being ponderous, thoughtful without being condescending, simply pointed out that our problems will always be with us.

As one from a country also with more than one language, he knows of what he speaks. As Northern Ireland is divided by religion, as Belgium is divided by religion and language, Canadians will always be scrapping and niggling and chewing over our differences.

Quebec is not going to separate. Neither is Quebec ever going to cease feeling left out, demeaned, nervous over being a minority in a sea of North American English-speaking louts who don't know how to make love and like gravy with everything.

Western Canada, feeling left out, refusing to acknowledge the mathematics of the reality that the power is where the population is—Ontario and Quebec—will continue to spawn the protest babes such as Presto! Manning (the Ross Perot of the Oil Patch), and the world will survive.

The Maritimes (the secret bedrock of the nation) will quietly go on doing everything quietly—mainly avoiding the dream of every yuppie to own a swimming pool the shape of his ulcer—and Newfoundland will remind us all that New York does not resent having to subsidize Alabama, and California does not complain about propping up South Dakota.

The solution, on our 125th gazing at the navel, is not to look inward but to look outward. While the editorial writers and the hotlines fulminate about the cost of the horse, look elsewhere in search of a land so lucky.

You can't find it. Take it from a chap whose employers, as punishment, force him to search out superior places of citizenship. As a five-year resident of the Excited States of America, as a three-year resident of Betty Windsor's plot, as a chap who makes the airlines of the world profitable, this here scribbler is an expert.

His advice to this birthday place of his birth: shut up and get on with it.

November 13, 1989

The national slogan is "Never complain"

Canadians deserve everything they get. They are the moral descendants of the Brits, who willingly queue up for anything and accept, at the butcher's, liver that is wrapped in tissue paper and bleeds all the way home on the bus. The slogan is "We never complain." It should be writ large on the compromise Canadian flag that was designed to look like a meat-packing emblem. Never complain. It is the national slogan.

You know this is Canada because at Terminal 1 at Lester B. Pearson International Airport in Toronto, the largest and richest city in the land, the newsstand is not open at 10:01 p.m. It is not open because in mighty Toronto, the world-class city, they lock the newsstand at 10 p.m. The rumor must be that in London and Paris and Rome and other world-class cities they lock the newsstands up tighter than a drum at 10 bells and therefore Toronto, being world-class, must do the same.

You know this is Canada because in Ottawa, the Sparta of the Tundra, when you get off a plane you cannot find a luggage cart. Why can't you find a luggage cart in this new, enlarged terminal that took only three years of construction to make it into the empty, lonely space it is today? Because—naturally—the luggage carts are cleverly and carefully in neat rows outside, out in the Arctic gales that sweep past the taxis that emit the stale odor of musk-oxen that have gone too long without shampoo.

You know this is Canada because at the stylish (and too small) Vancouver airport, it took only 15 years after it was opened before the brilliant minds running it ventured into the daring proposition of opening a second newsstand. This thus eliminated the situation wherein you could read *Maclean's* from front to back before you got to the end of the line where you could pay for it.

All this is Canada, and only Canada, because no one ever complains. Terminal 1 in Toronto, one of the great disasters of this or any other age, was conceived with the brilliant concept of building the multilayered parking lot on top of the terminal itself. This has resulted in famous occasions—motorists trying to wind their way down the circular ramps—of gridlock lasting up to four hours, drivers expiring from carbon monoxide, babies being born *en route* (and several others conceived).

No one complains, because it is Canada. Once the brains who run such things in Transport Canada figured that stacking a parking lot, layer-by-layer, on top of a terminal was possibly not the brightest thing since Leonardo da Vinci, they came up with Terminal 2.

Terminal 2 eliminated this problem. Terminal 2 was laid out horizontally—as opposed to its vertical predecessor—with the thoroughly logical idea that aged grandmothers just love walking up to 200 yards to get to their gate for the flight to Thunder Bay. As an added attraction, one of its more engaging features is that when 350 passengers emerge, their legs crossed, from a 747, there is a men's facility that accommodates one (1) urinator at a time. It takes some doing, but Ottawa is up to it.

The people in Ottawa who run our airports are not only stupid, they are firmly against literacy—which one supposes is the same thing. It is not only the newsstand in Terminal 1 in the obscenely rich world-class city that is shut down tight at 10 p.m. So is the bookstore. If those who move their lips while they read *People* magazine must be deprived, so should the fans of Hemingway and Atwood. It's only fair.

Being one of the world's leading experts on airports, I know all the secrets. Such as the fact, the smaller the airport, the more obscure the town, the more diligent are the geiger-counter people who massage your more delicate parts with their electronic prods. The champion of all is Kelowna, British California, a well-known haunt of international terrorists. One more trip through there and your agent will be singing soprano.

The ineffable Terminal 2 in the world-class city, designed by a guy with a ruler and geographical dyslexia, very astutely has situated its newsstand on its departure level in a spot where both domestic and international travellers develop spavined backs while lugging their luggage in search of it.

A chap getting off a plane on the arrival level immediately discerns that this is a city (an airport, a country) that not only discourages reading but in fact may be ready to ban it.

It is called the Pearson International Airport, but is actually the Pearson Bush-league Airport, as witness any European or Japanese traveller who arrives on his own time zone and is told that he cannot get a drink until noon, bar none.

Never mind that it happens to be 5 p.m. according to the body clock of the German businessman trying to shmooze a deal with a Mexican financier. This is tight-assed Ontario, after all. There goes world-class.

In Edmonton, the airport is twice as big as the city and twice as empty and is situated halfway to Calgary. You can hitchhike to Calgary faster than it takes you to travel by taxi to the Edmonton airport. In foggy Halifax, the Ottawa brains brilliantly built the airport half a day's journey out of town, cut down all the trees for the site, thus clearing a large enough area that now attracts the grateful fog.

It has been said that people get the politicians they deserve (as they get the newspapers they deserve). In general, Canadians get what they deserve—because they're afraid to complain. Or riot.

It's very strange what one discovers in the detritus of past columns, when ordered to rummage by the cruel editor.

Here it is, in 1981, a paean to the genius of Eugene Forsey, the Newfoundlander whose wit was lively as a flea, famous for his letters-to-the-editor of the Grope and Flail, *Canada's almost national newspaper.*

Here, his discussion of a Supreme Court decision on the constitution, is a classic Newfie dissection of the learned judges' opinion that, well, it might be yes, it also might be no. As the English say: if my aunt had balls she might be my uncle.

Forsey calls forth our ancient friend John Milton, who warns about "that Serbonian bog ... where armies whole have sunk."

Hello there, Bill Clinton. Hello there, NATO. Hello there, Art Eggleton, whoever you are. Amazing what you find when you go back to 1981, and find wise Eugene Forsey.

November 9, 1981

Phantom of delight in a bog

The greatest thing Newfoundland has ever done for Ottawa (the opposite is nonexistent) is to ship it Eugene Forsey. The crusty little man with the limber pen cuts through all the persiflage of the town like a destroyer cruising through fudge. At 77, he is still the most famous letter-to-the-editor artist in the country, flaying columnists who stray from logic and challenging ponderous editorial writers. Born in Grand Bank, he was a Rhodes Scholar, helped draft the Regina Manifesto, taught at McGill, Carleton and the University of Waterloo and is *the* self-appointed expert on the Canadian constitution. Forced out of the Senate two years ago at the mandatory retirement age (while intellectual inferiors slumber on), he is still an active figure on Ottawa streets and watches the Commons most every day from a corner seat in the Senate's gallery.

Eugene Forsey should be given a medal, for he is the only man to find something poetic in the most boring subject of the year: the Supreme Court decision on the constitution, where the good judges managed to say maybe yes and, then again, maybe no. Asked to analyse the decision by the Government of Canada, Forsey came up with one of his typical terse and pithy papers. (People who get their letters-to-the-editor printed learn to be short and quick.) More miraculously, Forsey plucked poetic imagery out of the weighty legal judgments. He doesn't think much of the Supreme Court finding that Mr. Trudeau is violating the conventions of the country by trying to sprint to London without the backing of all the provinces. Six of the judges themselves admit the conventions are "political," and should be worked out by politicians. Once people have grasped what the court's ruling on the convention really means, he argues, it is unlikely it will carry much conviction. It may

turn out to be for the eight protesting provinces, says Forsey, no more than "a phantom of delight/A lovely apparition sent/To be a moment's ornament." Further the mess left us by the judges is a "vast Serbonian bog, where armies whole might sink."

Now here we're on to something. A town stultified by the mumblings of Eugene Whelan or the verbal meanderings of Allan MacEachen has no poetry in its soul. It takes a Forsey to reveal to us that Wordsworth was interested in the constitution. A little research uncovers the source:

She was a phantom of delight
When first she gleamed upon my sight;
A lovely apparition sent
To be a moment's ornament:
Her eyes as stars of twilight fair,
Like twilight's, too, her dusky hair,
But all things else about her drawn
From May-time and the cheerful dawn.

That indeed is the constitution—a phantom of delight. A cottage industry only three years ago, it is now a multifaceted conglomerate, giving work to reporters, parliamentary committees, television technicians, otherwise-obscure back-benchers at Westminster, making well-dressed provincial deputy attorneys-general into national figures, keeping an entire government obsessed while children go unshod, mortgages are snatched from widows and stamps have to be bought with a down-payment. A lovely apparition sent to be a decade's ornament.

Now for that vast Serbonian bog. It was old John Milton, as it turned out, who—on his studies on future Canadian constitutional problems—came up with the best description yet of what will befall politicians so foolish as to venture into constitution-land:

A gulf profound as that Serbonian bog
Betwixt Damiata and Mount Casius old,
Where armies whole have sunk: the parching air
Burns frore, and cold performs th'effect of fire.
Thither, by harpy-footed Furies haled,
At certain revolutions all the damned
Are brought, and feel by turns the bitter change
Of fierce extremes, extremes by change more fierce ...

There. Is that not Ottawa as ye know it? A Serbonian bog where armies whole have sunk, vast legions of obscurantists disappeared, regiments of idealists who were going to reform the tax system, elevate the poor, punish the bloated rich—all gone, invisible. It is a Serbonian bog where the agriculture minister wants to be prime minister, where the minister in charge of acid rain fancies himself as prime minister, where the minister in charge of interest rates covets the job, where the minister in charge of railways chops the railways and the minister in charge of housing invites troubled mortgage-holders to live in his basement.

The harpy-footed Furies would like to hale these chaps before the fierce extremes, except that by law they are exempt for four more years and we can't get at them. It is also not helped that the guys opposite are in a bog and a fog all their own. Our problem is that we need Wordsworth and old John Milton with us today, to update their deep interest in the constitution blues. Irving Layton is still concentrating on sex in print, Mordecai Richler is fighting with his mother and Pierre Berton is liberating us into our past. Mick Jagger might do well. Or Ogden Nash, if he were still with us. Since Bill Wordsworth and Mr. Milton are no longer in the press gallery, perhaps we should call in Dennis Lee, author of *Alligator Pie*. Ottawa needs a poet laureate. Deserves it.

Nothing ever changes in Ottawa, except the salaries for the swivel servants. It is noted here, in this 1976 column, that top mandarins made $66,000, more than Henry Kissinger did as American secretary-of-state.

It is now 1999, and assistant deputy ministers are paid $140,000. What deputy ministers make is known only to God.

March 22, 1976

Dullsville-on-the-Rideau: if Ottawa were a woman, nobody'd invite her to parties

It happens as soon as you get off the plane, walk stiff-legged across 20 yards of frigid tarmac and enter the Ottawa airport terminal. It hits me in the face each time as surely as if it were a tepid facecloth. It is the miasma of Ottawa. My blood congeals, my heart sinks, my pulse rate slows, a melancholy lassitude overcomes me. I know, sadly, that once again I have been immersed in the all-pervading blahs of the capital of the country. *Ottawa.*

You may think I exaggerate, but most all other refugees from the outside world report the same symptoms. There is something about the town—the atmosphere, the people, the palpable *feel* to the air—that is discouraging, that is disheartening. If you wish to understand why the government that governs you doesn't govern very well, you have to understand the dismal backwater that is Ottawa. The main problem, of course, is its isolation from reality. That very quality is endemic to the mind of the civil servant, as we know, but silly Queen Victoria reinforced it by perversely plunking the capital down in a spot on the globe where no one really wants to go and no sensible soul would stay. One of the reasons why British politicians have such sense is that every day as they leave Westminster they shove their way onto the tube or wrestle for a taxi with the common folk. They actually know what a taxpayer looks and smells like. Other, less intelligent countries seek to place their lawmakers in sealed cocoons in sylvan settings as if the clear air would purify their tiny minds. Washington is bad enough, but at least it has a certain power link with New York. The worst example is Victoria, otherwise known as God's waiting room, floating adrift on a fantasy island, oblivious to real life. Brasília, naturally, stands as the ultimate monument to planned irrelevancy, but our own little Ennui-on-the-Rideau runs a close second for a capital out of touch with the land it is designed to serve.

The problem with Ottawa is that it is inhabited by only three types of people: civil servants, who have no interests; politicians, who have no principles; and journalists, who have no manners. They all talk about the same things, the same gossip, the same stale speculation, the same jokes. They drink their own bath water so much their innards, not to mention their thought processes, grow rusty. After about three straight days in Ottawa I tend to develop the ying-yangs, a condition brought about by running into my own rumors that I had started several days previously. In Ottawa you continually bump into yourself coming round the corner. The torpor spreads out as if in ripples from that depressing airport terminal. The place is impervious to outside influence. None of the verve of Montreal, only 120 miles away, seeps through. None of the grasping voraciousness of Toronto (not a New York, as someone said, but a failed Boston). Nor even, on the other hand, any essence of what Judy LaMarsh calls the "happy sluggards" of Vancouver. Instead, it is merely the blahs.

The amazing thing about Ottawa is that over the past few years it has become a more interesting place to *live*. Journalist Doug Fisher states that in terms of middle-class affluence, Ottawa is now "the top large community in the world." There are now 16,000 civil servants making more than $20,000 a year. Top mandarins make $66,000 (Henry Kissinger gets only $60,000). There is skating on the Rideau Canal, 50 miles of bicycle paths laid down by the National Capital Commission at a cost of $1.25 million, the $46-million National Arts Centre to bring culture to the civil service mind. As Fisher says, it is now an almost obscenely "secure and comfortable city" where one has to be a cretin to lose one's job. The sad fact is that none of this material cushiness has improved the personality of the town. It has resulted only in a more expensive type of dullard, even more smugly reluctant to stray once one's nose is securely in the public trough. There's no flux, no movement. If you leave the press, you move into government flackery. If you are defeated at the polls, you are fixed up with a job. (When the voters disagree with the Liberals, the Liberals prevail.)

Ottawa has a cachet all its own: every place in town seems just too far to walk but not far enough for a cab. The Sparks Street mall, a brave idea, is lined with second-rate restaurants. There are no decent shops, as every guilt-ridden conventioneer trying to buy a salving gift for wifey has discovered. That faded Disneyland, the Château Laurier, is suffering the lingering death of all railway hotels. Its basement Canadian Grill, where a few of the cabinet still dine, reminds me of some faded flower of cuisine in an Adriatic port. Upstairs, in the Cock and Lion bar, executive assistants lunch on martinis and bile. Can we understand, in retrospect, Pierre Trudeau when we recall that he lived for years in a single room in the Château while he was a Privy Council adviser? No wonder the social life at 24 Sussex Drive is so dull.

At the base of Ottawa's dullness is the beastly weather. If Jim Coleman described Winnipeg's climate as 10 months winter and two months hard sledding, Ottawa's is masochism raised to public ritual. It is flagellation by Mother Nature. No wonder Mackenzie King fitted in. As Sharon Churcher of the *Wall Street Journal* proved in her celebrated (and accurate) critique, Ottawa is colder than Lhasa, Tibet, colder than Helsinki, colder than Moscow. In summer, thanks to Queen Victoria's genius in picking a swampy area at the junction of the Gatineau, Rideau and Ottawa rivers where mosquitoes can breed unmolested, an oppressive blanket of moist air hangs over the city. Mandarins keep fresh shirts in the desk drawer so they can remain kissin' sweet until cocktail hour. God did not intend man to live in a city with two bad seasons.

In the end, it is the calcification of the mind that does it. I arrive from Toronto, 50 minutes away, and have to wait three days for the locals to get the current magazines so we can talk about the same things. I feel in a space lag, waiting for Alley Oop's time machine to decompress me. The city is largely unaware of the *Toronto Star*, the biggest paper in the country. Marc Lalonde, one of the most powerful men in town, has been commuting from Montreal since 1967. Ottawa does not represent Canada since nothing in Canada is so dull. If there is lack of reality in the legislation emanating from your capital it is in large part due to the influence of Ottawa itself, yesterday's city tomorrow.

March 4, 1980

The parties on The Rock

W hen I become Prime Minister (as I may), there will be enacted a new law applicable to all Canadians. It will be that all citizens of the land not already living there be compelled to visit Newfoundland at least once before they croak. You cannot really be a Canadian until you have seen The Rock, where it all started, have talked to the Newfs and had your sinuses cleaned out with a little shot of Screech. Newfoundland reminds us that there is something older than a shopping plaza in Edmonton, that there are more serious things in the land than Harold Ballard, and Canada is not, as a bitchy Fleet Street paper dubbed it, "The great white waste of time."

St. John's harbor is timeless, appearing today as it must have when John Cabot or whoever sailed in around 1498. Cabot's real name was Giovanni Caboto, and he was born in Genoa, but I digress. Water Street is the oldest street in North America, as some of the fish and chip shops seem to testify. High on the hill sits Joey Smallwood's legislature building, looking like a miniature version of an early New York skyscraper, the only legislative building in Canada built on the vertical scale, as if Newfoundlanders yearn to struggle toward the sky, out of the bleak reality of The Rock.

We are, for purposes of research, at Murray's Pond Fishing Club, a spot of roast beef haven outside St. John's where the gentry retreat when the cares of the week fall on their foreheads and gentle relief (i.e., raucous behavior) is the only solution to the torments of the soul. The occasion is a St. Valentine's Day costume dance, the event attractive to the lawyers, doctors and stockbrokers who allegedly fish at Murray's Pond. The event is a magnificent success, highlighted by the prominent and wealthy St. John's lady who comes dressed as a stripper from a military base in West Germany, ahem. In her fright wig, above the neck she looks remarkably like Cher. Below her neck she looks like, well, a stripper from a military base in West Germany, with accoutrements that Cher has only dreamed about. Her husband is dressed as an Arabian sheik, as only he can afford the chandelier-like diamonds that dangle from her erotic earlobes. Robin Hood and Maid Marian are here, as is the Queen of Hearts and her tart—who turns out to be her stockbreaking husband in purple wig, bee-stung lips and tight pink corduroy miniskirt.

There is only one disconcerting factor. Sifting through the costumes, early on, are a number of beards, a number of tweeds. They do not fit. They are, it turns out, headed for another party upstairs, a party hosted by Clyde Rose, publisher of Breakwater Books. Rose, with a bushy beard and a curly personality, is an interesting character, as is almost anyone who lives in Newfoundland. He has spent all his life, save three years in Montreal and a short stint in London, here. He was born in an outport, a fishing village that clings to the cliffs of The Rock, his ancestors there for 300 years. When Rose and other Newfoundlanders from the outports arrived at Memorial University they were required to go to classes to "unlearn" their dialects, to learn how to "speak English" or Canadian or whatever it is called. "Imagine!" Rose howls, "Wiping out 300 years of oral tradition. It was like brainwashing."

Downstairs, it being full of lawyers and therefore incipient politicians, there is much talk of Dick Hatfield and Bob Coates. The jokes have a Newfoundland twist, and therefore are unrepeatable. Everyone admires the hooker from Lahr, the hit of the dance floor. Someone paints with lipstick the navel of the Queen of Heart's tart. Bonnie and Clyde are here, Clyde being someone who once offended his partners by defending Greenpeace in their court battles over the seal hunt; the winsome Bonnie, who looks like a younger Julie Christie, in real life is a PhD student in English. She packs a mean machine-gun.

Upstairs, the beer flows. A poet in a flattened black cowboy hat and beatific smile tears the music out of a fiddle. An actor with a munificent belly holds forth on a tiny flute. There are several accordions and much mirth. All the old Newfie songs are dragged out, and most everyone knows the words. It is dark and close and intimate. You can feel the culture of the island, sniff it like the salt air.

Downstairs, the scotch flows. As the music rises and slips into boom-boom time, a young schoolteacher with the clean good looks of a Hollywood teen idol seizes the lady from Lahr and does a mock bullfight with his jacket as cape. Encircled and encouraged by the throng, he attempts to remove—in syncopated fashion—the fashionable lady's fashionable dance-hall array. It is a wild adagio, garter belts peeking, a game that is a little more than a game, everyone wondering just how far it can go. The fish, slumbering outside beneath the ice of Murray's Pond, seem blissfully unaware of the contrast within, but the two floors of the late-evening revelry illustrate perfectly layers of Newfoundland society, one affluent, the other pensively trying to consolidate something. Upstairs, the fiddle squeaks and the accordions moan. The respectable stripper whirls and escapes, only to return for another escape. The teacher rips off his shirt. His wife dives at him to restrain him. The poets upstairs chant their sea shanties. This is Newfoundland, 1985. The country club set waiting for the riches of the Hibernia oilfields to arrive. The other set upstairs desperately trying to hang on to the past. So they won't be "unlearned."

The Wild West really is wilder. Someone once said that if you imagined the United States as a table, and if you lifted it on one side and all the junk fell to the end, then you would end up with California. Where all the skate-boarders, topless beach-volleyballers and freaked-out New Age religious nuts end up.

That basically is British California, also known as Bennett Columbia, Lotusland where it never snows and all the kooks end up. The reason it has so many social problems is that if you're a drunk, you can lie under a bridge all winter with your vanilla extract in a brown paper bag and never freeze to death. It's a treat.

It's the same reason why the last four B.C. premiers have all been enveloped in scandal. Most of it because of plain stupidity. Wacky Bennett, ruler for two decades, 1952–72, was succeeded—after a short three-year interregnum with the socialists and Little Fat Dave Barrett—by his son, MiniWac.

Bill Bennett never stole a dime in office but, after leaving it, destroyed both his own and his family's reputation by taking a phone call one morning from a horsey friend.

Friend, owner of a timber fortune, tipped him off that a merger proposal with an American partner had fallen through. MiniWac called his broker and made millions with his brother Russ in the brief minutes before the Toronto Stock Exchange halted trading in the relevant stock.

After a clutch of lawyers in Vancouver made another million or two in legal fees through marathon appeals to the highest courts in the land, Bill was found guilty of insider trading and there went the family heritage.

This was followed by the next Social Credit premier, nutball Bill Vander Zalm, who wears wooden shoes so as to keep the woodpeckers away from his head. He was unhorsed after being caught accepting a large and fat envelope, filled with cash, at a suite in the Bayshore Inn in the middle of the night, the donor being a Taiwan billionaire.

His saintly successor was the NDP's honest Mike Harcourt, who eventually got sick of the pressure after a previous party finance minister, Dave Stupich, couldn't really explain where all the profits from the blue-rinse faithful in Nanaimo bingo games had gone.

The loyal horsemen of the RCMP still haven't quite figured that one out, though they did raid the suspiciously lavish Stupich home on an island where he resided with a new squeeze.

Not to be outdone in the realm of home invasions, Glen Clark—Harcourt's successor—made all the national TV highlights when the fuzz

*scared the bejeesus out of his terrified wife and kids when they knocked on
the door one night with a search warrant and went ruffling through his
underwear in search of no one knows what.*

It is Lotusland. These things happen.

December 1, 1975

Never mind who's going to lead B.C., who's going to make it laugh?

I t was Angus MacInnis, a founder of the CCF, who once said that in the Maritimes politics was a disease, in Quebec a religion, in Ontario a business, on the Prairies a protest and in British Columbia entertainment. Outsiders must understand this simple fact of life before plunging into the subtle aspects of a B.C. election to be decided December 11.

Does the most affluent section of the world ever to vote in a socialist government dare give Premier Dave Barrett a second term? Can a regional movement, Social Credit, which is attempting the difficult task of passing on the succession from highly successful father to untried son—Wacky Bennett to Miniwac, Bill Bennett—make a comeback? Such pedestrian questions pale beside the main issue: who can supply the entertainment quotient sufficient to induce B.C. voters to crawl out into the rain for a December polling booth?

To understand, you must remember it was no surprise that within a year of Barrett taking power a cabinet minister had to be sacked for being caught *in flagrante delicto* in a car within a 50-yard view of the Premier's office window. Or that the social hostess of the stately Empress hotel complained about the two NDP ministers, installed in a suite close by the one reserved for Prince Philip, who were cooking their meals by hotplate and leaving the beer bottles rolling about the Persian carpets. Or the Social Credit lady MLA who had to request the Empress management that her room be switched because of the steady tattoo of passion exerted on the wallboards of the adjoining room due to the amorous nightly adventures of one particular randy NDP minister.

All of this, of course, is in keeping with the great traditions of BC politics. Voters in the nethermost province have been weaned on kooks, from the day 100 years ago when an itinerant from the California goldfields, William Smith, felt his name was too commonplace. He changed it to Amor de Cosmos (lover of the world), became B.C.'s second premier and once delivered a speech lasting 20 hours. Down through the years, the longing for slightly deranged statesmen has persisted. There was the famed Socred MLA Lydia Arsens, who fought fluo-

ridation and once proposed to the legislature that all householders be required to have three garbage cans, in three colors, to make life easy for the dustman—since the red can would contain tins, the white one waste paper and the blue one such mundane things as coffee grounds and soggy tea bags.

All of this is pertinent in the important matter of Bill Bennett, who is attempting to muster the combined free enterprise vote of what essentially is a rigorously free enterprise province against the socialist horde of Premier Barrett.

Young Bennett is energetic, alert, rich, dedicated—all those necessary boy scout things. But he also, in the words of a visiting female journalist subjected to two hours of his good looks, has "a relentless dullness" and is "eminently forgettable." Recently another female reporter, in the midst of a TV profile on Bennett designed to reveal the real man behind the political mask, in frustration demanded, "Don't you ever indulge yourself in anything?" "Well, yes," replied Miniwac solemnly, "peanut butter sandwiches." He held his fingers apart before the camera to indicate the sinful thickness of the crime.

It really just doesn't rank with the crowd-pleasing antics of Phlying Phil Gaglardi, the evangelical speed freak, who while upholding the law as highways minister also was convicted of speeding and careless driving offences, had his licence suspended, was fined $1,000 for contempt of court and once sped away after running over a dog, only to be overtaken by an irate motorist (and voter). The Reverend Gaglardi, in a passionate plea for understanding in the legislature, one day cried, "If I tell a lie it's only because I think I'm telling the truth."

There was Wacky Bennett himself, an abstemious teetotaler who dressed in black homburg and a funeral director's suit but who in some perverse way collected around him a Technicolor retinue of flacks, touts, rounders and sycophants. One went to jail for forging his signature, another used his name to call phony press conferences for mining promoters and a third wrote a fawning book that was so dreadful it almost won, unentered, the Leacock medal for humor.

Bennett's successor regularly saves voters from wasting their time watching *Hee-Haw*. Barrett on stage is something fit only for a home movie: wrenching off his jacket, then his tie, on one occasion even his shoes. Short, fat, profane—a socialist Buddy Hackett—he has John Diefenbaker's timing crossed with Lenny Bruce's vocabulary. He quaffs Chinese food by the bushel, plays rugby (where he is in constant danger of losing his pants) and tells lady reporters to *bleep* off.

The B.C. demand for balminess affects even those hired to represent the Queen's dignity. Speaker Gordon Dowding, an NDP lawyer, got into a row in the House after it was revealed he used the legislative dining room to cater a private party and the telltale cherry tomatoes were sprinkled down the legislative steps. Barrett, watching the robed Dowding march stiffly down the corridor in his tricorne one day, cracked, "I think the job has gone to his three-cornered head."

Attorney-General Alex Macdonald, in kilt and sporran, plays tennis with Bobby Riggs on the Empress lawn, doing a striptease throughout until he emerges in his shorts. The powerful doctrinaire socialist, Resources Minister Bob Williams, likes to smile sweetly at reporters' mean questions and reply, "Kiss my ass, daddy."

And there was the celebrated Agnes Kripps, a gushing Socred who one day aroused snoozing MLAs with a speech explaining there were too many sniggers about the word "sex" and that she proposed replacing it with an entirely new word—BOLT—for biology of living today. There was a thunderous clatter as MLAs of all parties sat up with a start. "I'm bolt upright just listening to you," cried an NDP backbencher. As poor flustered Mrs. Kripps tried to flounder on, a Socred shouted, "It's okay for the bolts, but what about the nuts?" Mrs. Kripps, refusing to quit when she was behind, finally attempted to silence the hilarity all about her by pleading to the chair: "Mr. Speaker, Mr. Speaker, won't you please bang that thing of yours on the table."

Conceded, the mathematics say Bill Bennett should be able to marshall the section of the population that is against socialism. But is peanut butter going to be *enough*?

September 12, 1983

Kind friends and gentle places

The best way to spend the dying days of summer is with friends and with that oldest friend of all, dignified old Mother Nature. Saltspring Island lies in that demiparadise in the Strait of Georgia between Vancouver and Victoria, a locale that takes on all the characteristics—and attracts all the characters—of any island. Leftover hippies from the 1960s still live in the hills with their marijuana crops, emerging in their shorts and thongs for the Saturday morning market in Ganges, the metropolis of the place. They mingle with the retired colonels from Poona and the dotty old ladies who find the island a welcome escape from reality. Reality, when you examine it, is quite boring. Better to live on Saltspring and meet real people. The market, mostly dispensed from the backs of camper trucks or from camp stools, has apples, honey, quilts, home-made cinnamon buns, a box containing "free kittens" and a local variety of kitsch. There is a raucous broadcaster, born in Glasgow and living out the fantasies of a Scottish laird on a mountainside farm full of cows and loving grandchildren and jibing friends.

On the island, deer dart in front of the car. There is a retired millionaire with the face of a cherub who made his money on used cars in Britain and who thinks Trudeau is a Commie. Debate beside a swimming pool looking out on paradise does not do much to budge him. At Booth Bay, where the guileless daughters of the owner wait on your table as you gaze out on the sculptured

English garden with the sea beyond, you can wade into the channel and pluck oysters like grapes. It is hard to keep one's mind on Herb Gray in these circumstances.

Bowen Island is a 25-minute ferry ride from Horseshoe Bay, which is a 20-minute drive from Vancouver. Early in the morning a man can make it from his summer cabin to his office in downtown Vancouver in an hour. An editor of a Vancouver paper lives there year-round. It is disgustingly beautiful and private. No prospect displeases. It is a 20-yard stroll to collect the blackberries that fill the breakfast bowl, as we sit looking across the water to a mountain profile that resembles the sleeping Charles de Gaulle. There is a lady from New Zealand who as a hostess is famed in Ottawa, Winnipeg and downtown Westwell, Kent. Her husband is one of those rare breeds, a silent lawyer, who is a mean force in the local version of grass hockey, played with ice hockey sticks and tennis balls and specializing in incapacitating soft-boned visitors. Flamboyant stock market millionaire Peter Brown, in case anyone doesn't know he has money, arrives at the tennis court in his electric golf cart which has a Rolls-Royce grille. In his deep mahogany speedboat, which looks as if it should be driven by David Niven off Monaco, he makes it to his summer home on Bowen in 25 minutes from Vancouver harbor. Off the aging wooden deck of the cabin, which started out as a shed at the turn of the century, the water is speckled with white sails and graceful yachts and log booms. Occasionally, a large freighter, like an unwanted stranger, oozes around the point, threatening to scatter the booms.

Deep Cove is near the end of Indian Arm, the final meandering of the fjord that cuts into the innards of Vancouver and separates the main section of Valium West from the North Shore. This is the home of a former judge who decided that livin' was more fun than judgin' and so she retreated to her law practice until the day when she will follow her hero, Judy LaMarsh, into politics. (As a card-carrying feminist, she would probably insist on "heroine.") She is famous for her parties, and her parties are famous because of the food. It's a good combination. Her sense of humor deserts her only when it comes to smoking, beloved guests informed via signs that they please spend the party out on the deck, where they are forced to inhale the backdrop of battle-green mountains and calm water. One of the guests is a big heavy from Toronto who is much in the Zena Cherry social column in the *Globe and Mail*, the bible by which the Toronto glitterati live. He complains, after several days in the area, that he wants to put his eyeballs on a sabbatical. They can take only so much. He is found one day rollerskating the 10-km seawall around Stanley Park—a man released from prison. There is much laughter at Deep Cove, along with the hostess's giggle, which has the effect of the tickle of a feather. There is gravlax beyond belief, with a sauce that should be banned and three gummy desserts that would be obscene in Boston.

Point Roberts is that funny spit of land south of Vancouver that is a lonely part of the United States. The host's way of greeting is to nod from his pool, which is as warm as Dolly Parton's heart and sits on a cliff that looks across the gulf to Vancouver Island and Japan beyond. The trees look as if they were painted by Tom Thomson. One could weep.

There is somebody's birthday party in one of those Vancouver condos that overlook the world. The teenagers this B.C. summer are booming with California health crossed with Ivy League preppiness. There are tons of kind friends, the only thing that counts. Late at night an author arrives on the flight from Central Canada with plans to live on a boat on the water. His worried Toronto comrades have warned him to bring enough razor blades. They're serious. Laughter is the key. His wife has brought along a guitar, so she can learn it. She knows authors. It is summer.

August 15, 1983

Life in southern Saskatchewan

The land around Avonlea, Sask., 80 km south of Regina, is as flat as Ronnie Reagan's intellect. On any day you can see forever. The faint blimps of clouds bump against the horizon a thousand miles away. There is, however, one anomaly. Hidden beneath this flat deck—invisible until you come upon it—is a leafy cellar, a meandering ravine that contains a small lake and comforting acres of trees that hide camper trucks and picnics and tents and nostalgic relatives who grasp each other around the memories and remember all the funny times and neglect to recall the bad times. In the telescope of time, we remember only the good parts.

They grow beef on the hoof here. A 17-year-old boy from British Columbia, a darting hockey defenceman and a gutsy rugby player, looks in awe and some trepidation at these brutes he is about to encounter in a touch football game in the sylvan glen. There is Brent, an intelligent young man who rises unimpeded well beyond six feet and who moves like a tight end out of the Minnesota Vikings camp. There is Greg, built the way they used to build outhouses, with a shy grin that melts hearts and muscles that tattoo opponents' ribs. Older men look upon him and weep, while their wives sigh and dream. He has a cast on the wrist he broke while losing a match with a punching bag, so, he lopes through the game on half-motor, merely threatening opponents with the brandished white weapon. Russell is merely menacing, a hunk who runs in a straight line. The groceries that go into the growing of these boys would feed Chad for a month.

Kevin is built closer to the ground, his centre of gravity around his hips, a dangerous moving object who hits you with the velocity of a bowling ball. He has rolled over his father's truck, denting the parts but not his confidence, and he has an infinite capacity for after-dark overtime. He does not lack for company.

Ruby is here, the pleasing crinkle lines around the eyes indicating a lady who has laughed a lot in her life—and plans more. She is just in from Vienna, where she learned the Austrians have more manners than the French. (Almost everyone in the world has more manners than the French.) Her husband, Lloyd, since they live in Georgia, has brought along a bottle of the finest bourbon, Rebel Yell. Ordinary bourbon is worse than bad rye whisky. Good bourbon goes down like a tart port. Lloyd is a popular man this day, as the mosquitoes arrange themselves in dive-bomber formations in the trees, picking out targets. Touch football has evolved into volleyball.

Harvey is here, a semiretired professional who has learned to his astonishment—and delight—that at the age of 59 he is a lazy person. His countenance gleams in pleasure at the realization. Edna, a lady in her, ahem, 70s, astonishes her grandchildren the night previous by breaking into the Charleston—a dance they regard as foreign and as freaky as the animated sleepwalk they later break into when the teeny-boppers are let loose in the blue suede ambience of the dance band in the hall in Rouleau. Her ankles are of the same quality that used to raise so much comment in the church choir. Dora has definite views on how the world should be run, particularly the segment of the world run by Premier Bill Bennett. He would benefit from an hour with her, although he would not enjoy the experience.

Dale, with good humor, provides the finest breakfast restaurant between Kenora and Banff. Ruby says the best bumper sticker she has yet seen is the one spotted in Florida: "We're spending our children's inheritance." She has further wise advice: "Stick with your kids while your hands are still warm. Then let them go." Jackie, the daughter of Janice and Jim, is an accomplished acrobat and tap dancer, exuding self-confidence. She will have no problem in life.

Neither will the 14-year-old from Vancouver, who dazzles the boys in her yellow-and-white mini. She watches Dale and another Lloyd play the piano and banjo as the family favorites roll out and asks in a logical question, "How can they play without music?" Life is too short to explain that in Depression days there was no money and, as Barry Broadfoot's *Ten Lost Years* explained, you had to create your own entertainment. Everybody played an instrument. (Mart Kenney, of Mart Kenney and His Western Gentlemen, now supposedly retired but still tootling in British Columbia, tells the story of starting his first band in the Dirty '30s, booking a date in a rural Alberta hall and ordering his sidemen to rent tuxedoes so they would look classy. The admission to the dance was 25 cents. His band began to play at 9 p.m. It was still playing, plaintively, at midnight. No one came. No one had 25 cents.)

Vaughn does not make the football game, luckily. He is bigger than any of them. His repertoire of late-night songs would not please Mart Kenney. Leslie of the luminous hair has a husband, Bob, who is a wise professional hockey player who got out early and has a profession. He tries to convince the 17-year-old with the impressive shoulders to do the same. Jim laughs like always. Dick does his Don Rickles one-liners, the Will Rogers of the Soo Line. Jack has the most sedate dancing style of all, cruising about the floor like the *Queen Mary* on a gentle swell. The women, as always, kiss you full on the lips with a smack that can be heard in downtown Saskatoon.

The only thing to do in summer, while we wait patiently to change governments, is to go to a family reunion.

The thing about Winnipeg is that nothing ever changes. It is the rock at the centre of Canada. The Winnipeg Jets get shifted elsewhere. The Blue Bombers get moved into the Eastern *Division of the Canadian Football League and no one blinks. Winnipeg survives.*

The point is that Manitoba is not really a part of Western Canada—as Saskatchewan, Alberta and British California so surely are. Winnipeg is the bridge between the central Canada that real Western Canadians so bitterly resent, and the real West.

Winterpegers would never dress up in fake cowboy gear once a year, as Calgarians do—almost all of whom have never seen a horse up close. Instead, they go the Royal Winnipeg Ballet in the most culturally solid city west of Montreal.

May 22, 1995

Winnipeg: a city of survivors

Everyone worries about Winnipeg. The hockey club is supposedly going, going, gone. The winter lasts forever. The town is dying. The Crow has been killed. The mosquitoes. The place is so conservative it has just voted conservative again. Oh dear.

If the truth be known, Winnipeg is the most stable city in Canada. It is stable because nothing ever happens there. Not for The Peg the wild booms and disastrous busts of Calgary, millionaires flying to Hawaii on their private jets one year and then selling the car the next.

Not for The Peg the airy arrogance of Edmonton, which once thought it was going to be such a surging metropolis that it built its international airport so far out of town that you can't afford a hotel room after you've paid the cab fare.

When the Oilers were winning all those Stanley Cups and the Eskimos were winning all the Grey Cups, the city erected huge signs on the outskirts: EDMONTON, THE CITY OF CHAMPIONS. Winnipeg is The City of Survivors. It can't be crushed if it loses a hockey team, but it has no ambition of becoming something other than Winnipeg. All youthful dreams died long ago.

The city where the Red joins the Assiniboine exists on good theatre, the famous ballet company, fur coats and concentric circles of friends who know they're all going to be around for the same parties a decade hence. There is no urgency. Time moves at a stately gait in Winterpeg.

One of the reasons for the serenity is that the city is not in lockstep with other regions. It is not really a card-carrying member of the Prairies, Saskatchewan and Alberta carrying the ball there. Winnipeg, so much older and more settled, has one foot in Central Canada.

This was proven when the CFL, which doesn't know what it is doing these days, on the death of the Montreal Alouettes moved the Blue Bombers into the Eastern Division, supposedly mates with Hamilton and Ottawa and Toronto. Winnipeg did not blink. Life goes on. Any city that can abide those mosquitoes can cope with anything.

Winnipeg was going to be the Chicago-of-the-North, the railway and grain centre of the nation that the 20th century was supposed to belong to. It was the headquarters of the Hudson's Bay Co., the oldest incorporated company in the world. The most influential newspaper editor in Canada was John W. Dafoe, advising and admonishing Ottawa from his desk at the *Winnipeg Free Press*.

His correspondents in Ottawa, Bruce Hutchison and Grant Dexter, were

closer than glue to the Liberal governing party, Hutchison even writing speeches for prime ministers, and that's why the Crow lasted as long as it did.

The reason for the quiet town's cultural maturity is its easy mix of the Ukrainians, the Jews and the Icelanders and—I guess we'll have to include them —the WASPs, from the Richardsons and the Heffelfingers and down to the rest.

An hour north on Lake Winnipeg is Gimli, where every single person is a descendant of the Icelanders who came in 1875 in search of fish and starved to death in great numbers. Despite this, the survivors have grown to enormous heights.

I know of one family, two lanky young men and four beautiful daughters, most of whom tower over nine feet, six inches. The youngest of the brood, a champion speed skater before she took up poetry, is known as Baby Stonehenge. You get the picture.

Winnipeg has turned out Larry Zolf, the most uncontrollable maverick ever weaned by the CBC. At summer camp his counsellor was one Allan Gotlieb, later Ambassador to Washington who—Zolf claims—sat up in a tree reading Schopenhauer while children drowned all around him.

There was also Babe Pratt, who was bigger than Eric Lindros and was a rushing defenceman before Bobby Orr was born and, leading the New York Rangers to a Stanley Cup, attributed it to "some hungry rookies and a lot of thirsty veterans."

Not to mention Jack Pickersgill, Mitchell Sharp, James Coyne, Trent Frayne and Scott Young, whose son Neil has apparently amounted to something south of the border.

Several years ago in the town that winter never forgets, I saw an improbable and hilarious play involving four women who had been playing bridge once a week through their courting days, their tired and droll marriage days, on to their grandmother days. Only last week do I discover it was written by Carol Shields, the American-Canadian who has just won the Pulitzer Prize and has spent her entire adult life in Canada and The Peg with her University of Manitoba professor husband.

(It is so typical of Canadian chauvinism that newspapers here never mentioned that she was actually an American and held dual citizenship. It was so typical of American chauvinism that papers there never once mentioned that she happened to live in Canada.)

That's OK. That's Winterpeg. No muss, no fuss. As a nationality-surfer who cruises in between the frenetic wanna-be Americanism of Toronto and the heyman-laid-back Starbucks lifestyle of Vancouver, Winnipeg is an oasis of calm.

Ain't nobody there gonna get their knickers in a twist. You got the winter, you got the mosquitoes. After that, Quebec in no way is gonna bother you. It is unflappable.

There is a reason for this. It is indeed the centre of the country. Don't worry about Winnipeg.

The problem with Toronto is that, essentially, it doesn't have any soul. It doesn't have a real feel to it, as do most interesting cities.

It is filled with people who have come to it from elsewhere with the sole purpose of making money. Nothing wrong with that, one supposes, but it leaves Canada's largest city composed of residents who don't laugh much and who ride on the subway in the mornings with grim visages in the search for moola. It does not make for a lot of fun.

Montreal has soul. A bit watered down these days, at the thought of another neverendum lurking around the corner, but Montreal still has soul. New York has soul—a very gritty one admitted—but a soul nonetheless. Like New Orleans, or San Francisco, Paris naturally, Rome absolutely, even Winnipeg in its own way. Toronto doesn't have soul. There is no substitute for it.

The problem with Toronto is that there is nothing to see. You wake up in the morning and you can see either blacktop, or towers. Nothing invented by nature intrudes. It's flat, on a square grid. Not, as mentioned, much fun.

The crazy thing about the town is that the only interesting visual bits are the ravines that slope down to the lake—the lake that nobody knows. When swooping down, for example, the Rosedale Valley Road, one can be swallowed by the green leaves of the forest—magnificent in autumn, when red and gold—climbing the slopes on either side.

That's the problem. You have to go down to look up. The town has been built upside down. It's the most unusual city I've seen since Venice.

Having no natural beauty, Toronto has further compounded nature's error by rendering invisible its only obvious advantage: it is built on a lake. Generations of Torontonians are born, live and go to their death not knowing this. It is one of the great hidden secrets of our time.

Toronto has done this by erecting one of the architectural monstrosities of all time. Something called the Gardiner Expressway, an elevated goofiness of concrete that acts as a curtain that shuts off Lake Ontario to the city.

The world-crass city, now realizing its mistake, is talking about burying the monster, but it won't do much good. Behind it, between the city and the lake, there has now been erected a picket-fence of apartment towers that shield from the denizens of this strange city the fact that they live on the water.

May 22, 1989

Protecting a city from its lake

Toronto, in its own way, is a very strange place. It is the only place in Christendom where the town's chief eccentric, every time he goes into hospital threatening to die, causes the price of the shares in the national sports shrine he owns to leap in glee on the stock market. It is about the only place left in North America that has three lively and competitive and profitable newspapers. It is also undoubtedly the only city in the world that lives on the water where you can't see the water.

It is one of the great secrets of our time that Toronto is situated on Lake Ontario. It can be detected if you look at a map or on an atlas, but you can't detect it if you live in Toronto. You might as well be residing in Yorkton. There are people who are born, live and die in Toronto, envying Vancouver's Pacific and Halifax's Atlantic and never once seeing the open water that washes on the city's shore.

To achieve the impossible—having a huge lake that no one can see—took some ingenuity, but Toronto has managed it. For starters, it built one of the esthetic disasters of the century as a sort of Berlin Wall to barricade the city from the water. It is called the Gardiner Expressway, named after the bulldozer of a civic leader who masterminded it. It is a concrete conduit of commuters high in the sky with enough pillars, on-ramps, off-ramps, barriers and broken truck tires to sufficiently obscure any possible view of the lake to anyone but a helicopter pilot.

In case there is any chance that a human being, as opposed to a car, might see over, under or through this monster, the city is cleverly allowing to be erected along the waterline a picket fence of massive condominiums for the 3,000 millionaires who wish to purchase a view of the lake. The old warehouses and docks on the waterfront have been deemed outmoded. Instead, a mini-Manhattan to shield from forbidden eyes the evil sight of water. Towering inhuman caves of glass and steel that house tax shelters rise to fill in the few precious glimpses of distant lake water. It has been a difficult task to block almost every view, but by diligence they have achieved it.

Toronto once had its chance. The SkyDome, to open on June 3, in fact sits on the land that was supposed to be Toronto's first public park—killed by political graft and railway greed. In the 1830s, there was a dream of a green park for the citizens on the lakefront. Watercolor renderings by Toronto's surveyor of the time show walking paths and trees and laughing children on slides. According to official city council minutes, aldermen talked about putting a park south of Front Street as early as 1836. This was two years after the city was incorporated. Population: 9,252.

Lt.-Gov. Sir Francis Bond Head commissioned a study for the park plan, but by 1850 (the true Toronto appears!) John G. Bowes was elected alderman on a platform of railway development. The population of the new centre of Upper Canada had zoomed to 30,000. Bowes also happened to be an owner of the Toronto and Guelph Railway, which obviously eyed the harbor for shipping and wanted its trains allowed into the centre of the city. By 1851, he was mayor and rich, selling his railway to the Grand Trunk Railway, and rail lines on the supposed park land easily got council approval.

Toronto seems to have learned nothing from Vancouver or San Francisco, where public outrage over loss of ocean views has killed off development. In

San Francisco, there is the magnificent sight of one elevated freeway that ends in the sky—construction halted in mid-concrete. In Vancouver, a brilliant plan by Toronto's Four Seasons Hotels chain to smother the entrance to Stanley Park was blocked after a long fight by some of us who cared.

Toronto, in its worship of bigness, is about to unveil the world's largest gridlock. On these once-parklands, it has packed right at the foot of the CN Tower a convention centre, the Roy Thomson Hall (funded by the family of that connoisseur of the arts) and now the SkyDome. (In a delicious example of retroactive guilt, Canadian National Railways, which took over the Grand Trunk Railway after the First World War, "donated" $25 million worth of land and services so SkyDome would be built where laughing children on slides were meant to be.) And they've broken ground on the same site for the new CBC headquarters. When everybody shows up at once, the traffic jam is going to start in Hamilton and end in Oshawa.

No one in the Toronto planning department obviously has ever been to a sporting event or a symphony concert. I await with amusement the reaction of the esthetes at Thomson Hall in the middle of Beethoven's Fifth when they hear the drowning roar, right next door, of 57,000 nuts in the open-roofed SkyDome greeting a George Bell home run or an Argo touchdown. I can't understand why these people don't check with me first.

Everyone in the world outside Toronto knows that, essential for the sanity of the populace, is the daily, calming view of water. You can't move in Vancouver or San Francisco without the Valium-like effect on the eyes. You can't go anywhere in London or Paris without crossing a bridge over the Thames or the Seine. All the great cities are built on water—which was the original reason, transport, for their existence.

Some day, somehow, Toronto is going to realize that it is built on a lake. Only it can't see.

October 21, 1985

At home with squirrels and gulls

This is to serve as a serious tourist guide for those strangers, especially Americans, who might stumble into Toronto in the eventuality that the World Serious has arrived. There seems a belief, from below the border, that the city is inhabited by arctic breezes. They should be assured that that temperature is enclosed only in the hearts of Bay Street bankers—the people who made the country what it is today: emotionally constipated.

Toronto is most proud of the fact that it has a large knob at the top of a large tower. This is known as the tallest free-standing structure in the world—that proviso added because there is something taller on earth, a communications tower in Poland that is supported by guy wires. If that's the type of competition you want to get into, feel free. Toronto also has the largest number of sea gulls ever to infest a baseball park. It is the only city in the world to arrest a ball player, David Winfield of the New York Yankees, for accidentally killing a sea gull with a thrown ball. Most people would have given him a Victoria Cross, but Toronto is different.

It is one of the very few remaining cities in North America with three independent newspapers. Each one of them feels superior to the other, and two of them are possibly right. The ignorant Americans are all upset about the necessity of wearing snowshoes to the World Series, if the Blue Jays make it that far, as they threaten to do. (By the way, the World Series has nothing to do with global domination, although it sounds that way. The title comes from a trophy originally donated by the old *New York World* newspaper. You could look it up.)

Back to the weather. Americans, you see, spend their lives seated before the evening news, ending with the weather forecast that explains that "a cold front is moving down from Canada." Canada comes across as a rigid lump of ice slightly larger than that which sunk the *Titanic*. As we all know, the temperatures in Toronto are basically those of Detroit, Chicago, Milwaukee or New York, all of which at last look had ball teams that did not play in mukluks.

Toronto, aside from lying south of Vancouver, also lies south of such cities as Seattle and Minneapolis. It is south of the states of Washington, Montana and North Dakota. It is south of much of Oregon, Idaho, South Dakota, Minnesota, Wisconsin and Maine. It is south of parts of New Hampshire, Vermont, New York, Michigan and Wyoming. It is difficult to say something nice about Toronto, but occasionally the truth must out.

Toronto is absolutely gaga over Yonge Street, which is the longest and possibly ugliest main street on earth. The most expensive women in Canada now reside in Toronto, hanging about the Courtyard Café and Hazelton Lanes, absolutely dripping in Gucci and Rolex until you need a geiger counter to force your way past their spritzers. Toronto also has a lot of trees, and therefore squirrels. I think we can say with some sense of certainty that Toronto leads the nation in sea gulls combined with squirrels. It is a good image.

As the world will find if the city makes it into the World Serious, Toronto has the worst baseball stadium in baseball. It was designed neither for baseball nor football but for an agricultural fair–cum–rock-concert. As a result, Toronto suffers severely from a bad case of dome envy, which is something like penis envy except that it is more rounded. Montreal has a dome that forgot a roof, and Vancouver has a real dome (the dumbest place in the world in which to play baseball), and, therefore, Toronto has an urgent need to shut out the sunshine. It will probably succeed.

If you must know, the average October temperature in Toronto is 49° F (so Americans can understand this), while Detroit is 51.9, Milwaukee at 51 and Pittsburgh at 53. What everyone remembers is that the very first time the Blue Jays played at home, on April 7, 1977, it snowed. That made all the wish-fulfilment newscasts in the United States, naturally, and the image has remained.

There are a lot of tall buildings in Toronto. This is because Canada was first settled by a group of Scots Presbyterians. Being Scots Presbyterians, they worshipped money and set up the Canadian banking system, which is the tightest labor union in Christendom, outranking the postal workers and the Teamsters. Canada is the savings-account capital of the world because of these pinch-faced philosophers. To make room for all this stored loot, which the bankers use to buy their six-piece, bulletproof suits from Harry Rosen, they had to build all these buildings, mostly on the same corner, all of which except one have the architectural originality of a Lego set. This is why there are a lot of tall buildings in Toronto.

Toronto is the home of many famous people, many of whom don't live in Toronto. It is famous for Pierre Berton, the one-man industry. He happens to live in Kleinburg, Ont. Toronto's most famous journalist is Peter Newman, who lives on Vancouver Island. And so it goes on.

The other matter about Toronto that matters is that it secretly wants to be part of the United States. It worships money and therefore looks to the source. New York has a boor called George Steinbrenner, so Toronto counters with Harold Ballard. New York has a disgrace called a subway system, so Toronto counters with its own bargain basement—the Maple Leafs.

There are many similarities, and tourists do not have to be frightened. The weather is not the problem. It is the frigidity of the natives. Careful not to nick yourself on the prickles of their charisma. The Perrier is safe to drink.

So Pierre Trudeau, the former idealistic Montreal professor who wrote in Cité Libre *in 1963 that Liberals were "men who tremble with anticipation because they have seen the rouged face of power," once in power as prime minister fixed up with plush jobs 26 of the 38 Grit MPs defeated in the 1972 election?*

His mantra of power-equals-patronage was simply improved upon by Brian Mulroney, who taught Jean Chrétien how to improve upon that.

Canada is a very simple country. It is very simple to divine, if you are a reasonably bright young man and reasonably ambitious, that there is one obvious way to the top. Become a Liberal.

The political historians record that Francisco Franco ruled Spain for 36 years. It is considered remarkable. What almost no one notes is the only other "democratic" nation that has been dominated for so long, so completely, by one party.

For 62 of the last 78 years, ever since 1921, the Liberals have ruled Ottawa. Save only by John Diefenbaker's tumultuous, cabinet-revolt 6 years, the juvenile 9 months of Joe Clark, the remarkable 9 years of Brian Mulroney and the 15 minutes of Kim Campbell.

The way to the top is to become a Liberal. Prime example would be Roméo LeBlanc, a decent and not-spectacular guy from a very modest back-ground in New Brunswick.

After a solid, honest stint as a CBC reporter, he became press secretary to Prime Minister Lester Pearson. And so on the rise. Press secretary for Pierre Trudeau for a bit. Then fisheries minister in, of course, the Trudeau cabinet.

Next, as it comes to all good faithful and loyal Liberals, the Senate. Jean

Chrétien, since it was the turn for a francophone in Rideau Hall, asked hockey icon Jean Béliveau to fill the slot.

Béliveau, a gentleman nonpareil but a political innocent, told friends in the press that he had turned down the invitation—a no-no. No one else in Quebec wanted to be known as the second choice, and Chrétien was stuck.

LeBlanc, technically a francophone since he was an Acadian from New Brunswick, was the solution. Only one problem. The lady he was living with, but not churched, sister of the Canadian ambassador to the United Nations, Bob Fowler, presented a problem.

Get churched immediately, and the appointment would be made. The church was found, the appointment was made. That's why it's great to be a Liberal, and you want to get ahead, and God's in His Heaven in Grit Canada.

December 15, 1975

Blessed are they who throw in with the Liberals, for they shall never want

So Franco is dead. There have been the usual moral cluck-cluckings from the editorial pages over the fact one regime ruled Spain for 36 years. What is strange is that no one draws the parallel with another regime that has dominated one country so thoroughly—the Liberal party of Canada. The Liberals have ruled Canada 38 of the past 49 years, 43 of the past 54. We all talk about Spain as the last great dictatorship, but is there any other "democratic" country in the world that has been dominated so completely by one party? The Liberals use a different method of sustaining themselves in power than Franco did, but it is just as successful and in its own way destroys the parliamentary system.

The Liberal method is to co-opt talent from the civil service, put it into political life, then return it safely to its own secure reward back in the civil service. It is Tinker to Evers to Chance, the taxpayer paying for it every step of the way. It accounts for the current bloodless technocrat cast to the Liberal front bench, since so many of its predominant figures are drawn from the civil service. John Diefenbaker says Pierre Trudeau is "not a House of Commons man" in that he has no real feel or respect for the chamber. He is entirely correct, of course. How could Trudeau have any essential feel for the House when his first choice in the governmental process was in the non-elected category? (He served as a Privy Council aide before being induced to put his credentials before the voters.)

Mitchell Sharp, who is one of the worst House leaders in history, comes by his ineptitude honestly. He had been a civil servant for 15 years before rapidly reaching his Peter Principle in politics. The aloof Bud Drury travelled the same route.

I was having some drinks the other day with Jack Pickersgill, who maintains the only reason the Tories haven't been able to achieve power more often is that they are stupid. I argued there might be more to it, such as the Liberal recipe of which Pickersgill is the outstanding example. He started as a third secretary in External Affairs back in 1937, was a sly aide to both Mackenzie King and St. Laurent, then came out front as a politician in 1953. As transport minister in the 1960s he invented the Canadian Transport Commission and then resigned from politics to become its first chairman. He now, thanks to various grants, writes entertaining books explaining why the Liberals were always right. In the world of Tinker to Evers to Chance, he's in the Hall of Fame.

Edgar Benson, when he grew bored as defence minister, was fixed up as the next president of the CTC. Gérard Pelletier became ambassador to France, a suitable rank that Sharp, Drury and Jean Marchand will soon fall heir to. It is generally ignored that the Liberals even have their own corporate pastureland for the care and feeding of out-of-work cabinet ministers. It is called Brascan (formerly Brazilian Light and Power), the conglomerate that controls Labatt

Breweries, Ogilvie Flour Mills and everything down to Laura Secord candy. Mitchell Sharp, a deputy minister under C.D. Howe, was recycled through a vice-presidency in Brascan before emerging as an authentic Liberal cabinet minister in 1963. The late Robert Winters, another Howe protégé, ran Rio Algom until he returned to Ottawa to joust for the 1968 Liberal leadership. He finished second to Trudeau and 31 days later emerged as new president of Brazilian Light and Power. Yet another Howe career man, Jack Nicholson, was a managing director of the same company for five years before surfacing as a Liberal cabinet minister. When he left politics, Ottawa made him B.C. lieutenant-governor. The present Brascan president, Jake Moore, is a former partner of Walter Gordon at Clarkson, Gordon. Energy Minister Alastair Gillespie was vice-president of another Gordon company.

And so it goes. The only time the internal railway raises attention is when the Liberals become absolutely too arrogant about it. The briefest immersion course in history belongs to Pierre Juneau, who resigned as CRTC chairman in August so he could be parachuted into the Hochelaga by-election to justify his cabinet post. Defeated in October, by November he had been handed a $50,000-range, unspecified job in Trudeau's office. Juneau, a heretofore honorable man, must blush a lot these days.

Most insulting of all was the payoff to Jack Austin, who served only 15 months as the PM's principal secretary and was rewarded with a $29,300 rest in the Senate. Since the clever Austin is only 43 and the law will not require him to retire until 75, it means a record payoff of $937,600. A fellow Liberal senator, as outraged at the appointment as were most B.C. voters, makes the point that the Senate is legitimately regarded as a slumber home for loyal party workers and dutiful bagmen. "Austin's total volunteer effort for the party," says this senator, "consists of 60 days—the time he put in running unsuccessfully for a seat in Vancouver-Kingsway years ago. Every other job he has had in government has been in the $40,000 to $50,000 bracket."

When Trudeaumania died after 1968, there were 38 government MPs defeated or retired in the 1972 election. The Liberals managed to fix up 26 of them with jobs. Calgary's Pat Mahoney became a federal court judge at $38,000. Martin O'Connell was fixed up in the PM's office. The charming John Roberts was taken on the PM's staff. Yves Forest became a judge of the Superior Court in Quebec. Russell Honey was appointed a county court judge. And on and on ...

There would be an instant outcry in Britain if the civil service were as abused. The Trudeau Liberals seem intent on destroying the clear separation of politics and civil service necessary in the parliamentary system. Trudeau even uses his own office as a reservoir for candidates. The brainy Marc Lalonde moved into active politics from there. Gordon Gibson is now B.C. Liberal leader. Francis Fox is an MP. Roméo LeBlanc, the former Trudeau press secretary, is fisheries minister.

We do not have the multi-party system so much as one-party rule. Do you think Franco seriously viewed that as much different from his own regime? Do not sneer at dictatorships when this country is ruled by a shrewd, cynical oligarchy that has arranged the control and passing on of power.

One of the little-known facts about René Lévesque, father of Quebec separation, is that he was born and raised closer to Halifax that he was to Montreal. New Carlisle, to be exact, on the underbelly of the Gaspé Peninsula.

He also (hello there, Pierre Trudeau) had a very good war. He joined the U.S. Army as a military journalist. He endured the Blitz in London with such as Edward R. Murrow. He arrived in Milan in 1945 in time to see the dead Mussolini hung by his heels in the city square.

On his celebrated Radio-Canada television show, he travelled Africa. And covered the Korean War for the CBC. Claude Ryan said René had travelled and knew Canada better than either Ryan or Trudeau. In person, he was unforgettable.

September 30, 1985

Another flourish of symbols

There are few enough symbolic gestures René Lévesque—the icon of symbols—can make these days. He was the symbol of the Quiet Revolution, nationalizing Quebec's hydro resources and signalling to the ruling Anglos that the rules had changed. He was the symbol of separatism, frightening the rest of the country out of its wits. And then, to the disgust of the Parti Québécois true believers, he became the symbol of sovereignty-association—perhaps, maybe, somewhere down the road, off in the fuzzy future. That shattered the party he founded, and now, his usefulness over and his tenure down to the last few days, he has just one symbolic gesture left: he makes his final political tour in the United States, to emphasize his point that he feels more comfortable and at home in that "foreign" country than he does in a Canada he does not believe in.

He is tracked down in Philadelphia—another symbol: Liberty Bell and

Independence Hall and all that. Is this deliberate, this final little show of affection for America in his dying days in power, one last cocking of the snoot at Ottawa and all those visions that hound him north of the border? "Of course," he says. He is relaxed and tanned, his health restored from those traumatic days when his party was disintegrating before his eyes. Women who recognize him are drawn, as always, to the tiny man—his nervous energy a magnet.

Can he say when he decided he indeed feels "more at home" in the United States than north of the longest-misunderstood border in the world? "I can pinpoint it for you precisely. When I decided to join the service, I had to decide who would kick me in the you-know-where." If he was going to be kicked around, he wanted to be kicked around by the American army rather than the Canadian one.

That would be after he was kicked out of his Laval university law class by Louis-Philippe Pigeon—later a Supreme Court justice—for smoking. René, one imagines, rather likes the kicks. The lady who was his family's neighbor in little New Carlisle on the Gaspé Peninsula, where he grew up, says he had to be tied to a tree on a leash because he fought so much with the other kids.

A grand and interesting war as a U.S. Army correspondent behind him, he has never forgotten his fond feelings for Americans. His government now has eight offices representing Quebec sprinkled through the United States, from

New York to Atlanta to Los Angeles. He muses on how he became almost too well known to Americans—chortling about the old panicky "Castro of the North" descriptions.

Claude Ryan once told this scribbler that he believed René Lévesque knew and understood Canada better than he. Lévesque enthusiastically agrees. "You know why? He never worked a day in his life. He knew more about the Constitution—that bum!—than I did, but I knew the country because I had to earn a living." He points out as an aside that he covered two wars—the big one and the Korean War. He symbolizes a lot of things, including the grand old days of the CBC.

One gets the impression that he is not excited at the prospect of Pierre Marc Johnson, the humorless doctor-lawyer, succeeding him as the second leader of the PQ. He mentions several times how Johnson "started fast," but seems more interested in the chances of Manpower Minister Pauline Marois and the potential inherent in having a woman lead the party that is shoving him out. The impression remains that it was Johnson, son of former Union Nationale premier Daniel Johnson, who initiated the PQ crisis early this year by threatening to undercut Lévesque with a pledge to shelve the independence theme. The PQ became just another political party when its inner machinations equalled that of its tired old rivals.

His beloved Quebec? It is like "spring is busting out all over." He goes back to the 1960s when "the basic infrastructure had to be laid down," not mentioning that he was one with Jean Lesage and Eric Kierans in those days. Back then, only four per cent of the Québécois went to university. Now, he recites proudly, the figure is 20 per cent.

Best of all, one in six is in business or economics courses. That compares with one in 10 in the rest of Canada. It is the "maturing of the Quiet Revolution." In the bad old days of the Westmount Rhodesians, the 82 per cent of the population that was francophone owned just 20 per cent of the economy. Now, the man who is bowing out says with satisfaction that the number has risen to 40 per cent.

He is too elfish and too impish—the little boy tied to a tree—to appear the statesman, but the pride and the perspective are there. He basks in the attention of American academics on this final tour, they seeing him not as a threat or a curiosity but as a historical figure who tried a brave experiment and, having failed, looks back with humor and no visible bitterness.

He is going to hand over his power immediately (when the cool Johnson is chosen September 29). He is going to travel in Scandinavia, one of the few places in the world he has never been. He is spending two hours every day at the typewriter, putting it all down. "But not—definitely not—political memoirs." The old energies seem to be returning.

"You know what I would really like to do? To take a Grade 1 class—the little kids—and teach them things." He pulls an American dollar bill from his pocket. "Teach them that this is an American dollar and this is a Canadian dollar and explain some things." That's René, ever the teacher, always the symbol.

The best-read politician in Canada is the man who would break it up. Lucien Bouchard, as a youth, devoured the histories of Alexander, Hannibal, Napoleon and Julius Caesar.

Son of a truck driver, he learned Latin and Greek. He absorbed Sophocles, Horace, Euripides and Plato. At 21 he had not tasted a drop of liquor. Monsignor Morin, the head of his diocese, one day, in the presence of the altar boy's parents, placed his red biretta on the youngster's head and predicted, "Lucien will be our cardinal."

There was one anomaly. When Bouchard graduated from Laval law school with his new friend Brian Mulroney, he still could not speak English. He retreated to a law practice in his native Kingdom of the Saguenay, so remote behind the mountain wall of the Laurentians that no decent road from the highlands was built until the 1950s.

Chicoutimi thought of itself as closer to Europe than to New York. Lucien's father, before he died at 70, had been outside his province only twice in his lifetime—both times to the United States.

Lucien's mother, at 90, was asked by an American magazine what she thought of English Canadians. She replied honestly that she had no opinion because she had never met one.

Lucien Bouchard, the best-read, most dangerous man in the country, is now 61. He knows his time—and Quebec separatism's time—is running out. He will be approaching pension age before the next Quebec election happens.

His young, second wife, who he met on an airplane between Paris and London when he was our ambassador to France, hates politics and wants to return to her native California and her family. Their two young boys, as is well recorded, "spit" whenever they hear the word "referendum."

She lives with them in Montreal; he sleeps in a monkish bunker in Quebec City during the week, Montreal only a weekend retreat.

A coupla years back, the provincial premiers had one of their usual windbag annual conferences at St.-Andrews-by-the-Sea, that lovely old half-timbered retreat for the rich, overlooking the Bay of Fundy from New Brunswick's underbelly.

As every reporter knows, these are mainly photo-op fakes, with allegedly serious closed sessions sprinkled more elaborately with golf games and, as this one, barbeque-by-the-beach where the real gossip and secrets are traded.

Bouchard was there, with his usual large entourage, and there was ample time over the weekend for serious conversation, if anyone actually wanted it.

Your humble scribe approached him with an idea. Dalton Camp, the only intelligent person left in the Conservative party in Canada, who lives in rural splendor in New Brunswick, writes a column for the largest-circulation news-paper in Canada, the Toronto Star. He happened to be among the bored gaggle of journalists hanging around on the grass outside the conference hall, waiting, well, basically for the grass to grow. (Camp, though I do not share his political philosophy, somehow over the years had become a friend. It is, I suppose, mainly because he has a sense of humor, is vastly intelligent —a rarity in his old party—and does not take himself seriously.)

Your humble scribe, as I was saying, suggested to Bouchard, that with my Maclean's column and syndicated newspaper column, along with the reach of Camp's Toronto Star, we could explain his separatism argument to a very large proportion of the Canadian population outside Quebec. Since nothing else was happening, how about it?

A polite man, he politely replied that he would have his people get back to me.

Some hours later, while nothing was happening but the network paparazzi watching the grass grow, Bouchard and his numerous camp-followers were observed relaxing in the lounge of the host hotel. One of his people, as promised, came over and relayed the information that the premier would be too busy with conference business to accept the invitation for a joint interview.

Nine hours later, of course, they were still there in the lounge, nothing happening, except the grass growing. He had no interest in talking to "foreign"—i.e., outside Quebec—scribes. His mind is made up. Foreign voters would never be voting in a future Quebec referendum.

There never will be another Quebec referendum on separation—at least not in Bouchard's political career. He always has been more interested in power than in principle, and the hard-core Parti Québécois apparatchiks know that.

No leader willingly commits political suicide, and he has conceded, after the second separatist loss at the polls, that he will call a third referendum only when the "winning conditions" are there. Meaning only when his polls tell him he can win.

The polls, alas, tell him that 75 per cent of Quebeckers are sick and tired of the argument and don't want another referendum during his mandate. With the province's, and especially Montreal's, economy finally coming back, they want jobs and political stability.

Lucien Bouchard, an angry man all his life—his brother Roch has confided that, because of their mother's intense religiosity, "we felt guilt in the simple fact of trying to enjoy life. We couldn't laugh much"—is going to end his career an angry man.

March 28, 1994

Understanding Canada's enemy

The most intriguing man in Canada at the moment is the man who would break it up. He's more important than Jean Chrétien, or any provincial premier, or any cabinet minister or high industrialist. Whatever one thinks about Lucien Bouchard's aims, one must first attempt to understand him. The man who would ruin the country deserves to be understood.

The politician who now leads Her Majesty's Loyal Opposition in the House of Commons began to write his life story, *On the Record*, on July 1, 1991, the day after the founding of the Bloc Québécois. It was published in Quebec in 1992 and has now been translated into English by Dominique Clift, the distinguished Quebec journalist.

What is most obvious is that this is an extremely intelligent man. More intelligent—in a cerebral if not practical sense—than Mulroney, his literary and classical references putting him near the Lévesque and Trudeau level.

Intelligence, of course, never excludes nonsense. In a foreword added for this 1994 edition, he writes: "Jean Chrétien cannot claim, as Trudeau did, to represent Quebec. Facing Chrétien's 19 federalist Liberal MPs now are 54 members of the Bloc Québécois who will speak up for the sovereigntist reality of Quebec, formerly hidden from view at the federal level."

All true, naturally. Then this: "Quebec sovereigntists do not want to destroy a country but to build another one"—the non sequitur of all time.

Bouchard's tale is a remarkable one, a man whose life has seemed to be in search of a cause. He tells of watching his father, who never went past the fourth grade, attempting at the kitchen table to write to the first of his sons who went to study in France and finally dissolving in tears and crumpling the sheet of paper in despair after a half-hour, surrendering to his inability to write and communicate "with the son who had left to follow his own dreams."

In remote Saguenay–Lac-Saint-Jean, the young Lucien would ride along with his father, exhausted by nightfall, on his delivery truck route carrying lumber, nails, cement and sawdust.

The religious undertone was established early. All five of his father's sisters entered a convent and stayed there. Lucien as an altar boy served mass at 6 a.m. Even before university, "I believed I was destined for the priesthood."

This is a man with a mission. The church called early, and he eventually rejected it. Now his mission is a new country with a seat at the United Nations, along with Zambia and Bangladesh.

Sent to a rigorous classical education from the Oblate fathers at the Collège de Jonquière, the son of the unlettered truck driver discovered literature—Jules Verne, Dickens, Balzac, Victor Hugo—sometimes devouring two books between 4 p.m. and midnight.

The pattern was set early. With a classmate, he launched the school paper whose name *Le Cran* (boldness) "said it all." Rushing to be in the front ranks on Charles de Gaulle's memorable visit to Quebec City, he was crushed by the crowd, fell face first into a steel wire barricade and in pain looked up at the general. "He held out his hand, I grasped it eagerly."

Entering Laval law school, the boy from the bush discovered a remarkable number of anglophones who had gravitated to Quebec City—Michael Meighen, Peter White, George McLaren. And Brian Mulroney.

"His most striking quality was his charm." Bouchard was prophetic even then. "His ambition had a romantic aura: he saw the world as something to conquer rather than to change."

His break with his 30-year friend, Mulroney, is well documented. What is interesting is his journey there. On his initial political speech as a Laval student: "For the first time, I experienced the unique sensation that comes from communicating with a crowd."

He was a prodigious reader, taking in Proust and Gibbon's *The Decline and Fall of the Roman Empire*, reading *Time* at age 15 with the aid of Webster's dictionary.

A Liberal supporter at first, he confesses to coming to "independence" and signing a Parti Québécois card by 1972. He almost ran for René Lévesque's party. He wrote speeches for Jacques Parizeau.

Before being "stupefied" by the No vote in the 1980 referendum, "It seemed logical for the revolution to find its quiet accomplishment in sovereignty. An aura of inevitability gave it the elegance Einstein sought of a mathematical equation describing the perfection of the laws of nature."

Since that time, he has been a bitter man. He does not seem to see the hypocrisy—while keeping his PQ membership alive for 15 years—of accepting Mulroney's gift of an ambassadorship to Paris, a safe Tory seat and passage into the federal cabinet.

The first Bouchard, with his stonecutter's tools, arrived in Quebec City in 1650. Lucien Bouchard's father died without ever seeing the old country and left Quebec only twice, to see the horse races at Saratoga and Maurice Richard play in a Stanley Cup final in Boston.

But three of his sons earned doctorates in France. Unfortunate that Lucien Bouchard cannot see that Canada proved not too badly for his truck-driver father. Anyone who wants to keep Canada together might read this tome. It is best to know well one's enemy.

July 17, 1989

Why the country is breaking up

T he most surprising things surprise newspapermen, supposedly the most worldly types of all. The most amazing things (i.e., the most mundane things) make huge headlines. The newspaper before me, the *Victoria Times–Colonist*, is the oldest paper on North America's Pacific Coast, older than anything in California or elsewhere. You'd think the chaps would have developed some maturity by now. But there it is, a story spread right across the top of page 1—revealing the astounding news that 45 per cent of Canadians are unable to locate Ottawa on a map.

So? So what else is new? The Gallup pollsters deliver this large scoop to us, as if we should be shocked, or concerned, or worried. In a geography test, they drew an outline map of Canada, with provincial boundaries marked. Numbers were placed on the locations of 23 towns and cities across the country. The 1,029 Canadians polled were asked to locate and identify a list of 12 cities. The results indicated almost half the citizens of this fair land couldn't find Ottawa.

I don't know where the dumb people at Gallup have been. Anyone else could have told them. Ottawa doesn't exist. It is strictly a state of mind. Taxpayers don't think of it as an actual place—like Kamloops or Chicoutimi or Medicine Hat. It is simply a black hole, situated somewhere, where the swivel servants live so as to milk the rest of the country. It's, well, somewhere, but its exact location is immaterial, since it is unconnected by its mind-set to any place where real live people reside and breathe and get on with life.

The Gallup result proves what we have maintained all along. Everyone knows where London is, or Paris or Rome and even Washington. Ottawa? Does it matter? You can't get there from anywhere and you can't get from there to anywhere. So it doesn't really matter that, for 45 per cent of Canadians, it rattles around somewhere off in the void, growing ever more forgettable now that Eugene Whelan and Jack Horner have left.

The Gallup types found that one per cent of Canadians questioned thought that the nation's capital was in northern Manitoba. I suggest they misinterpreted the survey. I think the respondents meant that it should be in northern Manitoba. Just outside Thompson would be about right. The polar bears drifting into town in winter would be the first actual contact the snivel servants would have with red-blooded inhabitants of this dominion since Queen Victoria plunked it up there wherever it is that the 1,029 taxpayers couldn't find.

Another one per cent thought Ottawa was in Labrador. Canada, if you must know, would be better governed if Ottawa were in Labrador. As it now is, wherever that is, it is a recession-proof enclave, with the highest family income in the country, a bottomless sump hole for our money. In Labrador, we would get some action, some movement, as the bureaucrats and the politicians raced through legislation so as to get to the Caribbean vacations.

I should not be too hard on the Gallup actually, since their meticulous information-collectors have come up with an even more revealing statistic. It seems 53 per cent of Canadians couldn't find the location of Toronto on the map. Four per cent thought it was somewhere in Western Canada, which would puzzle anyone who went through the Depression, not to mention those living in Tofino, Gimli, and Climax, Saskatchewan.

The reason I suspect this survey is accurate, after all, is that 29 per cent of Toronto residents couldn't locate their own city on the map. This figures. On any given day, if you walk down any downtown Toronto street, or enter any Toronto office building, there are some 29 per cent of the faces you encounter that are oblivious as to where they are. They are in pursuit of The Buck. You can detect it on their visages, their nostrils palpitating in lust for a deal, a contract they can pull off over lunch that will ensure a $600,000 bungalow that is only a 90-minute drive in the morning from the slurbs.

They could be in Cleveland or Dallas or Pittsburgh or Atlanta. It wouldn't make any difference. They couldn't be in San Francisco or Montreal or Vancouver or Positano—but that's another subject for another day. The location of their own city, in the context of Canada, doesn't matter.

It's why the country is breaking up, Toronto concerned only with its baseball rivalry with Boston and the Yankees while Swift Current and Truro and Grand Forks are trying to figure out how to pay taxes to a black hole on the map that, in reality, doesn't exist.

Quebec (sadly) is going its own way as sure as God made little green apples—the survey showing the most dismal response from Quebecers, 67 per cent from that province locating fewer than half of the cities. They can be forgiven, in a way, because of their indifference, but Ottawa cannot escape being the main culprit. A capital that is unable to establish itself in the minds of Canadians as an actual location must, perforce, disappear in a Gallup poll.

To be noticed, one must have a personality. It applies to cities as well as individuals. The town that fun forgot ain't got any personality, since the people who live there are essentially selfish, revelling in their recession-proof, highest-family-income insularity, and so Canadians when asked where Ottawa is actually located come up with a blank and their eyes glaze over and they answer honestly to the pollster at the door.

The end result of the feminist movement—was it Germaine Greer who said it? —was Dutch treat. It certainly hasn't resulted in major changes in Canada's Parliament.

Judy LaMarsh was actually quite a powerful cabinet minister in the Lester Pearson government—and personally forced the powers-that-be to build a ladies' loo within sprinting distance of the cabinet's weekly meeting.

Flora MacDonald was the foreign minister of the Joe Clark government, as Barbara McDougall was in the Mulroney government. Jeanne Sauvé (born in Saskatchewan, by the way) was Speaker of the House of Commons under Trudeau, and then Governor General. Pat Carney was the only minister of the Mulroney regime—being Irish, as he was—who was allowed to shout at him in anger across the cabinet table, he allowing it since they shared the same emotional genes.

Today Sheila Copps, deposed from her previous deputy prime minister role because of her irrational behavior, is the only influential (and that problematical) female member of the Chrétien cabinet.

Alexa McDonough, the shrill heiress to her father's millions, is no more effective as the NDP leader than Audrey McLaughlin was. Deborah Grey, the witty and brassy Reform backup to Parson Manning, only emphasizes in Question Period each day a reminder to Canadians that she has the wit and brio that he lacks.

The feckless Bloc Québécois, the home of all that province's women who have that great flair and passion, has never yet produced a single female on its front benches who can light up the TV screen with her intelligence and separatist religiosity.

It's strange, but when I sit in the Ottawa Press Gallery, looking down at this dull bunch, all I see is a sea of blue serge, pinstripes and bad ties.

There ain't been much progress.

October 17, 1994

A woman's place is in Parliament

W hen Audrey McLaughlin first entered the House of Commons, she sat watching the men bellow at each other in the farce known as Question Period. After several months of observing the posturing and insults, she was reminded of her favorite episode of the *Murphy Brown* TV sitcom.

"The men in the newsroom are having a huge fight that's all about their egos," McLaughlin recalled. "Murphy watches them in disgust for a while, and finally she bursts out, 'Oh, why don't you all just drop your pants and I'll get a ruler?'"

The anecdote is recounted in *The Gilded Ghetto: Women and Political Power in Canada*, a new book by Calgary journalist Sydney Sharpe. To be published this month, it details the strange, isolated ("unspeakably lonely," in Kim Campbell's phrase) life of women sent to serve their country in Ottawa.

Even in retrospect, the numbers (or lack of them) are remarkable. The first female MP, Agnes Macphail, sat alone among all the blue serge from 1921 to 1935 before another woman, Martha Black, joined her. For five more years, they could at least see each other, but there wasn't much chance of co-operation, Macphail being a CCFer and Black a Conservative.

In the four decades from 1921 to 1964, only 17 women were elected to Parliament. And seven of them got there only because they inherited the ridings of their dead husbands.

Sharpe is good at recording the sheer anger of the women trapped in the boys' club. When she wrote Iona Campagnolo asking for an interview, the former Liberal cabinet minister fired back a furious response, asking why "a man" would dare write such a book. The author had to explain that she was burdened as a woman whose name was Sydney.

Sharpe is sharp at setting the historical scene. Women in France weren't even allowed to vote, since they were still not considered citizens, until 1944— in recognition of their war effort, after the Hun had been expelled. British women finally got the vote in 1928—15 years after a suffragette threw herself under the horses at the Derby at Epsom Downs and was trampled to death "in a ghastly example of appropriate symbolism" by the steed owned by King George V. (Women in New Zealand got the vote in 1893.)

The author notes shrewdly that all the symbols of parliamentary government are still drawn from the manly arts of war. The chief official in the Commons is the sergeant-at-arms, who carries the mace. His counterpart in the Senate is the gentleman usher of the black rod.

Campagnolo notes that all the paintings in Parliament's corridors are of men and war and swords and blood. The few female images are British queens, including Victoria, whose statue apparently was first guarded by an imperial lion "in a state of too-obvious virility." In deference to shocked females and curious children, his bronzed penis was sawed off in 1908—"the only emasculation known to have occurred on Parliament Hill."

What is a girl to do? For one thing, on Parliament Hill where hundreds of women work for MPs, Tory Barbara Greene demanded better lighting after she was physically assaulted in a dark parking lot. Sharpe says the highly respected *Toronto Star* columnist Carol Goar was also mugged in the same area.

The new band of women MPs, cutting across party lines, got a tuck shop carrying things women need—pantyhose and sanitary napkins. Writes Sharpe: "Within the bustling community of Parliament Hill, with its myriad services aimed at males, women were given less consideration than they would receive in any rural Canadian town with a drugstore."

She has an interesting theory of one defensive mechanism that lonely, talented women—trapped in a male preserve—mount in the isolation. From Judy LaMarsh to Kim Campbell, they gain weight. Monique Bégin, slim and attractive when first arriving in the Commons from Quebec, confesses that she gained 60 pounds in six months after going into Trudeau's cabinet.

She devotes an entire chapter to Brian Mulroney, the classic MCP in youth, being educated by his wife and his female Tory mentors, eventually doing more than any PM to advance women in Ottawa. In his first cabinet when only nine per cent of all MPs were women, 21 per cent of his ministers were female.

She has the perceptive detail. Of all the calls received by Barbara McDougall's constituency office during the crucial FTA election, there were more about her hair than about the trade pact. She tells the reality: of all the women who have recently hit the top reaches in Canadian politics, they've all been either divorced or single—from Charlotte Whitton to Sheila Copps, Pat Carney, Flora MacDonald, LaMarsh, Bégin, the widowed Judy Erola and McDougall and on and on.

She ends on hope. While 66 Tory women candidates lost, meaning that with the NDP two of Canada's major parties had elected a grand total of two females, there was another side. The Grits ran 64 women; 36 of them won. Eight of the 10 Bloc Québécois women became MPs. Even the Reform, where the broads are supposed to serve coffee, elected seven of its 23 female candidates.

The percentage of women in Parliament rose from 13.4 to 18. In less than a decade since Mulroney signalled his approval, female participation has nearly doubled.

In 1968, at the height of femme fascination with Trudeaumania, exactly one woman, NDP's Grace MacInnis, was elected.

June 25, 1990

The Yanks have all they want

Why does everyone always look at the dark side of things? Why doesn't everyone take the positive side of things, a well-known feature on the back page? In every cloud there is some silver. We must look for it. The Meech mess has some silver in it. It is that the Americans, watching this incomprehensible mishmash from the outside, will be further dissuaded from any aspiration of acquiring our troubles.

Canadians, in their conceit, always assume that the voracious Yanks want ever more territory and cast covetous eyes this way. In truth, Americans are very insular people. They simply want to be left alone. They are isolationists by nature, being formed by peoples who left other lands because of their troubles and unhappiness there. Having founded the home of the rave and the land of the spree, they know they have discovered Nirvana and are content.

Americans did not seek out world leadership. It was thrust on them, willy-nilly, after the 1945 war because of the collapse of British energy and the rising threat of the Soviet Union. Most Americans resent the burden of foreign aid they have had to supply, just as a previous generation didn't like Woodrow Wilson's championing of the League of Nations. Most Americans, if they had their way, wish the United Nations would get to hell out of New York and go off to Geneva so the Swiss could figure out what to do with foreign diplomats with wall-to-wall limos who refuse to pay parking tickets.

Americans have yet to figure out what to do with their black population, which, although only 12 per cent of the 250 million total, gives more than 12 per cent trouble. Because Americans can't figure out what to do, their inner cities are being destroyed, drugs and crime are rampant, and a permanent underclass is being formed. You think Americans want to inherit Quebec too, not to mention Newfoundland?

The surging Hispanic population is bringing increased pressure on the idea of Spanish as an official second language. Do you think Americans want to wrestle with the problem of assimilating seven million proud Québécois who are accustomed to official language status? Canada can't figure out Quebec after 123 years. Do Iowa, Mississippi and New Mexico want to have a try?

The standard theory up here is that the Americans lust after our water and our resources. Yes, do they know they would have to take Bill Vander Zalm too? That should frighten them. The thought of having to listen to Jean Chrétien's eloquence—in either language—would give them pause to think.

One of the hilarious things about the innocent arrogance of John Buchanan

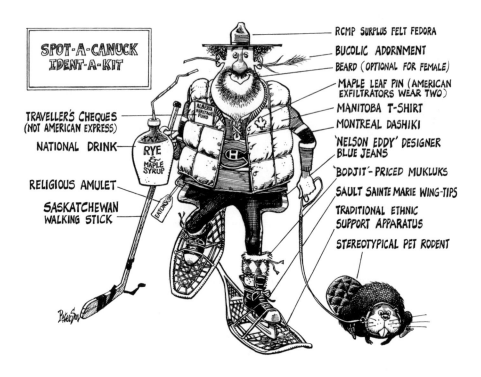

SPOT-A-CANUCK IDENT-A-KIT

RCMP SURPLUS FELT FEDORA
BUCOLIC ADORNMENT
BEARD (OPTIONAL FOR FEMALE)
MAPLE LEAF PIN (AMERICAN EXFILTRATORS WEAR TWO)
MANITOBA T-SHIRT
MONTREAL DASHIKI
'NELSON EDDY' DESIGNER BLUE JEANS
'BODJIT'-PRICED MUKLUKS
SAULT SAINTE MARIE WING-TIPS
TRADITIONAL ETHNIC SUPPORT APPARATUS
STEREOTYPICAL PET RODENT

TRAVELLER'S CHEQUES (NOT AMERICAN EXPRESS)
NATIONAL DRINK
RELIGIOUS AMULET
SASKATCHEWAN WALKING STICK

RYE & MAPLE SYRUP

was the assumption—given the leaving of Quebec—that the Atlantic provinces could just automatically join the United States. Who says the United States would want the Atlantic provinces?

Heavy-water plants that don't work? Fish stocks that have been plundered? A welfare-based mentality? K.C. Irving, for God's sake? And, thrown in to boot, Clyde Wells? The Yanks have troubles enough of their own.

Besides all this, there is the simple reality that the Americans don't have to try very hard to own Canada. They do that anyway, thanks to the lie-back-and-enjoy-it compliance of their hosts. The Prime Minister of the country proudly announced on his election that Canada was "open for business again." Meaning, rape. After one of the periodic spells of nationalism, in trying to repatriate its pride, Ottawa was now telling the Americans to revert to their usual role: running this country as a branchplant, frozen-banana republic.

When you can get the milk for free, why buy the cow?—as a million mothers have warned their daughters. The present government doesn't take this as a warning; it takes it as its credo of life. View its servile attitude to the instructions of Jack Valenti and the Hollywood film industry. View its (jump? how high?) attitude to American Express moving into Canadian banking. View its every-one-makes-mistakes attitude towards the U.S. invasion of Panama. If there is one thing Canada, in its hour of discontent, does not have to worry about, it is American intentions of expansion northward. America at the moment is turning ever more inward, as the developments in Germany and Eastern Europe diminish American power.

There are no longer any superpowers. Moscow is in terrible trouble with its economy and recalcitrant republics. America is worried about Japan and its own economic future. There are now no giants, just fears. Canadians are smug—more smug than they usually are—if they think Americans are spending their time at this point in their troubles wanting to invade Saskatchewan.

We should be content. Content in our knowledge that we just have the small problem of Quebec (and Clyde Wells) to deal with. The country will survive, warring as usual.

To a scribe who has recently been five years in Washington, viewing the American problems (and virtues) rather as a bemused visitor from Mars, one regards an American love for Canadian property as remote as a complete sentence of English from George Bush.

They have got much better things to do with their time, and so do we. Such as adapting to the never-solvable riddle-within-the-enigma of Quebec. Besides, the Americans don't have to buy us: Brian Mulroney is leasing us out, week by increasing week.

The American swallowing of Canada, following the American bullying of Canada, of course has advanced apace since this piece on bully boy Jack Valenti a decade ago. (Valenti is still with us, still bullying.)

The aborted Bill C-55—"stillborn" perhaps a more apt description— early this year simply reveals the supine Liberal government that blusters so much under Sheila Copps and then folds like a five-dollar suitcase when Washington shouts.

When the Cretenites ran for the hills under U.S. trade threats on the split-run magazine issue, it was estimated that the Americans had grabbed at least $100 million in concessions and might take 40 per cent of the Canadian industry's advertising market.

(There are some who might charge that this scribbler is in a certain conflict-of-interest position because he writes a little-read back page column in Maclean's. *You betcha!)*

October 30, 1989

No flying buns for a bully boy

O nly in Canada would we offer a platform to a bully from another nation to tell us how to run our country and our economy and our life. Only in Toronto would compliant hosts sit dutifully and listen to a foreigner lecture them about why their tentative ideas on their independence are incorrect. Only Canadians would sit silent, rather than pelt him with buns and boo him from the stage. We are so polite. So chicken.

Jack Valenti is a short, white-haired bully, one of the most powerful lobbyists in the United States, representing one of the richest lobbies in the United States, that being Hollywood's film industry. He is a fixture in Washington, welcome at the right White House parties, playing tennis with the right people, ever-ready to leap upon the subservient cousin called Canada.

The problem is that subservient Canada would like to gain just a teensy bit of control over the film industry in this country that the United States—being the United States and Canada being Canada—controls. (It is mean and picky to object, of course, the United States having controlled our oil industry and tire industry and auto industry and Mulroney industry for so long—but we try.)

Jack Valenti is frightened. He is frightened because little Canada is making motions of actually allowing some domestic control of film distribution. Hollywood, being Hollywood, feels Hollywood should be allowed to treat the rest of the world as Hollywood. Valenti has allowed that if little Canada is to be allowed what Canada wants to do, it would be "the thin edge of the wedge." Those sleeping Europeans might awaken and then, who knows, Asia. There goes the neighborhood. There goes monopoly control, and you know what that means?

Jack Valenti's salary and tennis club membership.

At issue is the nervous Ottawa attempt over years to suggest some Canadian control over the film distribution industry in this country and—a shocking proposal!—to increase the showing of Canadian movies in Canadian theatres. Since we have spent our lives watching Hollywood portrayals by Nelson Eddy in the Rockies, the cliché of our time, this indeed is a remarkable suggested innovation.

Marcel Masse, the current Valenti enemy, being the communications minister and cultural czar of all of Canada, has in process, somewhere through the Hampton Court Commons maze, legislation that would give domestic distributors a decent shot at bidding on films for showing in Canada. American distributors, being of good cheer, have always regarded it a hoot that they can dominate what is shown in Canadian flick parlors.

Hollywood distributors don't put a nickel into Canadian productions and they take about $1 billion a year out of this country. Valenti, as chairman of the Motion Picture Export Association of America, is paid to ensure that lovely ratio.

That's okay, but why does the Empire Club of Toronto not throw buns at him while, in his mellifluous Texas drawl, he piles on the bullying bafflegab? The Empire Club, one of the last refuges of what is left of the Toronto Establishment, is not a club at all but a speaking platform, the emanations from which are collected under red-leather covers at the end of the year, somewhat like the received speeches of Rudyard Kipling.

The Empire Club, being pristine and virginal, does not pay its speakers fees for their Olympian thoughts, and I have once received, at year-end, a leatherbound volume. I do not think, however, this excuses the appearance of Jack Valenti, who doesn't need the money, being the highest-paid hit man in the famed Elysian fields of Washington flackdom.

There are definitive reasons for Valenti's nervousness. The European Community, which supposedly is to become one chummy bunch in 1992 with the knocking down of borders and passports, has, despite the white-haired bully's frenetic lobbying, ruled that its TV stations beam at least a majority of European broadcasting.

There is the faint possibility—despite the Yankmania of this current government in Coma City—that something tentative can be laid down, if Ottawa has the courage. The bully Valenti killed off, with great vigor, the previous domestic film policy proposed by Flora MacDonald, the lady who could never hold great sway around the Mulroney cabinet table. The Tories allowed it to die on the agenda while they called an election. Flora died before the voters.

There now have been eight successive Ottawa communications ministers—twitchy and never backed up by the Prime Minister's Office—who have tried to strike a deal with the Hollywood studios that would result in plowing something back into Canadian film production. Canada, in its struggling film industry, has resembled East Germany to Moscow. The analogy is the same.

Jack Valenti, being a great free-enterpriser, of course would resent the comparison, would be appalled by it. He would be expected to do so. Nations that dominate and bully lesser nations are always astonished when it is pointed out what they are in fact doing.

The United States has dominated so long the cultural outfall of Canada, through films and magazines and other detritus, that it has no idea of its dominance. Canadians, because they are so used to the dominance, never think to object. And our timid, timid government does not have the guts to stand up to the obvious.

Which is why no one at the Empire Club had the wit to lob a bun at a bully who was insulting our integrity.

February 20, 1978

Only in Canada, you say? Pity ('cause you can't get there from here)

There's the story about the couple in London who, with blitz babies being evacuated due to German bombs, shipped their two children to stay with relatives in Vancouver. "They're landing at some place called Halifax," said their wire. "Please meet them at the dock."

The return wire from Vancouver contained the classic geography lesson: "Meet them yourself. You're closer than we are."

The poor Brits can be forgiven an understandable ignorance of this strange, freakish country that is 4,000 miles wide and basically 200 miles deep. They're foreigners. The galling thing is that the mandarin minds in Ottawa do not seem to appreciate the vastness of this land. (Why should they? They seldom budge.) That's the only conclusion that can be drawn from the ludicrous policies of the Canadian Transport Commission that have kept domestic air fares higher than international ones. It's cheaper to fly from Toronto to London than to visit Aunt Ermitrude in Vancouver.

It's one of the reasons why this disparate country is in danger of flying apart: the fractured regions in fact are encouraged—by Ottawa airline policy—to travel abroad rather than mix internally. Thus the north–south links are strengthened while east–west barriers go up. Toronto and Montreal flee to Florida and the West Indies. Prairie farmers head for Arizona. British Columbians go to Hawaii and California. There's more than just weather: it's more economical. This must be the only country in the world where the government stands aside while national air policy actively discourages domestic travel.

How hilarious is Ottawa? Public demand for domestic charters (since international charters have revolutionized air fares) was opposed before the CTC by Air Canada and CP Air but supported by Wardair, the big Edmonton-based charter firm. And the result? The CTC reluctantly gave in to the demand—and gave the nod to Air Canada and CP Air, while denying it to Wardair. Brilliant! Only when the Consumers' Association of Canada got into the act did the nervous Liberal cabinet, its days numbered, order the CTC last month to let Wardair in too. (The CTC is independent, except when the vote-hungry Liberals decide it isn't.) It's a tentative concession, with the government giving way to public demand.

The two major airlines claim there won't be that much demand for a 45-day booking, giving you a return fare for the price of a single trip plus $31, between any two points more than 700 miles apart. I'm not so sure. I suspect you could fill several jumbo jets full of superior Ontario and B.C. denizens who would like to jog their childhood memories of Saskatchewan and, in spring, the purest water in the world, the water that collects in shallow ponds in wheat fields. The ponds are the reflected blue of the unending Prairie sky and are always scalloped by little ripples from a breeze, origin unknown.

There is the hum—long forgotten—of telephone wires in the silence. One has forgotten there is such silence anywhere. In summer, the road in front of a car melts into liquid with the heat haze. One does not need a map since a route ahead can be devised in geometric patterns, the whisper lines of far-off telephone poles providing a key to where the roads intersect. In the distance, the next town can be detected from the wavering forms of two grain elevators that dance and sway through the heat.

I suggest anyone from the West would find useful a look at St. Jean Port Joli, one of those postcard river towns out toward the Gaspé, with thin slivers of farms and road marching perpendicularly from the river, right out of the history books. Visitors from the Prairies, accustomed to strict north–south bearings, feel disoriented and grow thoughtful as the fathomless St. Lawrence sweeps Canada to the sea.

I can mention the soothing beach, which dwarfs Waikiki in size, at Shediac, New Brunswick, one of the quiet wonders of that modest province. Or the view in the autumn from, say, about Ludlow, across the Miramichi River (not to be confused with the Restigouche, the Wapskehagen, the Upsalquitch, the Kouchibouguacis or the Tomogonops.)

The very best view in Alberta, if you must know, is from the town of High River, which spawned Joe Clark and is such a deceptive 30 miles from the soaring ice cream toppings of the Rockies that innocent tenderfeet, fooled by their eyes, have actually set out to stroll the "several miles" to the seductive range. It is one of the biological oddities of our time that Jim Coutts, Mr. Trudeau's principal secretary, comes from 18 miles down the road. (Nanton, Alta: home of "Canada's Finest Drinking Water." Coutts never touches the stuff.)

I can tell you about the tiny fishing village in Newfoundland where the children are like wild ponies and the trees grow no bigger than vegetables and the men come in from the sea with nothing and an anthropologist named Elliott Leyton writes and welcomes stray visitors. It would surprise most Canadians, who think of the Prairies as a sterile Sahara, that it abounds with water. That would be Manitoba and one of the eerie experiences of our time is floating along the Red River, above Winnipeg up to Selkirk, in a huge paddle steamer on a spring evening, a live Prairie schooner in full flight.

For Ontario I would pick Marmora, one of those never-changing towns east of Peterborough. Stolid, square brick houses with ample verandas, generous trees shielding the sun, a town out of Norman Rockwell epitomizing all that is Ontario, conservative, moral, stable, unimaginative.

I have never been to Prince Edward Island, but I understand they have potatoes. I've never met a potato I didn't love.

The main tourist sight in Nova Scotia, to tell the truth, is Harry Bruce, a scribbler who lives in Halifax. He is so grateful to see anyone from Nanton, or Marmora, that he will buy you a drink. Tell him I sent you.

In B.C. the most heavenly view north of Las Vegas is the vista out of the window of the beer parlor in a small hotel in a town called Kaslo, out across Kootenay Lake. There is a sight in the Okanagan Valley, on the highway between Kelowna and Vernon, when a swerve on a high cliff gives the first glimpse of Kalamalka Lake which, for some reason arranged by God and the tourist board, emanates bands of purple and blue and green from the rocks underneath one of the most stunning lakes in the world.

All this, I would suggest, is worth as much as yet another subsidized tour on a subsidized bus to Anne Hathaway's cottage. But Ottawa, being intelligent, undoubtedly knows better.

March 16, 1998

What a visitor from Mars would discover

A visitor from Mars, you see, arrives in Canada and can't figure out this debate on whether Quebec is going to separate or not. On examination, the puzzled visitor would find:

1. For 29 of the last 30 years, the prime minister of Canada has come from Quebec.
2. The current prime minister of Canada, in his second term, is from Quebec.
3. The chief justice of the Supreme Court of Canada is a francophone from Quebec.
4. Three of the nine justices on the Supreme Court of Canada—or 33⅓ per cent—are, by law, from Quebec, whose population of Canada is now down to 25 per cent.
5. The head of the Canadian Forces is a francophone from Quebec.
6. The Governor General of Canada in Rideau Hall is a francophone.
7. The Clerk of the Privy Council is a francophone from Quebec.
8. The Canadian ambassador to the United States in Washington is a francophone from Quebec.

9. The head prosecutor of the International War Crimes Tribunal in The Hague
   is a Quebec-born francophone.

10. The finance minister of Canada is from Quebec.

11. The perplexed visitor from space would then go to the history books. The
    visitor would discover that the problem goes back to the early morning of
    September 13, 1759.

12. Louis-Joseph de Montcalm-Grozon, Marquis de Montcalm de Saint-Véran,
    was a soldier at 12 and was severely wounded and made prisoner at the
    Battle of Piacenza. In the Seven Years' War, he assumed command of the

French troops in North America in 1756, and captured the British post of Oswego and also Fort William Henry, where some of the prisoners (men, women and children) were massacred by the Indian allies. In 1758, with a small force, he successfully defended Ticonderoga and then moved to Quebec City with 5,500 troops and prepared to defend it against a British attack.

13. James Wolfe, born in a vicarage in Kent, served against the Scottish Jacobites at Falkirk and Culloden. As a major-general, and commanding 9,000 men, he sailed from England in February of 1759 and in June landed below the cliffs of Quebec. His attack on Montcalm's strong position was completely foiled. Until at dawn on September 13, when he scaled the cliffs at an insufficiently guarded point with 4,500 men and found himself on the Plains of Abraham.

14. The French were routed, Quebec capitulated and, as the history books say, "its fall decided the fate of Canada." Wolfe died in the hour of his victory. Montcalm, mortally wounded, expired the next morning.

15. In most all historic struggles—the Battle of Waterloo, Trafalgar, the U.S. Civil War—there is a clear winner and a clear loser. What happened on the Plains of Abraham that September was that the French thought it was a TIE!

16. The distinguished American historian Henry Steele Commager once wrote that "never in the history of colonial wars has the victor treated the vanquished so generously."

17. The English, as we know, gave the French special protection for their Roman Catholic religion, their language, their civil law. Montreal, today, must be the only place in Christendom with a Protestant school board and a Catholic school board.

18. The result is that, in 1998, for the first time in recent memory, we have a leader of Her Majesty's Loyal Opposition in the House of Commons—Joe Clark taught himself French quite well—who cannot express himself intelligibly in French.

19. Every separatist in Montreal can swear that they personally know someone who, after the war, went into Eaton's on Ste-Catherine and was told to "speak white." They were probably correct.

20. We are down to a situation where we are told that the only way for the country not to be destroyed is for the curly-headed leader of the federal Conservative Party of Canada to give up his principles and give in to the overwhelming pressure and become the provincial leader of the Liberals in Quebec.

21. It recalls the old stand-up line: "I'm a politician and I have principles. If you don't like them—well, I have other principles."

22. Daniel Johnson Jr. should be given a Victoria Cross for, knowing he simply doesn't have the personality or verve to compete with St. Lucien, valiantly falling on his sword, thus preventing the Parti Québécois from calling a quickie spring election.

23. The Great Unwashed, out there before the voting booth, may not have IQs up there with Einstein, but they have great common sense and fairness. They know that any government that tries to take advantage of the confusion and weakness of the Opposition seeking a new leader would be punished mercilessly at an election. St. Lucien, knowing as much, has admitted as much.

24. He perhaps knows that a Manitoba Tory government, trying that gig, was astonishingly unhorsed by a young Ed Schreyer of the NDP who had been a leader for barely 18 days and hadn't had time to unpack his Ottawa bags.

25. The visitor from Mars would find this a very funny country. The visitor from Mars would be right.

The Dolorous Doomsayer

*One of the more chilling experiences of a columnist's life is being forced,
which no sane man wants to do, to go back over the output of 24 years on
Maclean's back page.*

*One shudders at some obvious miscalculations and overstatements, finds
on occasion a long-forgotten gem that one remains proud of, wonders why
this particular column was written and wishes that particular one could
have been improved—with a little more thought, and time.*

*One of the surprises, among the columns chosen out of the 1,000-plus
written, is the surprising number featuring the ineffable Joe Clark. Why, for
example, more on his resoundingly mediocre career than on, say, John Turner,
who promised such greatness and seemed to lose it all on that eight-year
exile on Bay Street?*

*On reflection, it seems, the answer is that Joe Who simply won't go away.
He first entered the House of Commons in 1972, when he was only 33. While
being re-elected three times, he became leader of the Conservatives in 1976,
and prime minister in 1979.*

*Tossed out on his keister in nine months because he couldn't count, he
resigned as Tory leader in 1983. And here he is, 1999, his non-existent chin
now sunk to his chest, at 60 trying for a comeback that will never come.*

*Chrétien once told me—when he was still speaking to me, that depending
on the odd years and what I had written about him—that as an ambitious
young MP he enjoyed a good relationship with the young ambitious MP across
the floor.*

*Both had a flippant, rather cocky approach to their party elders and so,
naturally, recognized an affinity, though they were, forever, party foes.
Parliament is more a club than voters will ever realize.*

*One day, in the autumn of 1975, Chrétien explained, he found himself in
the Commons men's room, standing at a urinal beside Clark. They were
alone. Clark allowed that he, almost an unknown to the public at large, was
thinking of running for the Conservative leadership, as Bob Stanfield had
just decided three defeats at the hands of Pierre Trudeau were enough.*

*The young Clark asked the young Chrétien for his advice. "Joe," replied
Chrétien, "I'll tell you one thing for certain. If you don't run, you can't win."*

*Joe Who burst into laughter at the obvious down-home, common-sense
logic of his adversary/friend. He ran. And he won.*

*Of all a scribbler's relationships with prime ministers, the one with P.
Trudeau of course would be the most interesting and—in the end—the most
disappointing. From the usual idolatrous young scribe in 1968 who loved the*

outrageous, sandal-and-cravat-wearing intellectual on the diving board, to the disillusioned columnist in mid-term, then to the sympathy over his sad marriage and tragedy over the death of his young son, it was never, as they say, dull.

As recorded in these columns over the years, he became intellectually lazy, "swallowed by the system … whittled down by the machinery … just another cog unable to move the bureaucratic wheel of party politics."

At one stage, of 85 ministers who had passed through Liberal cabinets, at least 52 could be traced to later patronage.

Close Trudeau friend Michael Pitfield, wealthy at birth, was lofted to the Senate at 45 and at retirement, if he reaches it, in 2013, will have pocketed some $5 million.

Most telling of all, all the brightest and most energetic of Trudeau's ministers had left him—Turner, Macdonald, Kierans, Mackasey. And we were left with—??—Chrétien.

Finance minister Chrétien, as newly released cabinet minutes have revealed, sat in silence while Trudeau announced startling new cuts in government policy that he had never discussed with his over-awed young fellow Quebecker, who had never, needless to say, ventured near the London School of Economics or the Sorbonne.

October 6, 1975

That Trudeau's such a lovely guy, so loyal to those who work for him

The British have a lovely word called "nouse." Nouse means intelligence combined with common sense. Horse sense. It is useless having a burnished intellect that sends out its own pure of light if there is no sense attached to it at the lower end. The lack of nouse is the outstanding feature of the Trudeau government.

People with nouse do not grant themselves 33⅓ per cent pay increases while attempting to exhort the grubby unwashed to a policy of restraint. People with nouse do not slip back into arrogance, with the ease of pulling on fireplace slippers, as soon as they achieve majority government once again. People with nouse do not insult the public with the cynical payoff to a prime minister's principal secretary, rewarding 43-year-old Jack Austin's 15 months of service by giving him a lifetime guaranteed income in the Senate—32 future years at $29,300 per for a total of $937,600.

The nouse-less Trudeaucrats. It is their shining characteristic, their neon-lit trademark. Run your eye down the list of Trudeau ministers and it is the consistent quality that pops up in this uniform cast of technocrats.

The image of the group of automotive technicians who run Ottawa has disguised a remarkable facet of Pierre Trudeau: he lacks the ability to be—in another British political phrase—"a good butcher." He cannot bring himself to prune and hack the congenital stumblers and fainthearted clots who clutter up his ministry.

It is generally unrecognized that Trudeau (mainly because of the artful change of life he goes through every few years: *i.e.*, the recycled swinger, the reincarnation of Laurier, the homebody and suburbanite daddy) has passed both John Diefenbaker and Lester Pearson in length of service. By the time his current term is up he will have passed Louis St. Laurent and will be well into the full gallop in pursuit of Mackenzie King (John Turner knows how to count too). This longevity through three elections (and four mental costume changes) has been established with a cast of characters that drifts on untouched by the supposedly tough hand of Himself. The intellectually rigorous product of Jesuit mental discipline finds himself unable to wield the axe even in the face of proven incompetence, even in the face of his proud boast, when he formed his first ministry, that his ministers would have to "produce or else."

We all believed it at the time. "Nothing is permanent," the new Prime Minister warned ominously in 1968 when he picked the largest cabinet in Canadian history, a collection of 29 supposedly nervous souls. Instead, we waited two years for his first cabinet "shuffle." Where was the chop, the famed Trudeau uncompromising lust for excellence? It produced not a single new face in the cabinet, with two of the ministers going back to the jobs they held under Pearson.

Ah, the Pearson years. Soft, nice guy Mike Pearson, who was too kindly and old-shoe to jettison familiar friends. Do you know that Pierre Elliott Idealist has existed for more than seven years with the core of his cabinet picked by Pearson? He has yet, despite the readjustment forced on him by John Turner's farewell, to put his own stamp on the cabinet.

After that coitus interruptus in the long-awaited 1970 shuffle, we had to wait four more years before there was a blood-letting. The ruthless one was six years in power, in 1974, before sacking *anyone*. At that, the only two of any note were the feckless Herb Gray, who has since discovered more bravery outside the cabinet than he ever did in it, and the handsome Bob Stanbury, terror of the Ottawa stenographic pool.

So what are we left with in 1975? Men who have long since proven their inability to shoulder the burdens thrown them, men who have bent and stretched the Peter Principle to unreasonable limits, men who—even taking into consideration the demands of regional, racial and religious quotas—have no business surviving in this government.

James Richardson, the poor little rich boy who will live forever in political folklore for Marci McDonald's description of him falling out of his bunk all night on one of his defence ministry ships because his naval officers "neglected" to tell him to strap himself in.

Judd Buchanan, the insensitive prize-winning insurance salesman, unleashed upon the native people of the land as Minister of Indian Affairs, regarded in the north as a beardless boy attempting to learn as quickly as possible the time-tested Liberal gifts of waffle, shuffle and mumble.

Can anyone take seriously a government that maintained for seven years dear old Mitchell Sharp, foot-in-mouth Mitchell Sharp, author of the famous reply when asked about the 1968 Russian invasion of Czechoslovakia: "Disappointing."

There are so many: Hugh Faulkner, who always appears as if he would be more comfortable in an Oscar Wilde play. Alastair Gillespie, that interchangeable TV face, the silver-haired executive from Central Casting who so pleases those interested in industry, trade and commerce. Robert Andras, the very image of a northern Ontario service club recording secretary masquerading as a manager of a very important Canadian ministry.

Even the heavies in the Trudeau cabinet have that bloodless, technocrat cast that forces one to look back with fond vigor on such as Judy LaMarsh. There is Marc Lalonde, an honest man who still can't understand what was wrong with Air Seagram, the only man in Ottawa, in the words of the Press Gallery's Marjorie Nichols, "with an IQ of 200 and the political judgment of Justin." There is Otto Lang, who can never concede he is wrong (as he was on Morgentaler) and who manages the formidable feat of appearing to be to the right even though he is surprisingly progressive.

Can anyone recall a single memorable phrase that will live beyond any of these ministers? Is "eat shit" to survive as the only quotable epitaph of this government? Those who leave, a Hellyer, a Kierans, a Turner, are allowed to sidle away. The strong resign. The weak are never sacked.

It is ironic that Pierre Elliott Trudeau, who came into politics and shook our minds as the greatest individualist within memory, ended up swallowed by the system, whittled down by the machinery, diminished, just another cog unable to move the bureaucratic wheel of party politics. In the art of jaded politics, he is a prime exhibit. He is demeaned. The system of cabinet tenure, squatters' rights, has not changed. He has changed.

September 18, 1978

For proof that power tends to corrupt look no further than Pierre Trudeau

What is so astonishing, in this sour fall of 1978, is the shift in mood and perception. The mood belongs to Pierre Trudeau and his face toward the public: it is cynicism. Relationships between the unwashed and those on high always are bound to alter, but the most remarkable thing about Pierre Trudeau's link with his subjects in this autumn of our discontent is that it is so diametrically opposed to the original understanding. The public can perhaps comprehend and absorb the fact that the leader chosen is not really as bright as first perceived—as in Jimmy Carter. Or that, for all his fire and idealism, he essentially doesn't know how to run anything—as in John Diefenbaker.

It is somewhat harder for a public to swallow the fact that its chosen hero has had a complete mental (more correctly, perhaps, ethical) reversal of field. That is the current view of the electorate toward the chameleon Trudeau, the man who captured the imagination of the country one decade ago because of his frankness, his appealing innocence in decrying personal ambition, his apparent honesty in allowing that he really didn't seek the job and regarded the whole exercise, in his own words, as a bit of "a joke" on the public and press. Now, 10 years later, we have the most jaded, insulting appeal for public support since the days of "Boss" Tweed. Some of the recent Liberal tactics appear almost a caricature of ward-heeler methodology. Look at the editorial columns across the land and you consistently come across one word: cynical.

What is so remarkable about the whole degrading process of the last few months is that the prime minister, encased in that intellectual cocoon that shields him from real life, appears astonishingly immune to the rising contempt of the electorate. He is vaccinated against reality.

There's a reason for this insularity. The Liberal party seeps through the underbelly of this country like a nuclear submarine in the deep. In 1955, when the Liberals modestly acceded to the 20th anniversary of uninterrupted rule in Ottawa, the shrewd political scientist Paul Fox noted that: "The Liberal government aims at operating noiselessly, like a respectable mammoth business operation which fears nothing more than making people aware that it is there. The shadows flit silently along the wall, as in Plato's cave, and the citizen is never sufficiently disturbed to turn his head."

In truth, a business operation. As a sample, in the 1935 election just five firms contributed 26 per cent of the campaign funds for the key Toronto Finance Committee: Labatt's, Imperial Oil, Laura Secord Candy Shops, Canadian General Electric, National Breweries. Forty per cent of the money came from just 12 sources. (Liquor and gold mine interests were the prime donors.) By the 1940 election, just seven donors provided 40 per cent of the slush fund.

By 1953, 50 per cent of the Liberal party financing came from commerce and industry, 40 per cent from businessmen linked to firms and only 10 per cent from private individuals. K.Z. Paltiel, research director of Ottawa's 1964 Barbeau Committee on election expenses, found that only some 350 donors piled up the $7.5-million war chest used by the Liberals in the 1957 campaign.

In this atmosphere of the Natural Governing Party, born to rule and steered by business, there has been the shrewd Liberal tactic—the recruiting of symbolic public relations figures from outside the grimy party system. Mackenzie King came from his duties as an employee of the Rockefeller family. Uncle Louis St. Laurent came from corporate law, Lester Pearson from the bureaucracy and Trudeau from the intellectual fringe. In the case of the latter three, a reasonable case can now be made that they were chips floating on the Liberal tide, the party machinery keeping them aloft. What is now becoming apparent about Trudeau, the innocent chosen over the pros, is that after a decade he has become a passenger on the vehicle. The party lumbers on and he flounders for a direction.

For a man of such inflexible personal standards, he is astonishingly pliable when the backroom operatives convince him that another tack is necessary to ensure the rule of the Natural Governing Party. Jack Horner was purchased in return for a cabinet seat. Key Tory Gordon Fairweather was lured onto neutral ground and away from the Opposition shadow cabinet with the Human Rights Commission appointment. Tory MP Bob McCleave was given a judgeship. Claude Wagner was purchased with the sweet of a Senate seat.

The spring buying of Opposition trouble spots over with, increasingly desperate plunges were needed to shore up the fall excuses for a vote. The prime minister, a philosopher seemingly taking a constant cram course in economics, decided that Helmut Schmidt, rather than Jean Chrétien, is his real finance minister. With the only strong personalities in a grey cabinet long fled—Turner, Macdonald, Mackasey, Kierans—the ebullient Chrétien was reduced to being a target for open derision from the press gallery when Trudeau's surprise "budget from Bonn" left the finance minister fumbling and naked. There is a whiff of the Keystone Kops to Parliament Hill, a smell of the last floundering Diefenbaker disaster days.

On Pierre Trudeau's first foray into Bennett Columbia to divine whether he had support for his whimsical bid for the Liberal leadership in 1968, his backers had scheduled a Sunday evening reception in the Hotel Vancouver's main ballroom. As he was upstairs changing his clothes, an expectant crowd waited for the ballroom doors to be thrown open.

Standing first in line was a vibrantly beautiful young redhead. She was literally jumping up and down, saying to her female companion, "Do you think he'll remember me?" Mr. Trudeau came down, fought his way through the crowd, she threw herself at him—somewhat like Bill Clinton and Monica Lewinsky—and yes, he definitely did remember her. It was their first meeting since he had met her in a bikini in Tahiti.

April 30, 1979

"Unwittingly, this scandalous lady has epitomized the election issue"

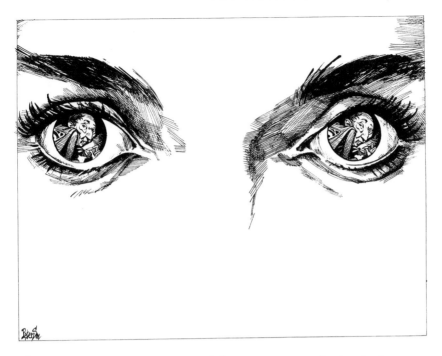

One of the strangest aspects of this very strange election is that no one dares mention the subject everyone is thinking about: Margaret. It is partially a measure of the grey, tentative Canadian nature and partially a measure of the supine Canadian press which, slavering, runs those truncated, jazzed-up, pre-shrunk hunks from her book but then refrains from discussing the larger issue. The issue, if you must know, is that Margaret's book reveals more about the prime minister of Canada than it does about Margaret. As such, it is legitimate matter for discussion, when we are about to defeat or re-elect that same private, protective gentleman.

A large myth has been allowed to accumulate that Pierre Trudeau has been harassed and harried about his private life by the vulgar Canadian press. In fact, the opposite is true. No other recent political leader—considering the provocation—has been so ignored, i.e., protected. The Australian public—still without sufficient answers as to how the late prime minister Harold Holt died (apparently) while swimming alone—would not put up with the way our press allows Trudeau to disappear to distant corners of the world while following his orders not to follow. The Americans would rebel. In truth, we have become intimidated by Trudeau. His threats and warnings and appeals about his personal life had, over the years, cowed those of us in the press—employers and employees alike.

The Margaret book by accident gives us a rare insight into the man we will encounter in the polling booth. Quite surprisingly, what emerges is a Pierre Trudeau far from the decisive autocrat who has banished all the strong personalities from his cabinet. Here is a tentative Trudeau, worrying before marriage (wisely, as it turned out) whether Margaret would remain faithful to him, saying "almost sadly, 'I know you'll leave me one day.'" We learn, as a semantic footnote to history, it was because a "nervous and jittery" PM was so jumpy about the upcoming secret ceremony that he blurted out the supposed "fuddle duddle" in the Commons.

There is, in a way, a more compassionate Trudeau who cries openly with Margaret during his marriage indecision, who cries shatteringly on getting the news of Pierre Laporte's murder, who so obviously loves his three sons and—slyly detecting which trees have rotting trunks—proves to his adoring tads that he can fell a tree with a single kick. But, always, there is that solitary soul that existed alone for 50 years and exists again alone. Concluded Margaret before marriage: "He was destined for eternal solitude." The millionaire who "inherited his mother's puritanism and frugality" insisted at 24 Sussex Drive on drying himself "with the smallest and meanest towel he could lay hands on." This superb athlete "won't play a single competitive game." He pits himself only against the elements. Does he dream in French or English? "He said, patiently as to a child: 'I don't think in words, Margaret, I think in the abstract.'"

There is, chillingly, the discussion on the FLQ crisis with the PM supposedly explaining to his young wife that if ever she or any baby of hers was kidnapped there would be no deal, no amnesty. Would that mean he would allow her and the children to be killed? If we are to believe Margaret, the stern answer was, "Yes. Yes, I would." There was the shock of the pitifully innocent (not in the biblical sense, thank you) bride of finding that the cerebral Trudeaus didn't exchange presents at Christmas.

There is the husband who arrived home "punctually" at 6:45 every night, swam "44 laps, never more, never less," and 17 minutes later was ready for his sons and then dinner "precisely at eight," followed by 45 minutes during which he would do nothing requiring deep thought while he "as he puts it, digests." Then: "I was absolutely forbidden to interrupt him as he worked. Time with Wifey was over." It sounds like downtown Etobicoke.

There is through the eyes of this politically naïve, incredibly vain young girl turning into a woman the poignant tracings of the marriage that her mother and all of us thought would never work. The flower child who doesn't want to grow up and still at 30 found solace in drugs (her generation's drugs, not Joan Kennedy's alcohol), found on becoming Mrs. Trudeau that "a glass panel was gently lowered into place around me, like a patient in a mental hospital who is no longer considered able to make decisions and who cannot be exposed to a harsh light." She never stops extolling her husband as a shy, gentle, loving man, but recalls what he told her solemnly when they were first married: "One of the best things about Mother was that she never disturbed me."

Margaret Trudeau—again, unlike the myth—is a very intelligent woman. Her insights (on Kosygin who cried on leaving her, on Brezhnev, on Ivan Head—"that pompous and somewhat self-important man," on Ottawa, on Chou En-lai, Nixon) are shrewd. She will have to answer to herself and her children for her silliness and destructive vanity. But it all gets down to Pierre Trudeau's motto: "Reason before passion." Unwittingly, this scandalous lady has epitomized the election issue. She left the marriage convinced that "Pierre's solution to subjugate everything to reason and will was wrong." A useful book, yet another small clue to the unfathomable puzzle that is one of the men you will find on your ballot.

June 25, 1979

After Trudeau's self-indulgent peacockery, a teen-age Eisenhower gets to run the store

Pierre Trudeau tried to lead Canadians out of the jungle, but they wouldn't come.   —Carleton University Professor Patrick McFadden

Would it be permissible, now that we've stood off a full ballot's length for a few weeks, to take a rather different look at a rather different man. Pierre Trudeau is a tragedy-within-a-mask: the most private man who disguised himself with public buffoonery and fuddle-duckery. The most quotable prime minister we've ever had (some of it even printable) never once in 11 years allowed the public to penetrate the mask. He leaves office as he entered it—a steely mind and unbendable personality that the voters, in the end, tired of trying to unravel. We like aloofness in our leaders, but eventually we resent being cut off entirely from some tiny peek inside the mind. That, in the end, is what doomed Pierre Trudeau. He accepted gratefully the power we handed him but he would not hand back the slightest insight into his soul.

Still, let us count the accomplishments. The current myth is that he was elected enthusiastically in 1968 by an anglophone Canada because he could "handle" Quebec but, in fact, in 11 years he made matters worse, producing only a separatist government in his own province. That is not true. He was fighting a rearguard action against history. Claude Ryan is the first to concede

that the Parti Québécois skirmish, when dealt with, is just one aspect of an evolving drama that will be with us long after René Lévesque is gone. Trudeau, through his bravery in going to Ottawa to prove a point to the people he even now will not call "Québécois," fought for time and won it for nearly a decade.

His comrades—Pelletier, Marchand—and his acolytes—Lalonde, Goyer, Chrétien, De Bane—destroyed forever the Uncle Tomism of the tired Liberal hacks endemic to earlier Liberal regimes. Whatever the movement-of-*indépendance* feeling among young intellectuals in Quebec, it would have been far swifter without the Trudeau insistence on a higher percentage of francophones in the sacrosanct WASP preserves of the upper mandarinate, without the valiant though fumbling dream of induced-bilingualism among the wooden-tongued snivel servants, without the pointed lesson that a Pepin could be trade minister, a Chrétien could be finance minister.

The lesson was pointed at Quebec, though it killed the party in Ontario and British Columbia. (The operation was a success, but the patient died.)

He knew, by 1968, that a gathering wave was chasing him in Quebec. Astute Quebec reporters know that by the aborted Victoria Charter of 1971, the Bourassa government in structure was controlled at the deputy minister level (Claude Morin et al) by the separatists. By 1976, when Pierre Trudeau swanned in the Olympic Stadium box with the despised Jean Drapeau, he had lost all touch with the creative forces in Quebec he once used to lead. The wave washed over him.

Other points. He forced people who regarded us as bores (essentially correct) to take a second look. *The Guardian* of Manchester says that events in Canada fall into the D category of news: neither important nor interesting. The Old World snobs, lumbered with the tired, cynical personas of a succession of grimly fingered Harold Wilsons, were perplexed, intrigued and mildly titillated by the fact this numbing land could toss up a stylish wit and fake roué who on examination had an intellect. Their minds whirled, momentarily, over their clichés of King of the Royal Mounted. For that small mercy alone, we are in tiny debt to Pierre Trudeau. Be honest.

He raised, for a time, a remarkable increase in public interest in government and the political process. Like Kennedy, he attracted people who previously thought politics was the preserve (as it was) of doleful men with large ponds for stomachs and large vacuums for principles.

In the end, style stuck him. Reporters marvelled over his guile in sweeping up to Rideau Hall to hand in his resignation in his Gatsbyesque Mercedes sports car. In fact, it simply reminded the sober voters gazing at their TV sets of the very reason why they dumped him. Self-indulgent peacockery. They wanted instead a teen-age Eisenhower to mind the store and now they've got him.

More? He made us think, in a way, of the two solitudes simply by being our first leader who could swear, so eloquently and so vulgarly, in two languages.

Just as much as he raised the hackles of those whose hackles hackle at the thought of cornflakes boxes, there has never been so much interest in night school and university and correspondence French. He is, in his own perverse way, the ghost of Riel.

In retrospect, he was a lousy leader, the definition of a leader being someone who can gather strong lieutenants around him, and Pierre Trudeau—in an astonishing confession to biographer George Radwanski—confirmed what we all accused him of. He felt no duty whatsoever to persuade wavering souls (Turner, Macdonald, whatever) to stick with him, nor did he think it was his task to seek out replacements. Those who felt it incumbent must come in obeisance to the Sun God. He was not a leader. He was the original ayatollah.

That was his fatal weakness. But he gave it a try. Give him credit for that.

December 3, 1979

"Say, who was that masked man anyway?"

"Why, that was the Lone Stranger!"

I said at the leadership convention at which he defeated me that Mr. Trudeau was the most remarkable Canadian of his generation, and that comment still holds.
—John Turner

The remarkable nature of the mask that is Pierre Trudeau is shown by the fact that he remains as much a mystery in leaving power as when he assumed it 11 years ago. He divided emotions as no other Canadian politician before him, mainly because he persisted in keeping his real personality in hiding, a hostage to his public life.

His longtime friend and confidant, Gérard Pelletier, once explained that while Trudeau gave the impression of a daring risk-taker, he was, in fact, a most cautious person. (His long delay in risking the perilous shores of marriage, if nothing else, proved that.) Pelletier pointed out that Trudeau would launch his canoe over a seemingly treacherous stretch of white water—but only after charting and checking beforehand on foot every bit of the route. He took risks, explained Pelletier, but only carefully calculated risks. In fact, little was left to chance. "Reason over passion" was the family motto. Which is why Margaret, in her own shrewd way, titled her still best-selling confession *Beyond Reason*. She thought there was something possibly more important than reason alone.

He was unfairly hanged by some of his own quotes. Other politicians, watching an unusual man get into trouble by trying to be more candid, retreated even more into their rote clichés. His "Why should I sell your wheat?" was badly ripped out of context, it having been merely a rhetorical opening to his long philosophical explanation of why he, as prime minister, did have a responsibility to sell the farmers' wheat. His fond professorial habit of musing out loud, holding his thoughts aloft as if gazing through a glass of wine, was intriguing to watch but deadly when translated into cold type.

When he asked reporters, "Where's Biafra?" it was actually intended as an arch riposte to reveal that the journalists badgering him did not know the map of Africa. His contempt for the profession of journalism was profound. I once cringed in humiliation when, on his introduction as an honorary member of the National Press Club (the scene of that mock self-strangulation with the club tie), he talked in disguised sarcasm of how as a young man he had "always looked up" to the envied reporters he had seen entering the Montreal Press Club, well-dressed, with always the prettiest of girls and the best of booze. He grew up in the Duplessis era when political reporters received a brown envelope present at Christmas, and the contempt he had learned from that particular time he was never able to shuck.

The first of our politicians to bring the element of the body to his role ("a physical fitness nut with a high IQ," as Charlie Lynch described him), he fascinated at first because he seemed to make the difficult look so easy. In truth, he was a terrible procrastinator who never in 11 years ever really fired any of his many cabinet fumblers. (Herb Gray and Robert Stanbury were the only ones he really "let go.") He forced all the myriad other ones to fall on their own swords: he wouldn't take the responsibility himself. He was defeated in the end because this supposed white-water man dithered for two full years over an election date, convincing the public finally that in his mirror he was indecisive, not the *High Noon* character they had imagined.

The chap who once rode a motorcycle with his silly German helmet and attempted to paddle a canoe to Cuba ended up with a strange, floating concept of leadership, refusing to persuade strong comrades to stay and unwilling to recruit new ones. Bemused at the beginning by his shrugging ascension to power, at the finish he watched as if mesmerized as the sand in the egg timer ran out. He seemed fascinated at the process as the clock wound down.

The man of masks, who told biographer George Radwanski that he was so sickly and insecure as a child that he purposely set out to build a physique and a steel will that would repel all outsiders, wobbled between the arrogance seen by the public and the shyness seen by his intimates. In his final, disconsolate days, he astonished even his most faithful by turning on Quebec electronic reporters who were having troubles with their equipment with the curse that "English" reporters never had such problems (not true). Despite the family connections, he never could figure out what made British Columbia tick, complaining that the nethermost, affluent province always seemed to be "bitching."

Radwanski, who as a reporter with a law degree and a similar "European" mind-set got closer to Trudeau than any other journalist, concluded that he was "unfulfilled" as a prime minister, a semantic delicacy that may over time be the closest approximation of the truth. He was not a natural politician, but an aloof amateur who was carried away by events and in the end disappointed his public by turning into a switch-hitter who dillied and dallied.

The most remarkable Canadian of his generation, he did more than anyone to make this country sit up and take notice of itself. Well, back to the mundane men.

March 7, 1983

The friends of Pierre Trudeau

The philosophy of the Liberal party is very simple—say anything, think anything, or better still, do not think at all, but put us in power because it is we who can govern you best.　　　　　—Pierre Trudeau, *Cité Libre*, 1963

The minor fuss about Alastair Gillespie—who, as chairman of Carling O'Keefe, hardly needs the money—is puzzling. The thought that former Liberal cabinet ministers and close associates do not regard their government in Ottawa as a friendly broom closet, a pit stop for welfare, is ludicrous. The Gillespie–Mickey Cohen–Marc Lalonde connection, for all the strange lapse of memory in the steely Lalonde cranium, is simply natural. That's the way we do things in this country, and since the Liberals are almost always in power it is their elastic morality (see P.E. Trudeau, above) that affects the conduct of their business. Complaining about Gillespie's friends in high places is rather like complaining about Bryce Mackasey, that famed aviation expert, being named chairman of Air Canada, another past and honorable move initiated by the man who once promised us the Just Society.

One might as well question why Jack Horner is the chairman of Canadian National. The reason is that he is a purchased Liberal, having been traded from the Tories for a low draft choice and a pair of Jim Coutts's old red suspenders. Why is Edgar Benson in Dublin? Because, as a reward for being Trudeau's first brilliant finance minister and after years of lounging in the pastureland as head of the Canadian Transport Commission (succeeding that other plutocrat of the pork barrel, Jack Pickersgill), he is rewarded further with an ambassadorship. Why is Ivan Head roaming the world as boss of Canada's international research aid program? Because he was once a Trudeau adviser and speech writer.

One of the more intriguing aspects of the former moralist from *Cité Libre* is that he has embraced without protest the Liberal tradition that owes its philosophy to Tammany Hall. Why is Gil Molgat in the Senate? Because he used to be leader of Manitoba's defunct Liberals. Why is Ray Perrault in the Senate? Because he used to be leader of the expired B.C. Liberals. Keith Davey is in the Senate because he runs Canada from there. And, after she had been Ontario campaign chairman in 1974, the present Mrs. Davey was appointed to the Immigration Appeal Board for a 21-year term at some $40,000.

Mitchell Sharp, who aided Trudeau's ascension immensely by withdrawing from the leadership race several days before the 1968 anointment and pledging fealty, has been kept on the public payroll ever since leaving the House of Commons, lately for a pipeline that has never been built. Bud Drury was put in charge of administering more privileges to the overprivileged Ottawa upper-middle-class ghetto at the National Capital Commission. George McIlraith went to the Senate because he was one of Trudeau's first cabinet ministers. Royce Frith is in the Senate because he is a former president of the Ontario Liberal association. Jean Marchand is Speaker of the Senate because he is an old Trudeau buddy. Gérard Pelletier is at the United Nations because he is an old Trudeau ally. Paul Manning is a vice-president of B.C. Place, Vancouver's new domed stadium, and a useful connector rod between Victoria and Ottawa because he is a defeated Liberal candidate and former Trudeau aide.

Don Jamieson is high commissioner to Britain—an appointment he was so sure of that he boasted about it to the *Globe and Mail* some six months before he was appointed. He emotes from the same podiums and dines at the same tables previously graced by Paul Martin. Andy Thompson is in the Senate because he was a leader of the Ontario Liberals. Davey Steuart is in the Senate because he is former leader of the dead Saskatchewan Liberals. Ron Basford is the coal czar expediting the export of B.C. coal through the federal port of Prince Rupert. Joe Guay is in the Senate because he is less harmful there than in the cabinet.

Iona Campagnolo is president of the Liberal Party of Canada. Don Macdonald is never-ending chairman of the never-ending royal commission into the never-changing economic problems of this rich country. Len Marchand now works for Indian bands by the grace of federal money. Pierre Juneau is head of the Canadian Broadcasting Corp. Stanley Haidasz was elevated to the obscurity of the Senate. Pat Mahoney was made a federal court judge. Jack Austin was sent to the Senate at 43, when his presence in the Prime Minister's Office became too embarrassing, for a total remuneration by retirement at 75 of $3,943,105. Jean-Pierre Côté was made Quebec's lieutenant-governor. Peter Stollery, one of the more obscure members of Parliament, was rewarded for his brilliance with a Senate seat so as to give a chance for Jimmy Coutts to lose Stollery's Spadina seat. Michael Pitfield, the Senator from Independence, was sent to the Senate at age 45, a son of wealth who by retirement in AD 2013 will have received an estimated $5 million.

Since 1965, of the 85 ministers who have passed through the Liberal cabinet, at least 52 can be traced to later patronage. It is interesting to note that of the high-profile defectors, only James Richardson and Paul Hellyer, two millionaires, and Eric Kierans and John Turner, two tough and proud guys, have remained untainted by the pork barrel. Perhaps that's why Trudeau doesn't like them. He hasn't been able to buy them.

Our personalities, the shrinks tell us, are basically set by the age of three and never really change. So it's no surprise, one supposes, to say that Joe Clark has never changed.

He's like a Brillo pad. Step on him, squash him, and he just bounces up and comes back for more. He's the punching bag of politics.

One myth surrounding him—and it has helped him—is that he received a low blow from the press on his now-famous round-the-world junket wherein his underwear, his luggage and his reputation went missing.

There was a backlash, meaning public sympathy for him, the constant mutter being that anyone who has travelled by air has had their luggage lost at some stage and why blame poor old Joe. This is an understandable feeling, but there is only one thing wrong in this case.

An airline didn't lose Joe's luggage and his underwear and his reputation. Joe did it himself. There was only one culprit and his last name was Clark. Therein lies a political lesson, the real story about Joe.

In December 1978, preparatory to the tour that was to take off in January, the office of the Leader of the Opposition sent the itinerary to those of us who were to circle the globe with the future prime minister. (Who, the record will show, was supported by this scribbler, who felt democracy was not being served when the Liberals were in power forever, give or take a century.)

This scribbler took one look at it and concluded, in about 90 seconds, that the trip was going to be a disaster. Aside from the fact that the minions in Clark's office didn't know how to spell Alitalia, it was clear no one in his office had ever been on an airplane.

The most obvious insanity was a flight on Egypt Air that was to take off from Tokyo, with a short stop in the Philippines, before transferring its passengers to Lufthansa in Bangkok, on the way to the destination of New Delhi. The itinerary showed 45 minutes for the transfer in Bangkok.

Any dolt who has ever flown knows that airlines insist on a minimum of two hours in bookings for passengers doing a transfer on international flights. This was a tour drawn up by the staff of the future prime minister that was destined for debacle.

In Vancouver, before the small media mob that was to accompany Clark took off for Tokyo, we took Clark's press secretary to the bar, where, as we know, all serious diplomatic arrangements are made. All of us assured said press secretary that we would buy him drinks the rest of the way around the world if this nutty schedule worked.

He wouldn't listen, having apparently been injected with the same stubborn gene pool that was lodged in the Clark brain. Joe himself had been sent to Hawaii to rest up beforehand, so he could be sharp in dealing with the sharp minds at the top he would meet in Japan, India, Greece, Israel and Jordan. He would join us in Tokyo.

Egypt Air, we discovered in Japan, had such a scary accident reputation that two of the better journalists in our troupe tried to arrange to fly direct to New Delhi on their own. Being older, and therefore wiser, I convinced them of the No. 1 rule of journalism: Stick with the story. If Joe Clark was going to die in the South China Sea, we had to be there to record it as we went down with him. They finally agreed, and have thanked me to this day.

Egypt Air lived up to its reputation. There were bullet holes, with stale blood, on the head cushions where the press sat back in the cattle section. The pilot, obviously a relative of the Flying Wilendas, took off on a climb rate that took the stomach away.

When the Bangkok airstrip finally appeared, there was barely time—as could have been expected—for the entire Clark party to sprint across the tarmac to the clean and efficient Lufthansa jet that had been held up waiting for us.

Left behind, of course—as could have been expected—was not only Joe's underwear but all the cameras and equipment of the TV crews and photographers who were there to record the triumphant world adventure of the future prime minister.

So inept and innocent were Clark's staffers that they didn't even have in their hand luggage an "emergency kit" for such occasions—shaver, toothpaste, whatever. An embarrassed Canadian ambassador in New Delhi had to hustle up such essentials.

So inept and innocent were his entourage that Ian Green, the advance man who was assigned to fly a day ahead to each stop to facilitate arrival, missed his flight from New Delhi to Athens. Now a high swivel servant in Ottawa, he is still known as "Suitcase" Green because of the incident.

On the final stop, in Amman, Jordan, before heading home to the laughter of Ottawa, Clark after meeting King Hussein allowed his one and only press conference on the whole tour. He was asked, naturally, who among his entourage would get the sack for devising the trip-from-Hell.

He, that stubborn streak rising as it often does in insecure men, loudly pronounced that he had a magnificent staff and was standing behind every member of his office.

And, wouldn't you know it, the future prime minister, after becoming prime minister, lasted just nine months because those very same people, every one of them, couldn't do simple arithmetic and discover that he didn't have the numbers to win the vote of confidence that he didn't have to call.

The lose-your-jockey-shorts tour changed my mind about the man I wanted to defeat Pierre Trudeau. I stood six feet away from him as he went through some of the oldest civilizations on the globe—Japan, India, Greece, Israel, Jordan.

He never once showed any curiosity. It was clear he was not interested in their history, their culture, their art, their theatre, even their food. His mind seemed forever rooted in High River.

And now he's back as Jurassic Clark, the new white hope of the dead old Conservatives. We think not.

January 29, 1979

Bayonets beware—Joe "Cecil Trueheart" Clark is loose among the landed gentry

The problem is that Joe Clark really is a nice guy. He is kind, he is considerate. He would never do anything intentionally rude. He is, in a way, a sort of sociological freak, a mutation from the 1930s in the way he acts. Watching him carefully at close range over an extended period of days, one gets the impression of Cecil Trueheart, the second lead in a Noël Coward play set in the landed gentry belt of Kent.

Clark himself, who in private is devastatingly analytical about himself, even knows the reason why. High River, Alberta, despite its Gary Cooperish-name, was one of those prairie towns populated in early days by remittance men—the semi-failed heirs of the English genteel, sent abroad to lose themselves so as not to disgrace the family name. In High River, of all places, they played *cricket* when Clark grew up. As he explains, it was a town where manners meant something. It wasn't Gary Cooper at all. It was Noël Coward, within sight of the Rockies.

Watching Joe Clark day in, day out, night in, night out, as he circled the globe on an indoctrination tour that may have been the worst political decision since Suez, one is reminded constantly of that self-description of his background. It is the vicar's tea party across four continents, a continual "thank-you-very-very-much" while stepping backward for fear of giving offence.

Thank-you-very-very-much became the catchword of the Clark tour. Within days, after hearing it incessantly directed at prime ministers, subway attendants, minor officialdom and any potted palm that twitched, the Clark entourage mocked it, imitated it, repeated it, set it into iambic pentameter and Gilbert and Sullivan rhythms. If it is not a star turn at the March Parliamentary Press Gallery dinner, along with poor Joe doing his Mack Sennett act plunging face-first into a military guard of honor, then satire indeed is what closes Saturday night.

There is something worth examining in that fullback plunge into the bayonets of the honor guard. Clark, as voters will discover during the spring election campaign, is a man who gives the impression that he is never quite sure what to do with his body.

Everything seems out of sync when he walks, his arms swinging to the beat of a different drummer, the wrists and hands only vaguely connected to the arms. He is one of those rare people who does not appear *comfortable* walking. You want to shove a chair at him to put him out of his agony. Those long spindly hands flit about nervously, rubbing one another, flying to the pockets, fitfully tapping on the table or whatever is available. One suspects his aides wish he would take up smoking, just as René Lévesque is hiding his habit.

All this physical awkwardness has nothing to do with the ability to govern, of course, but it may affect his ability to get elected. Mackenzie King did not rule in the age of television. Clark never really appears at ease in public; once he senses the cameras are on him, he freezes even more and tends to bump into things, including bayonets. A Gerry Ford image, once acquired in the press/public mind, is a difficult albatross to shake.

The other factor that became revealing on Clark's snapshot tour of the globe is his difficulty in speaking English. It must be understood that, as a high-school debating champ, he grew up in the era of Diefenbakerese and, whether he realizes it or not, talks in the convoluted, Rotary-impressive style of that genius of circumlocution. A query for directions becomes the Gettysburg Address. Clark to a guide in a Jordan farming area: "You are not anticipating a significant cereal production?" Clark to a guide in impoverished India: "What is the totality of his land?" Clark to doomed women in a dismal Indian village: "I very much appreciate the very cordial greeting."

The ingrained habit of parliamentary pomposity could not be diluted by poverty, travel, illiteracy or informality. One of the TV cameramen who recorded his every motion from close range for two weeks concludes: "He's got no street smarts at all." One of his own entourage, after Clark visited the sick bay at the

Canadian peacekeeping camp on the Golan, side-mouthed: "Watch out. He walked into the needle."

His surprise in discovering that he needed translators in Japan meant conversations were "a bit like an arthritic ballet." The searing experience of an Israeli exhibit showing how the Nazis exterminated six million Jews showed "the utter carelessness of human life." That's not what he really meant, but those are the things that come out of a mouth conditioned in teen-age Diefenbakerese. His twitchiness of tongue and body was contrasted even more in the late stages by Maureen McTeer, genuinely pretty, now stylish, relaxed and pleasant, chattering away in French to a Canadian soldier, possessing just the right touch of light banter needed for these stiff occasions. Her presence emphasized the stick-man image of her uneasy husband.

He is a creature of the parliamentary system, painfully uneasy once outside the formal structure of the high-school debating atmosphere. Voters will make up their own minds over the pressures of a 60-day, camera-saturated campaign—especially considering the insufferable arrogance of the Trudeau gang —but I think for a start we should hide all the bayonets.

Thank-you-very-very-much.

June 4, 1979

Here comes Hunkie Power! For Joe Clark, suddenly the tongue is on the other foot

There is a certain crescendo, an ultimate, an apogee in all our fumblings through life. For the wooden-tongued WASPs of the land (and one should never discount their linguistic guilt) it came in the 1972 summit hockey meeting of Canada vs. the U.S.S.R. It was then that Foster Hewitt, the embodiment of all that was fine and true about Depression-age Canadian youth, revealed before the embarrassed nation that he could not pronounce "Yvan Cournoyer." René Lévesque had hardly been invented, Robert Bourassa was not yet a public joke, but even the sports columnists were smiting their foreheads at the thought that the Moses of Maple Leaf Gardens was so befuddled by the other tongue that he mangled the moniker of the fastest skater in the fastest sport of all. It was a strange and useful scene: frozen into the memory of sports fans out there on the tube was the realization that a living legend in broadcasting had never bothered himself enough to wrap his tongue around a foreigner who lived as far away as Montreal.

Inherent in that lesson was a bit of a guilt trip that trickled through the beer parlors. One end of the country, in the wake of Trudeau, actually began to accommodate itself to the pronunciation of such semi-household names as Chrétien, to learn that André Ouellet had some faint but distinct relation to omelet (though balking, in Anglo-Saxon stubbornness, at the glottal dexterity needed to master "Fabien Roy").

All this is a clearing of the throat to bring up the fact that with Joe If the tongue is on the other foot.

Fair is fair, and one of the useful things about the election of Joe Clark (along with the destruction of the theory that Canada, along with Zambia and Tanzania, had lapsed into the realm of one-party democracies) is that the country is going to be confronted with names that will conjure up images.

It will do Quebec good (not to mention Toronto's Primrose Club) to have to master the pronunciation of Ray Hnatyshyn of Saskatoon, who surely will be in Clark's cabinet, and the cool, competent Don Mazankowski who has never been heard of around the martinis in double-breasted Winston's in Toronto, but has been an observer at the United Nations, at conferences in the Caribbean and Poland and most assuredly will be Clark's transport minister. Steve

Paproski? The burly ex-Edmonton Eskimo lineman who is a director of the Banff School of Advanced Management? One day, when he was a bachelor, Steve Paproski was drinking with his buddy Gene Kiniski, who is the world professional wrestling champion (in selected arenas, on selected nights). Paproski, somewhat emboldened by the liquid, allowed that if ever he married and had a son he was going to call him Paddy. And Kiniski, pouring another beer, ventured that if ever he succumbed and had a son he would call him Kelly. And they weakened and they did, and so there are two young males now trodding the land called Paddy Paproski and Kelly Kiniski.

What we're trying to say here is that a country that has been long on trying to master the other tongue and culture is going to find itself under a Clark government faced with the reality of the ethnic underground that has always (shyly, but a bit embittered) felt itself ignored. We're going to find in the Commons such names as Bill Yurko (the former Lougheed housing minister), Paul Yewchuk, Stan Schellenberger, Stan Korchinski of Saskatchewan, and Alex Jupp from Toronto, an Elzinga, a Vankoughnet.

It will take a while to sink in, but the elitist link between Rosedale and Westmount (which reveals more than anything that the similarity between Grit and Tory is keyed to private-school wives) is shattered by the ascension of Clark and his ethnic troops.

What is even more ironic is that the last-ditch Trudeau ploy, of destroying the WASP–francophone swap of the Governor General's post by appointing a Teutonic Canadian from Winnipeg, merely falls into the Clark scenario.

Ed Schreyer, with his sparkling chatelaine who was a farm girl named Schulz, formed his first cabinet in Manitoba with men called Cherniak, Uskiw, René Toupin, Rev. Phillip Peturson, Burtniak and Borowski. In his current pleasant retreat at Rideau Hall, his excellency has a press secretary by the name of René Chartier (imported from Manitoba) and a personal aide called Dave Chomiak. The next premier of Manitoba, an election or two down the road, could be an MLA with the schizophrenic name of Wilson Parasiuk.

What is so amusing so far is that the tight-mortgaged denizens of southern Ontario and upwardly mobile British Columbia—who provided Joe Clark with his minority victory—have supplied the bottom glue for the section of the populace that previously has never been allowed access to power. We have had, previously, in our Ontario–Quebec trade-off for power and concessions, a belief that the ethnic minorities were to be milked for votes.

Joe Clark, in the words of Dalton Camp, may indeed signal the beginning of The Age of the Klutz. Very possibly, but while he struggles for an accommodation with a Quebec he clearly does not understand, Ottawa for the first time will have to adjust itself to a minority that has been patiently waiting its turn. It is called Hunkie Power.

How crazy, in this crazy country, that a party elected by good safe-mortgaged WASPs in fact is secure in power because of a new ethnic power game—some time zones to the west of the Quebec border.

March 17, 1980

Don't shoot the messengers! We didn't do Joe Clark in

The anthills are alive with the sound of outrage. Pick up any letters-to-the-editor section in the country and there are all these fomenting Tories, stewing in their own juices, having discovered the reason their Quixote of the oilfields fell on his own lance several weeks back. The reason, mirabile dictu, has been unveiled. It is all because a clutch of nasty commentators, mainly armed with typewriters, did a number on poor, young Joe, and a slavering nation, meekly falling into line, marched to the polling booth and voted the way your favorite columnist dictated.

Oh what balm. What salvation. What a convenient escape route. For the sins and stupidities of the Tories, look not inward but at the scapegoat—the all-powerful press that decides elections and toys with the fate of the nation. Rationalization is a great art form. The present Conservative party navel-gazing, contemplating the illusion of the press rather than the reality, is a rather pitiful spectacle to behold.

It is all doubly puzzling, this viewing of the facts of politics through the wrong end of the telescope, because there has probably never been a time when the press was less powerful in its ability to affect elections. Every major English-language newspaper in Canada, with the exception of the *Toronto Star*, backed Joe Clark and the Conservative party in this election. Practically every single commentator on the campaign trail, not to mention the meat-and-potatoes reporters, was openly contemptuous of the cynical, insulting Liberal campaign run by Pierre Trudeau and his packagers. Little good that did anyone. The voters went their own blissful way, as always, and did what they were going to do in the first place.

The abiding myth that the powerful press (and powerful press personalities) somehow hold sway over a simple-minded electorate is one of the astonishing fairy tales of our time. The belief that a Hearstian decision, arrived at over the press club bar, can affect in the teensiest way the polling booth is the thumb-sucking refuge, the Linus blanket, of the immature Tory party. In 1974 the newspaper proprietors of the land, in their infinite wisdom, stood shoulder to intellectual shoulder in support of the dignified (to the point of petrification) Robert Stanfield. We know what happened to him—destined to finish his days wandering the sands of Arabia.

There are examples cluttering the landscapes of history. Franklin Delano Roosevelt, the raging pinko of his time according to rock-ribbed traditionalists, was vehemently denounced for four elections by 95 per cent of the American press—owned by good Republican owners. For four terms he laughed his way to the ballot box. W.A.C. Bennett, the shrewd old con man, for 20 years in power courted the enmity of the four daily papers of Vancouver and Victoria. It was, he explained, like flying a kite. You can't fly a kite in dead air. You had to have the wind going against you. For a politician to succeed, he explained with a delicious chortle, you had to have the foaming press against you.

The delusion, so believed by the frustrated and furious Tories, that the press can make or break a politician, is a hoary hangover from those days when press magnates were shamelessly partisan and a public could get its information and views from practically only one source. But one of the funny things about modern journalism is that the increasing concentration of ownership has not—unlike other industries—been accompanied by increasing power.

It may help the profits and the orderly balance sheet, but it doesn't influence the public decision-making process one iota. They read it and then do what they were going to do anyway. The days when a single journalist could swing or sway votes, a Westbrook Pegler, a Drew Pearson, a John Dafoe, went out with Rudy Vallee. I blush to inform you, but journalism these days is one big service industry. Any readership survey will show you that the columnists with the boggling ratings these days are the ones who tell you how to change your snow tires or where to find canning lids. Ann Landers, with her meatloaf-and-menopause formula, tops the pundits every single day. To suggest that six Canadian columnists (who voted four different ways on February 18) can overthrow—or anoint—a PM is highly flattering but, in truth, a vast insult to the body politic. The system, she just don't work that way.

Of more importance is what this currently popular myth reveals about the Tory party. It has very serious problems—and will continue to have—with the public perception of Joe Clark as a man capable of sitting in the prime minister's chair. The press didn't create those doubts. It only reflected them. The party, of course, would rather not face up to the serious consequences of the fact that it may have made a big mistake in its compromise choice back in 1976.

One of the sad things about the Tories of 1980, a professional, full-time Opposition party which could benefit Canada by being in power for a good stretch, is that it persists in this futile bleat that it was defeated February 18 because of a few nasty critics. Oh Lord, if only we had the power ascribed to us.

On the day he was elected Liberal party leader in the Ottawa ice rink, and thus Prime Minister, his mother, stricken with Alzheimer's, was placed in front of a TV set in the senior's home on Saltspring Island in British Columbia to watch the triumph of her life's dream. She did not recognize him.

August 8, 1988

One fateful roll of fortune

There is always fascination when history sets a deadline for men. When the time and the individual come together for a fateful match, rather like a long-awaited prizefight. The spectators rub their hands together in the glee of anticipation. Churchill grumbled away in various second-stage roles at Westminster, switching parties, underestimated by all, until Britain finally made its date with destiny with him in 1940—at age 65. De Gaulle pottered away in his village of Colombey-les-Deux-Eglises for 13 years, secure in his ego that a tottering France would have to call on him again as savior, as it did—at age 68.

Not to give this quite the same importance, but there is a confluence of time and event at the moment with John Napier Turner. A man who seemed destined for the stars all his life, and who has seemed to disappoint, has now gambled all on one throw of the dice. The history books are going to award him the title of either hero or bum on his audacious brinkmanship on free trade.

He has, by playing his Senate card, in effect called the election—a privilege that heretofore was assumed to belong to the prime minister. Brian Mulroney, who opposed free trade in the campaign that got him elected, has been trying to noodle the issue past the electorate quietly—if necessary, but not necessarily, before an election had to be called. Turner has now snatched that opportunity from him. By announcing that the some-doddering, some not so, Liberal majority in the Senate will block the Commons decision, Turner has pretty well dictated that Canada will go to the polls before Santa arrives.

It's a gutsy decision. Most of all, it's a decision, plunked down by a reluctant

Hamlet who has puzzled even his most ardent admirers for decades. John Turner, aware at 59 that his time and his polls are running out, has decided to go out (or into) office with one bodacious flip at the start. If the Tories won't let the electorate decide free trade at the polls, then Turner will. Seldom in our history has an Opposition used the abiding rules of Parliament in such startling fashion.

Startling is not John's style. His political problem (explained here before at boring length) has always been that he is a basic conservative trapped with a Liberal party. He is a captive of circumstances, a prisoner of accident. He never knew his father, a British journalist who died when John was still a tad. Which is probably why he gravitated to the strong Ottawa mandarins (C.D. Howe et al) who gravitated to the table of his brilliantly minded and forceful mother (Canada's first feminist?), who was the strongest female presence in that legendary war-time government mandarinate around Mackenzie King. (The cowards in Turner's back bench who attempted that abortive putsch earlier this year used his absence, at the funeral of his brave mother, as the timing for the attempt to stab him in the front.)

John's route to the top has always been the standard, conservative route. Top boy at school. Most popular student at university. Oxford. Marriage into the right socioeconomic bracket (no incipient Margaret Trudeau ever loomed in his riflescope). The right law firms. He has always dressed, since youth, in the clothes of someone 20 years older, sort of Victor Mature crossed with Anthony Eden.

It has always been suspected that the Pierre Trudeau distaste for Turner was rooted in the belief of the former that the latter never really belonged in the Liberal party. He doesn't, really. Just as Mulroney, a natural seeker of consensus in the middle, without any real philosophical cellar, is far more a liberal person than the conservative John.

John Turner has always been connected with the right people. He was made a Canadian director of Bechtel, the world construction giant, by a firm friend and admirer, Bechtel's George Shultz. Shultz is now the secretary of state, one of only two stable elements in the Ronald Reagan cabinet, and stout backer of the Reagan belief in the free trade gambit that assumes the mouse getting further into the bed with the elephant will not harm the mouse.

And so it's fitting, dear reader, that the John Turner who has been accused of never making a tough decision in his life is now making the toughest decision for us. The last time he made a tough one, resigning as finance minister with tears in his eyes after the cruel Trudeau offered him the Senate or the Bench, after languishing on Bay Street at the corner banquette in Winston's on Adelaide and having a salad named after him, it was assumed that he was merely playing out dauphin-in-waiting.

Even then he didn't make a decision, failing to keep up with new press trends, ignoring his speechifying and bum-patting problems, thinking the old Oxford-and-fraternity Turner charm would suffice—defects that an "image consultant" is now trying to eradicate.

John, all of a sudden, with one last roll of the dice, has a better solution. Since the government won't do it, he is going to force the public to come to grips with the trade issue. He's always been conservative, and conservatives are supposed to go by the rules. The rules say that the Senate can block or obstruct a Commons decision it doesn't like. John Turner is invoking the rules, as a good Tory always does.

At the end of his famous soliloquy, Hamlet says, "From this time forth, my thoughts be bloody, or be nothing worth." John knows that he's going to be a hero or a bum. At the age of 59, after a rather tortured existence, that's quite exciting.

The second column I ever wrote for Maclean's *coincided with Robert Stanfield's announcement that three straight electoral defeats by Pierre Elliott Himself were enough, and he asked the Regressive Convertible party to mount a leadership convention in Ottawa in February 1976 to pick a successor.*

I assayed the obvious candidates and advised that Jack Horner was too stupid and Paul Hellyer was too stubborn and Joe Clark was too young and yada-yada. If the Tories had any brains, I advised—as they had shown they hadn't—they would figure out that the reason they had been shut out of power in Ottawa for most of the century was that they could never break into Quebec.

Why not, I suggested, take a flyer on someone I had never met, but had been keeping an eye on from afar. Name of Brian Mulroney, fluently bilingual, good record as a prominent Montreal labor lawyer who had achieved provincial television attention as a star on the Cliche Commission inquiry into union corruption. He came with a beautiful young wife whose prominent father, Dr. Dimitrije Pivnicki, originally from Sarajevo, was the Montreal psychiatrist who had accepted Margaret Trudeau into his hospital's care and, after she left on her own accord, observed that there was a young lady who needed a lot of help.

Two weeks later, my secretary at the Vancouver Sun—*the best ever, English—buzzed on my phone. (I used to call her "Miss Framsham," because of a plummy Brit accent. Friends would call and say, "Her name can't really be Miss Framsham?" I would tell them, "Of course not. Her real name is even more dangerous. It is Mrs. Robinson.")*

She said, "Allan, there's a Mr. Mulroney on the phone from Montreal." I picked up the phone and didn't even say hello. I said, "When did you decide to run?" The deep baritone at the other end of the line answered, "The second time I read it in your column." That was the start of an interesting relationship that really has not been resolved to this day.

Mulroney said he would be coming to Vancouver in several weeks for the usual "fact-finding mission" to see if he would run for the leadership—something he already planned to do, since he had been waiting for it all his life. Or at least since he was 17 (as had the same-age Joe Clark, when they met as wary adversaries even then at a Tiny Tory Youth Parliament).

He suggested we have a drink when he arrived. Certainly, I replied, by this time having dubbed him in my Vancouver Sun *column "The Candidate from Whimsy" since he was my own invention. He loved it, for years after announcing "This is Whimsy" when I answered the phone.*

The day he arrived on the Wet Coast, he phoned and invited me down to the Hotel Vancouver at noon. It was a lavish suite. He was surrounded by buddies from Montreal and acolytes. A waiter approached and asked for our drink orders. The Jaw That Walks Like a Man paused a little too long, and said, "I think I'll have a beer." That struck me instantly as wrong, trying to impress, and I ordered my usual gin mit *tonic.*

We talked for about 10 minutes, the acolytes as always chewing the drapes, and I remember thinking to myself—Is That All There Is? the old

Miss Peggy Lee song. Is this the future prime minister I have invented? All Irish charm and bullshit? Being Irish myself—despite my stepfather's Scottish surname—I recognized it immediately.

Brian certainly had street smarts (now corporate smarts). On his way to the top, he figured the most practical thing to do was to get an influential journalist who had a national audience into his hip pocket. For a while, he thought it was Peter Newman (as Conrad Black once did, until Conrad read the Newman book that was based on open access to the formidable Black brain, and mouth).

I therefore became—the teacher's pet at 24 Sussex Drive. There for all the banquets, all the parties, and a great friend of Mila, who can work a room better than anyone I have ever seen, including her husband.

Buddies in the Ottawa Press Gallery began to suggest that I was getting a little too close to the prime minister of the land—and started to refer back to the revered Bruce Hutchison who used to help Lester Pearson frame his major speeches (and then report on them from his Press Gallery seat above).

The moment seemed judicious to remove myself to Washington with Southam News for five years to, as it were, "launder myself" from a too-close association to someone I had supposedly invented.

This became even more clear, in the interim, when one noonish Sunday at a private cottage up the shore on Harrington Lake, there arrived by speed-boat a waiter with champagne, smoked salmon and Eggs Benedict. I thought I had to get back to Georgetown in Washington, most wisely.

Brian has since moved on from Peter C. and mineself, to William Thorsell, editor-in-chief of Toronto's National Newspaper, the Globe and Mail, *who has been the most obedient sycophant to the sibilant whispers of Brian since Cleopatra phoned Richard Burton.*

February 13, 1984

Mulroney the fondler and stroker

The other day Brian Mulroney got up from his front-bench seat in the House of Commons and cut out of Question Period five minutes early. As he headed for the back curtains, he passed the desk of Tom McMillan, the Hollywood-handsome young Tory from Prince Edward Island. He stopped for a word and squeezed his arm. He leaned over Bud Bradley of rural Ontario, whispered something and squeezed his arm. He stopped with a remark for Gordon Taylor, the grim-faced veteran from Alberta, and squeezed his arm. By the time he had slipped through the curtains, all three were smiling. Here, on display, were the gifts of Martin Brian Mulroney, the greatest fondler and stroker of egos since Lyndon Baines Johnson plied the trade.

LBJ was a hugger and squeezer, a politician who believed that if he could get you in his grip, the overwhelming logic of his pitch would become apparent. He worked on people, feeding personalities and massaging wounded feelings, a leader who was actually a masseur. The boy from Baie Comeau is cut from the same mould, an old-style politician in a modern age. His hero as a politician is the late Daniel Johnson, a Union Nationale premier of Quebec who taught the young Mulroney that there was no match for Irish charm mixed with Gallic shrewdness. As a tiny Tory at Laval law school and as a young lawyer in Montreal, Mulroney always courted those at the top, and Johnson taught him that people politics is the only politics. Policies will follow.

It's one of the reasons why Mulroney is accused of being so fuzzy on where he stands. At the 1976 leadership convention he actually had a reputation as a bit of a Red Tory, on the same edge of the party as Joe Clark and Flora MacDonald. Now he is painted as a tool of the business community thanks to his stint as president of the Iron Ore Co. of Canada. It's unlikely he has any hard and fast course or purpose; he's a pragmatist who wants power first of all. After that he will trim and shift, stroke, massage, reward and punish, his main target to stay in power.

Mulroney has a favorite story involving Bobby Kennedy's fated run for the presidency. Kennedy always travelled with his favorite dog, a huge beast that took up an inordinate amount of space on his campaign jet. One of Kennedy's entourage was a handsome and debonair New York millionaire who, at every stop, would walk the dog on the tarmac at the end of a long leash. At one stop, R.W. Apple Jr., the celebrated *New York Times* correspondent, upbraided the dog-walker. "I always thought I respected you," he said. "You're highly successful. You can retire in your 40s. You have a beautiful family and a good reputation. And here you are—walking a dog on a leash." The millionaire Democrat turned to the reporter: "You've got it all wrong. I don't look upon this as a dog. I look upon it as an embassy."

That is Brian Mulroney, roaring at his own sardonic humor, taking great delight in the side of politics the public never sees. Raised in the seamy backwaters of Quebec politics (and somehow surviving as a lonely Tory), he views patronage upfront and views those who grow prim and sanctimonious with the same puzzled attitude that Catholics view an abstemious Baptist.

He has horrible "rabbit ears." He reads everything written about him or his groupies, never forgets and never forgives. He is like the Kennedys in that if anyone attacks any member of the pack, there is an instant circling of the wag-

ons. It's why he inspires such loyalty—he gives it back, even to some aides who should be back on the farm. It's why some of us label him "MulCrony." He has sent private word to some Ottawa journalists that he has sacrificed one of their targets and they can now lay off, since he vows not to jettison their other targets. His staff has drawn up a "hit list" of some 350 flunkies appointed by the Liberals who will be first on the chopping block if and when the Regressive Convertibles are elected.

Since he decided three years ago that he was drinking too much and indeed wanted a second try at the leadership he has not touched a drop. It is soda water over ice every time. He mainlines on coffee and packs of du Maurier. The Liberals in the Commons call him Smoke Throat because of his bottom-of-the-rain-barrel delivery. The NDP calls him Myron Baloney. Tory friends call him Muldoon. Old pals from school still call him Bones because at university he was thinner than a rake. He is still thinner than a rake.

He is lost without Mila. She is his rock and his balance wheel. They are the only old-style nuclear family at the top of our political heap, Ed Broadbent divorced and happily remarried, Pierre Trudeau currently going through the country's most-watched divorce, the ratio perhaps reflecting accurately the populace as a whole. Mila Pivnicki Mulroney, who goes snap, crackle and pop once in a crowd, will slash into the Liberal monopoly on the ethnic vote.

He is billed as a Montreal businessman, but that was mere fill. He is, above all, someone who made his reputation as a labor lawyer, a cute operator who knew how to cut a deal in a hotel room over coffee and cigarettes when he felt the two sides in a dispute were ripe. Thus his outrage at a devious Marc Lalonde intimating that he, as a lawyer, would be so dumb as to leave some incriminating evidence in a letter to a rival government. Mulroney is too careful for that. He may prove to be too careful, but that's his business. It's back to LBJ politics, squeeze and cajole, the carrot and the stick. This is Brian Mulroney, the man who wants to be prime minister. You're welcome.

February 19, 1990

Why friends fall from high places

There is a rolling of the eyes in the body politic when yet another of Brian Mulroney's close friends takes the gas pipe. Here we go again. That's the popular opinion. That was the feeling when the latest bosom pal, one Brian Gallery, had to vacate quickly as vice-chairman of CN when bothersome reporters revealed he couldn't quite discern the difference between public duty and private interests. It is rather a pattern among the Prime Minister's pals, but there is a reason—not that anyone wants to listen.

Unless you have spent years in the wilderness, you do not know what the wilderness is like. Those chaps consigned to the French Foreign Legion in the Sahara—banished for whatever sins—know what it is like. So do—see the Prime Minister's pals—those wretched figures who stubbornly persisted at being Conservatives in Quebec through the Long March.

To be a Conservative in Quebec when the Liberals invented the word patronage was to be a lonely heathen in the land of Christians. While slush funds and paving contracts and lawyers' fees and real estate allotments went to faithful Grits who delivered the province *en masse* to Mackenzie King and St. Laurent and Pearson and then Trudeau, the bitter Brian Mulroney and his pals sat and watched.

To keep from being completely bitter, since that way lies death, they had a better plan. They would have fun while relegated to the wilderness. They would party and delight in the visions of the vengeance they would wreak upon their tormenters once they—in the sweet by-and-by—eventually came to power.

Mulroney and Gallery and their pals were the best party people in Montreal. Partially because their cause was hopeless. Partially because they believed that

Tory fortunes couldn't possibly become worse and therefore blue skies—somewhere, somehow—must be in the future.

Mulroney, the boy wonder who went out to Saskatchewan as an aide to Diefenbaker guru Alvin Hamilton, tried to cajole Dief as to how he could cosset his astonishing 1958 sweep of Quebec, but to no avail. He returned to the wilderness as Dief's charisma expired, boy Brian healing his wounds eventually in the Maritime Bar of the Ritz-Carlton.

Those decades when the bloodless, efficient Liberals ruled Canada mainly through their effortless rule of Quebec laid the basis of Mulroney's present troubles. Because there were so few Tories in Quebec—impossible to elect—they formed a coterie, devoted in their isolation, sworn to revenge when their time eventually came.

It did, of course, in 1984, and Mulroney set forth rapidly to do what his Liberal friends had been doing for most of all this century: fixing up friends. His best-received line, throughout his triumphant 1984 election campaign, was a proud boast to gleeful Conservative audiences that certainly he would appoint some Liberals to patronage posts—"after there is not a single living, breathing Conservative left in the land."

The euphoric Tories, eager for succor after so long in the desert, whooped and hollered at that line. They loved it. Especially since their bitterness over the obsessively fair Joe Clark, never forgiven for the fact that, on the night of his suicidal and goofy Commons nonconfidence vote that ended his career after only nine months, there were some 100 patronage appointments sitting on his desk unsigned.

Brian Mulroney, coming from backroom Quebec, was not to make the same mistake. Gallery, a large Irishman with an expensive wardrobe, was to be given the acting chairmanship of CN and then—when a permanent chairman was chosen—eased into a newly created job as vice-chairman, while retaining CN duties in France. Buddy Michel Cogger went to the Senate. Friend Yves Fortier went to the United Nations. Pal Jean Bazin went to the Senate—and mysteriously resigned recently, pleading that he didn't have the time to devote to the job, an oxymoron of our age.

Mulroney is held up against a hard standard. Pierre Trudeau has never been detected as having real friends. Those he has are not exactly eligible for government posts. Barbra Streisand as transport minister or Margot Kidder as external affairs minister were never in the running. John Turner's close friends are aging jocks, never in need of cushy jobs, and his mind never works that way.

But the Montreal gang, their coat collars turned up against the world, regarded 24 Sussex Drive once they got there as Valhalla. Of course, Gallery, with his CN largesse, complained in writing to CN advertising people who, ordered to cut costs, were cancelling ads in his own little shipping magazines. Of course, Gallery, a major Tory fund raiser, couldn't see anything wrong with throwing parties on his private CN car for Tory biggies. Chief fund raiser David Angus made such open boasts about his imminent Senate appointment that a nervous Mulroney never did make it.

The Québécois vote is a tribal vote each election, and in our time decides the election. The Mulroney friends—mainly stalwart anglophones who braved the francophone majority at Laval's law school—have their own tribal protective blanket. They resented the Liberal establishment that reigned over this country for too many decades.

They were shut out for too long and now, once in, have been so unused to the nuances of nudging rather than crassly pushing that they continually get into deep trouble in the headlines.

The people who were responsible for Kim Campbell, if you must know, were Isabel and John Bassett.

When Brian Mulroney signified his intention to leave 24 Sussex Drive, a Conservative gathering of the faithful at the Albany Club on King St. East in Toronto—where all Tories go to die, or drink, whichever comes first—had as guest speaker one night this sprightly blonde unknown from Vancouver.

Kim Campbell, in her salad days, could have been on late-night TV as a stand-up comic. She is very bright, very funny—and absolutely dazzled the Bassetts, Isabel being a committed feminist, and her husband, John, a charming male chauvinist pig of the finest order from another era, adoring his young wife, who was teaching him new things, especially about the idea of a woman as prime minister.

The Bassetts, kings of Rosedale and Tory fundraising, rounded up the troops and introduced the ebullient Campbell to everyone who counted and could write a cheque. Before anyone knew it, Barbara McDougall for one, Michael Wilson for another, divined there was no way they could mount the leadership campaign money that the Bassetts had already sewed up.

They withdrew rapidly, the innocent but energetic Jean Charest left alone to battle the Toronto Establishment imprimatur.

Kim Campbell, for all her brightness and charm in person, was never a politician. She was an opportunist, leaping—like a mountain goat from ledge to ledge—from university lecturer who never quite did get the reputed gradu-

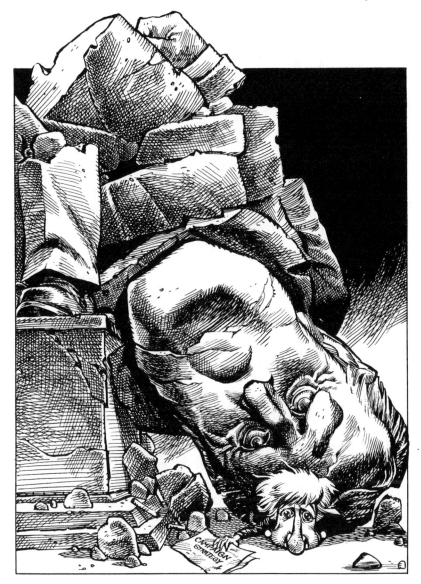

ate degrees credited to her (nor the foreign languages), to school trustee to law firm (temporarily), to Social Credit wannabe, to Conservative MP *boosted along by mentor Pat Carney, whom she never thanked once.*

She was a very interesting flame-out, the worst disaster the Conservatives ever invented. And Liberal Jean Chrétien sent her off to the posh job as Canada's consul-general representative in a posh Los Angeles mansion, since he above all really knows what patronage is worth.

October 11, 1993

The panic in the Kim Campbell camp

The terrified Tories, who have ruled the Dominion of Canada for the last nine years, have a genie in a bottle and are afraid to let her out. They are trying to win this most discouraging and unappetizing election with a candidate they hardly know and are most nervous about.

This is the woman who said, on silencing journalists: "I mean, it's a perfectly legitimate technique to seal them off from communications to try to force them out, perfectly reasonable." This is a politician who tells it like it is—and her handlers are petrified.

Kim Campbell, the Prime Minister of all of us (thanks to the votes of 1,800 high-priced Conservatives) is indeed a new brand of politician—as she is the first to advertise. The only problem for the party that chose her, very precariously, very narrowly, over the predictable and manageable Jean Charest, is that the senior mandarins of Torydom are absolutely panic-stricken that she will escape from the bottle.

"I will sell my soul to get re-elected." The battered and discouraged voters don't need to be told that; they have just about come to that conclusion. Sheila Copps says Queen Kim is "Brian Mulroney in a skirt." That's not the Tories' worst dream. It's that she's Pierre Trudeau in a skirt. Capable of saying anything, anywhere. They're petrified.

This is the woman who, as a backbencher in Victoria, told her NDP opponents one day that she sympathized with the scabs on their knuckles resulting from them dragging on the sidewalk.

Now this is good stuff. We haven't had this sort of straightforward political discourse since Sir John A. was on the stump. Who needs the Jean Chrétien bafflegab, the man who announces on CBC Radio that he wants an election "the better the sooner"?

Kimmy, her tongue working faster than her brain, gives good quote. On relating to people on Vancouver's skid row: "I know that a lot of you have faced disappointment and loss in your lives. I have, too. I wanted more than anything to be a concert cellist."

This is the best material since Sir John A., addled by too much firewater and the hot sun, barfed his cookies over the edge of an outdoor stage and then wiped off his chin and continued his speech: "So much for my opponent's platform...."

The genie in the bottle the Conservative high poohbahs, tremulous lawyers and agitated pollsters are worried about comes with other baggage. They are palpitating over the latest revelations that might emit from the mellifluous lips of the Prime Minister's first of two husbands, the chess genius from the University of British Columbia, Nathan Divinsky, the utter gentleman who announced to the *Vancouver Province* that he didn't want to comment on his marriage and divorce from the lady, but allowed that if she achieved the highest office in the land he was going to display a bumper sticker: "I Screwed the Prime Minister."

He has now been dining out on the story of how private detectives photographed him and Kim to aid his unamused first wife's divorce suit. Tory headquarters in Ottawa are on Mission Control alert, gasping at the next possible revelation as election day approaches.

"A lot of people that you're out there working for are people who may sit in their undershirt and watch the game on a Saturday, beer in hand. I suppose these people would find me as boring as I would find them." A Trudeau-in-a-skirt? This is a leader who speaks her mind.

Who's the last one to do it? R.B. Bennett? A woman at a White House reception excitedly upped to Calvin Coolidge and said that she had just bet $10 with her friends across the room that she could make him say more than two words. Silent Cal: "You lose."

What this confused nation needs is a leader who speaks the truth, the unvarnished truth, the real stuff. Kim Campbell: "I don't need to be loved by the public." Get down and dirty, Kim. Lucien Bouchard would never have the balls to say that. Presto! Manning? Forget it.

Queen Kim, 1986: "I'm a sucker for highly intelligent men."

Queen Kim, 1988: "I am five-foot-four and an undisclosed weight."

Queen Kim, 1993: "I've got a strong streak of wood nymph in me."

"I'm a very warm, affectionate person."

"I can still recite all the books of the Bible off by heart and sing all sorts of rousing hymns."

"I think I'm a pussycat. Do you find me abrasive?"

Not at all. If you must know, Kim, I find you the combination of Hillary Clinton—your brain is about equal—and Eleanor Roosevelt, with your mission and ambition, and Maureen McTeer, with your contempt for scribes who cannot comprehend your sardonic wit.

That's not my problem. My problem is that your ambition and brain has outstretched your experience; your handlers realize this and don't want to let the genie out of the bottle.

Your problem, Queen Kim, as the election slips away from you, is that you don't tell all the babysitters to get stuffed, that you are going to wing it.

There was a very significant, though little-noticed, death in the United States in April of this year that has serious bearing on Canada.

The death was that of Roman L. Hruska, who served in Washington for 22 years as a conservative Republican senator from Nebraska. He wielded considerable influence on the powerful Judiciary Committee. He was 94.

He was a leader in opposition to gun control. In 1974, he was one of the main figures in the U.S. Senate who engineered restoration of the death penalty for certain federal crimes.

He was a fierce opponent of what he regarded as excessive violence and pornography in films and on television, and sponsored many bills to curb them. He fought to maintain criminal penalties for marijuana.

But his relevance to Canada, and dutiful Canadian voters, came in a memorable speech to the Senate in March 1970. There had been considerable controversy over President Richard Nixon's nomination, for a vacant Supreme Court seat, of Judge G. Harold Carswell of Tallahassee, Florida.

Judge Carswell, a member of the 5th U.S. Circuit Court of Appeals in Florida, was—to put it mildly—a political hack. Dumb to boot. The liberal end of the Democratic Party loudly complained, contending that he was too "mediocre" to deserve a seat on the nation's highest court.

Senator Hruska, in a peroration that that will last through the ages, rose on his hind legs and asked why mediocrity should be a disqualification for high office.

"Even if he were mediocre," he stated to an enthralled Senate chamber that would later try to throw Bill Clinton from office, "there are a lot of mediocre judges and people and lawyers. They are entitled to a little representation, aren't they, and a little chance? We can't all have Brandeises, Frankfurters, and Cardozos."

In other words, there are a lot of stupid people out there, and they deserve to have their representatives in high office.

This was a brilliant concept, not heretofore expressed publicly, and has a lot to do, some 30 years later, with Canada's dilemma in Ottawa.

We have there, an elected dictator for each five-year term, a man who by any measure is mediocre. No one, not even Jean Chrétien himself, would claim that he possesses an outstanding brain.

He is, as the saying goes, possibly the only man in the country who can't speak either of the two official languages. In Dalton Camp's celebrated description, "He always looks like the driver of the getaway car."

He is—mainly because of the ineptitude of the Opposition parties, mere regional rumps—surviving in power while being decidedly mediocre.

No wily and mysterious Mackenzie King this one, no cerebral Trudeau, no aristocratic Laurier. Just the kid from Shawinigan, as mediocre as the carpenter down the block.

Senator Roman L. Hruska, though he never met him, would have liked him as an example of his unanswerable theory.

(Judge Carswell was dumped as the nominee.)

One idle Sunday, Jean Chrétien found me in a hotel newsstand and kindly invited me to his home and the family Sunday dinner. We had a lovely evening with his gracious wife, with all the usual lies and gossip.

I guess I must have been hard on him in a few columns after that. At the Parliamentary Press Gallery black-tie banquet a few years later, those who were not active members of the gallery—I was working in Washington—sat in a separate room. Chrétien wandered in to natter a bit with Charlie Lynch and Bruce Phillips and a few others he knew.

He looked down, saw me, and said, "And here's Mr. Fotheringham." I didn't think that a particularly wise thing to say to a national columnist who appeared coast-to-coast when the speaker was attempting to become the next prime minister.

January 13, 1993

No one wants to talk about it

The following probably should be labelled X-rated—in the current politically correct mode. It will be construed as anti-Quebec, racially motivated, probably even as a slur on the handicapped. All the political insiders talk about it— especially the nervous people within the Liberal party. The reporters talk about it, but nobody writes about it. Because it is supposedly sacrosanct.

What no one wants to bring up publicly is the matter of Jean Chrétien's failing battle with the English language. No one paid much attention to it when he was a minor, if charming, figure on the national stage. Now that his party leads in the polls and he supposedly might be the next prime minister, the uncomfortable subject keeps coming up: why can't he do something about his tenuous grasp of the second official language?

There is one specific reason why Brian Mulroney, trying to shake off Sawatsky, believes in his Irish confidence that he can win his third election. It is his little secret. He knows that our outmoded electoral rules specify that a Canadian federal election campaign extends over two months (if the Brits can elect a government in 30 days, why can't Canada?).

He knows, which works for him, that for some 60 interminable nights Canadians are going to endure 90-second sound bits of Mulroney and Chrétien and Manning and whoever laying out their plans for the universe and our greater good. He knows that Canadian voters—fed up with politics and Son of a Meech as we all are—will only then concentrate on the weary choice they will have to make come election day. And he knows that, TV night after night, Canadians will begin to ponder Chrétien's mangling of the language that most

Canadians think of as their own.

The Mulroney strategy, the Tory strategy, is that a lot of Canadians are going to contemplate all those dese's and dose's and wonder if that is the chap after all that they want representing them in White House conferences, in speeches before the United Nations. The Mulroneyites think their secret gift is the Chrétien inability to speak English in an acceptable manner.

It was Lester Pearson who asserted, quite accurately, that there would never be a prime minister who would follow him who was not bilingual. We accept that now as a truism. John Crosbie, who has the highest IQ of anyone in the Conservative party, is proof of that incontrovertible fact.

Pierre Trudeau, with his effortless fluency and eloquence in either language, dazzled Canadians with our potential. John Turner, cleverly building his first political base in a Montreal riding, knew whereof Pearson spoke and mastered the language. Brian Mulroney learned his colloquial French on the rough streets of Baie-Comeau.

Which leaves us Joe Clark, the other prime minister since Pearson. He too could see the future, and the lad from High River painfully taught himself French, knowing Pearson was right. As have any ambitious politicians from the wooden-tongued Michael Wilson to Barbara McDougall (hello there, Clyde Wells) who know that to aspire to high office they must master both languages.

That's the point. If Joe Clark could make the effort to spend endless and excruciating hours to make himself fluent in an unfamiliar language, why couldn't Chrétien? Every Canadian politician raised with English as his mother tongue knows that to succeed in Ottawa means gathering an acceptable grasp of French, both in listening and in speaking. Why has Chrétien never comprehended that simple truth, in the opposite direction?

When Turner, waiting in his Elba on Bay Street for nearly a decade for Trudeau to part the scene so he could be coronated, finally came back to the spotlight, he was a disaster before the cameras. Political pros and the press were astounded at his nervous mannerisms and coughing, stuttering performances that left the public wondering what had happened to the golden boy.

Why, muttered all the insiders, with all that time to wait did he not take some television training and coaching to adapt to the new demands of media? The same insiders now puzzle over why Chrétien—who also waited almost the same amount of time to succeed Turner—did not do something about his struggle with the English language.

The answer would seem to be a combination of conceit and complacency. There was a time when the little guy from Shawinigan was an absolute rage in such as Alberta and British Columbia, confessing from platform to platform that he put the wrong em-PHA-sis on the right syl-LA-ble. They loved it in the boonies, the cuddly charmer who made fun of his own troubles with the lingo.

That, then was not a future prime minister. That was a Trudeau outrider, who wanted to prove he was just one of the boys. (Quebec, meanwhile, decided he was an Uncle Tom, which is why he had to run in New Brunswick.)

Charm is not enough anymore, as we realize that Lester Pearson was right. Canadians are confused as to their political future, but they wonder about a party leader who—as Turner did—simply sat and waited it out without working on his weaknesses, assuming that the prize would simply fall in his lap.

The little guy from Shawinigan seems these days to have lost the other thing that went along with his charm—his confidence. It may very well be because he has belatedly realized that he didn't do what Joe Clark and others have had to do—reach out and seriously work on becoming truly bilingual, the only solution for leaders who want to save this crazy country.

November 8, 1993

Jean Chrétien's route to power

Joseph Jacques Jean Chrétien is where he is today because of two women. One wonders whether they know it.

On the evening of June 16, 1984, Iona Campagnolo came to the podium at the liberal leadership race in Ottawa and announced the vote that made John Turner the new leader of the party. She then, in offering commiserations to the runner-up, praised Jean Chrétien as second on the ballot "but first in our hearts." The convention roared in tribute.

It was an astonishingly silly—if sentimental—thing for a president of the party to say: perhaps the final revenge of a strong feminist for the bum-patting controversy she had gone through with Turner. It indicated that while one guy won we really liked the other guy better. And Chrétien became convinced that he had been somehow cheated of the crown. To this day, the two men have never made up.

The second woman is publisher Anna Porter. She came to a certain reporter one day and asked if he thought there was a book in Jean Chrétien. This brilliant scribe assured her there wasn't, that he was dead meat. She didn't agree, having just met Chrétien for the first time and, over lunch, was bowled away by his rough-and-ready personality. She saw something there the political expert didn't.

She hired Ron Graham, a felicitous writer, to tape-record Chrétien and then turn out a book in his name. The result, *Straight from the Heart*, became the best-selling political confession ever "written" in this country, selling 100,000 copies for Key Porter Books. On his nationwide book tour, Chrétien was treated like a hero and by the end of it he had forgotten Graham's name, having convinced himself he had actually written it. Good for him.

So he waited out Turner, he waited out Brian Mulroney, he waited out Kim Campbell and today he's boss of the land. Good for him.

Chrétien, son of a machinist, was the 18th of 19 children, only 13 of whom survived childbirth. He was kicked out of four schools until, at 18, he met his tranquillizer. Her name was Aline. She was 16, guarded by the chain-link fence around her convent school. He would walk on the outside, she on the inside, their fingers tracing a trail of love through the fence. He plighted his troth through wire mesh.

When Chrétien first went to Ottawa as an MP in 1963, he was practically unilingual French. Mitchell Sharp spotted his spunk and later made him his parliamentary secretary. After Chrétien became a junior minister, the finance minister escorted the young MP to his first cabinet meeting. When they emerged three hours later, Sharp remembered that he hadn't warned his neophyte of the rules on strict cabinet secrecy. "Doan worry, Mr. Sharp," said the rookie, "I didin understand a God-damned ting."

Once a junior cabinet minister, Chrétien found himself one day flying with his social opposite, the worldly and intellectual Pierre Trudeau, a man he held in awe. Chrétien sat by the window, Trudeau on the aisle. Trudeau immediately buried himself in his briefing papers. A half-hour went by in silence.

Raindrops began to speckle the window, and the nervous Chrétien, trying to get something going, said: "It's raining outside." Trudeau, never lifting his eyes from his papers, said: "If it's raining, it has to be outside." The flight finished after another half-hour in silence.

When Robert Stanfield announced in the summer of 1975 that he wanted out of the Conservative leadership after three successive defeats to Trudeau, Chrétien bumped into Joe Clark in a House of Commons washroom. They were both young MPs, near the same age, and respected one another though on opposite sides of the House, probably because of similar combative styles, two kids from two small towns.

Clark allowed as how he, for all his inexperience, was toying with the idea of running for the Conservative leadership. He wanted Chrétien's advice. "I'll tell you one thing for certain," Jean replied, "if you don't run, you can't win." Shocked into common sense by Chrétien's rough logic, Clark ran and of course won. I wonder if he's ever thanked him.

In Ottawa, Chrétien is famously impatient over detail, every department he has ever worked in reporting that his attention span won't go beyond three pages of written text. Is he in fact a Ronnie Reagan, who delegated everything, didn't want to know the boring facts on the issues because he wanted to watch an old movie that night, but was loved by the voters because he had about three simple ideas and stuck with them?

Churchill, while running a war and saving the world, would not even read a memorandum until it was returned to him "on one side of one page." Does Chrétien possess Trumanesque simplicity? The man who made the decision to drop the bomb on Hiroshima and never missed a minute's sleep that same night?

Or has he reached the heights, politics being his life and his only interest, purely by hanging around so long that all others have dropped from the vine from fatigue? He can't cancel all the helicopters, he can't reverse the Pearson airport deal, but he pretends he can—and sounds believable.

Like Ronnie Reagan, he suspends disbelief. Any man who can make Ron Graham disappear in his own mind may be capable of astonishing things. After all, Doug Henning, the magician, made the Conservative party disappear.

Considering where Joseph Jacques Jean Chrétien came from, he done good.

February 19, 1996

A novel of politics and passion on the Rideau

Washington, the most powerful city in the world, is agog. Nothing much fazes this town, but someone has stumped it. This would be the mystery author of *Primary Colors*, the hottest book in the country —and penned by Anonymous.

The "novel," brilliantly written, is about a slick governor of an unnamed southern state, a chap who has an eager eye for an ankle and who has a wife who is tough and smart. As a presidential candidate, "Jack Stanton" is easily recognizable.

So is "Cashmere McLeod" (Gennifer Flowers). So are the stand-ins for Hillary and top aide George Stephanopoulos and Mario Cuomo and every one of Clinton's insiders in the 1992 campaign.

The publishers, Random House, say they are as mystified as everyone else; they dealt only with an agent and a lawyer. As Clinton himself says, "It's the only secret I've seen kept in Washington in three years."

The mystery of course has made it a runaway best-seller, which is all to the good. I am in favor of best-sellers. As a matter of fact, I am working on a book at the moment that I plan to publish under the byline of Anonymous.

It involves a lad from a small Quebec town who is so slippery and clever that he faked an appendix problem and actually went through the operation to have it removed so he could get out of a residential school he hated. His name is François Lalonde.

He marries his childhood sweetheart and is so eager to climb the political ladder that he forgets to learn how to speak either of Canada's two languages. He convinces the voters that he is a populist and manages to disguise the fact that—during a spell out of politics—he became a millionaire through advising a Bay Street firm.

With the money, he buys the golf club where he once caddied as a youth. Almost no one knows this, so nobody believes it. One night he is almost killed by a nutcase invader because his home is guarded by rejects from the RCMP Musical Ride. There is no sex involved in this chapter.

One of the prime characters in this piece of fiction is chap named Delbert Suitcase. He is from Alberta. His father was raised on the Bible and embraced a political philosophy called Social Credit wherein every citizen would be given $20 from the government treasury. This was called a flat tax.

Delbert goes to Ottawa but is handicapped by the fact his voice squeaks and he always looks as if his aides have just sent him out for a haircut that doesn't quite fit. He has been introduced to button-down shirts but looks not only uncomfortable but embarrassed at wearing them.

His main platform is that he wants to bring back the strap. He is taking French lessons but so far has not got beyond the appetizer list on the parliamentary restaurant menu. There is no sex involved in this chapter.

There is also a fiery orator by name of Fleury Champlain. He has no sense of humor. He thinks Canada is not a real country. So far, he has belonged to every single political party in Canada except the Rhinoceroses. He apprenticed for politics as an ambassador in an unnamed European nation where he had a steamy affair with a CBC girl reporter.

He later meets on an airplane a much younger woman who is from California and they are married. He considers becoming mayor of a small town in Orange County but instead decides to break up Canada. François Lalonde says he is no threat but then goes on national TV with his face whiter than a tablecloth and says we should do something, sometime, about this. There is a lot of sex involved in this chapter.

There are side players in this novel. There is Finance Minister Pierce Fisher, who tells Canadians to tighten their belts while his blind trust manages his shipping empire that is registered offshore so as to avoid taxes.

There is a premier of Ontario, Elmer Gauntry, who says only the private sector—not government—can provide jobs. He has spent most of his adult life as a teacher, school trustee, member of the legislature and now premier.

Because François Lalonde cannot compete with Fleury Champlain in the oratorical leagues, he brings into his cabinet a young academic by the name of Robespierre de Gaulle. He immediately calms the nation by proposing that the crisis can be solved by Quebec being divided into four sections. They would be called Bosnia, Serbia, Croatia and Herzegovina. The country relaxes.

The romantic element revolves around a dynamic politician called Sandra Shots, who spends most of her time trading insults with elderly backbenchers from New Brunswick who think a condominium is a method of birth control.

There is a cameo appearance of a former prime minister, Candy Tableau, who is soon coming out with a book of her own in which she will reveal which well-known journalists chew snuff and have been caught with typists in the overhead baggage rack on the press bus.

There is a Newfoundland figure, Clark Turbot, who becomes a sensation on European television because of a telescopic camera lens that catches him conducting interactive diplomacy with Brigitte Bardot on an ice floe.

There is a surprise ending involving François Lalonde and Fleury Champlain, but we won't spoil it for you.

Coming soon to a bookstore near you.

Around the World with Dr. Foth

This scribbler, as my mother once remarked, was one of the lucky ones. Born in 1932, too young in 1939 when the war started and, the war ending in 1945, not yet old enough to be drafted.

So wars could be observed, as an adult, from afar. As these two columns observe, the military brain has not much improved from Vimy Ridge and the Somme, old men still making decisions to send young men to death.

What the military mind has learned, however, is the art of obfuscation. When reporters in Saigon won Pulitzer Prizes for proving that American generals—and American presidents—were lying about what was really going on in Vietnam, the military mind decided to correct that mistake in the next American war, against Iraq.

Reporters were rendered mute, kept so far from the action that their only information came in those celebrated Stormin' Norman's pointer-on-the-map TV spectaculars about "smart bombs" that proved out to be never so smart as claimed.

Like a replay of an old movie, the tragic nonsense in Kosovo replicates what nobody learned in Vietnam or Iraq. You can't bomb people into submission. Saddam Hussein is still in power; George Bush is not.

Historians tell us that the real turning point of the Second World War was when the maniac Hitler, with lone Britain at his feet, became enraged when Churchill sent a long-distance bombing raid to Berlin—a geographical feat no one had ever contemplated.

Hitler overruled Hermann Goering's Luftwaffe, which was on the cusp of destroying RAF bases, and ordered Goering to concentrate on killing London's civilians. That led to Churchill's "Finest Hour," the valiant Brits simply stiffening their spines and bringing on the admiration of the world.

When the Allies, gaining control, then carpet-bombed German cities— the Americans every day, the Brits every night—the result was, interestingly, about the same. At the end of the war, German factory production was higher than at the start.

As the nonsense in Kosovo and Serbia showed, the military mind never learns.

February 4, 1991

Bafflegab in a living-room war

Your agent, by nature a pacifist and a coward, liked the last war better. It involved sitting in the rooftop bar of the Caravelle Hotel in Saigon in 1962 and watching the gunfire bursts in the jungle across the river. Of the other occupants of the bar, *The New York Times*' David Halberstam won a Pulitzer Prize and almost stopped the war on his own; Malcolm Browne aided him and can still be seen on your screen covering the Iraq insanity; Peter Arnett, the New Zealander whose brother used to sit beside me in the *Vancouver Sun* newsroom, won a Pulitzer and of course is the CNN hero in Baghdad; and Neil Sheehan won a Pulitzer two years ago for the book on Vietnam that took him nine years to write. It was the best way to cover a war, especially with talent like that sitting at the next table.

There was also the (now-dead) sense that what you wrote had some relation to the truth—which is why Halberstam and his colleagues turned the American public against the war. They told the truth—i.e., that the United States wasn't winning—while the military and the politicians lied and told the opposite. In Iraq, in the Nintendo War, the military authorities have made sure that the Vietnam mistake will not be made again. The military will control the information, not the scribes. In an incomprehensible computer war, fought seven miles high where sensors and lasers rule, there has scarcely been mention made of a single Iraqi dead body. Science has sanitized war. Missiles and rockets knock out only buildings and never touch human beings. Sure.

Phillip Knightley, the British journalist who examined the official lies in his book *The First Casualty: From the Crimea to Vietnam*, interviewed a number of distinguished war correspondents on their retroactive feelings. Among them was Canada's Charles Lynch, who confessed that, in retrospect, the dispatches he and his buddies were filing weren't even "journalism." They were cheerleaders.

Peter Gzowski was reminiscing the other day about his hero, Ralph Allen, who like all the great ones, came from Saskatchewan, Oxbow being his cradle. Allen came back from the war and edited *Maclean's* to wean the pups like Gzowski, and he told them one of the most astonishing things he learned was that honorable men—generals and colonels and other officers—lied to him. They lied to him and other war correspondents because it was their duty to lie, although they were honorable, decent men.

A reporter, of course, does not need to go to war anymore to find official people who lie in the guise of duty. A high-placed aide to a prime minister promises a columnist aboard a campaign plane that an interview with Himself is just around the corner, day after day, with the full knowledge that no interview will ever take place.

There is one disadvantage, to the military and political obfuscators, in a living-room war that, thanks to satellites, can be viewed live, ranking right up there with the Stupor Bowl and the weather reports. It is that the public—for the first time—has as much information as the reporters.

The scribbler in the field in his Banana Republic safari jacket is, because of the circumstances, getting his news from CNN just the same as Aunt Mabel at home in Dauphin, Manitoba. Soon it becomes apparent to the folks in Dauphin as to the gaps in the dobs of information being ladled out.

The precision hits of the "surgical" bombing is in the ration of news allowed on the screen, but there is no blood, no shattered limbs, no corpses. There has never been a war but this one without corpses, but when the military controls all the information, corpses can be dispensed with.

Eventually, the good burghers in Dauphin divine what the reporters on the scene already know. It's a sitcom version of war, somewhat like *Cheers*, where everyone laughs at the one-liners from the guys who sit at the bar all night and no one comments on why they drink so much.

The amazing production of the Television War, in which Israeli casualties can be seen in Technicolor, while the Iraqi dead are somehow invisible, should rate for high nomination in the Grammys. The public, for itself, can be educated in Orwellian grammar, where "ordnance" in fact means death from the sky and "sorties" are in fact not bombing raids but just the number of planes that have taken off that day.

Those who live by controlled information are doomed to die by controlled information. Lying to the David Halberstams and Charles Lynches and Ralph Allens of previous wars is one thing, mutually acknowledged subterfuges off in some war tent. When you lie on television to a roomful of restive reporters in Saudi Arabia, or Washington, or Ottawa, what is forgotten by those in charge is that all the nation is also watching, peering for the first time over the shoulders of the scribblers they once despised.

Instant war, live in your living room, leaves little room for bafflegab. The Pentagon spokesman who says too many times that he can't answer that question is revealed to Aunt Mabel as a chap who doesn't want to answer that question—probably because he knows the answer.

Television reveals phoneys, as it revealed Richard Nixon and as it makes Brian Mulroney so obviously uncomfortable before its unrelenting gaze. The more the military and political pooh-bahs attempt to control the news out of this war, after letting it escape them in Vietnam, the more they are revealed in their true aim.

As a modest chap, as faithful readers know, I would suggest that if I ever were to be proud of any column I have written, it would be this one on Dieppe, a disgrace that lies on Lord Mountbatten's brow even in his grave.

August 13, 1979

Behind the myths of bravery and pluck, there was no pride or glory at Dieppe

Engrained in the memory bank of every Canadian adult are those epic battles: Iwo Jima, Guadalcanal, Midway, Corregidor, Guam. They are, of course, famous American war names, drilled into our compliant minds 30 years ago by a barrage of Saturday afternoon movies featuring those celebrated soldiers in the foxholes, Errol Flynn and John Wayne. Because we did not have a propaganda movie industry, Canadians even now know little about one famous place-name associated with Canadian troops: Dieppe. In the mythology it is considered a sterling example of Canadian bravery and pluck. In truth, it was a disaster, a slaughter, conceived for political reasons, not military, and botched up from beginning to end. It was not glory.

On August 24 to 26, The Dieppe Veterans and Prisoners of War Association will hold a reunion at Port Hope, Ontario. There aren't too many left to attend. Out of 5,086 soldiers who landed on the Dieppe beaches that August day of 1942, only 1,443 made it back across the Channel to England. By contrast, the Germans had only 597 killed or wounded. Yet there has never been any serious examination in this country as to the blame, the spectacular (and cynical) horrors in the planning. We have no Errol Flynn, no John Wayne, to conduct a military autopsy.

On examination, Dieppe proves to be the modern-day version of the Charge of the Light Brigade. Richard Lamb, a British war historian, flatly labels it "the worst-planned battle in military history." The essential problem is that it was concocted for nonmilitary excuses, a ploy devised for high political reasons. As a result, Canadian casualties were an incredible 68 per cent. This wasn't war. It was execution.

In 1942, the Russian armies were in great danger. Leningrad was surrounded by the Germans. Stalin was insistent on an Allied attack somewhere in Western Europe to divert the Nazis, but the Allies had already decided to delay a Channel invasion and land instead in North Africa. Churchill and Anthony Eden, fearing Stalin might strike a deal with Hitler, pressed for this Canadian raid on "lightly defended Dieppe" to impress the Soviets.

Ordered by their political bosses to attempt a dubious task, the military chiefs indicated their lack of enthusiasm in a strange way. Army planners said three essentials were necessary for the one-day raid: airborne troops, heavy air bombing, bombardment from a battleship. All three were denied. As incredible as it seems even to a layman, the main beach assault was planned for broad daylight—30 minutes after the defenders were alerted by assaults on the flanks.

Even the dress rehearsals in Britain were fouled up, the units landing miles from their objective. After another false start, General Montgomery recommended that the Dieppe raid be cancelled forthwith. But Churchill was due to fly to Moscow August 12 and wanted to placate Stalin with plans for a major assault on Fortress Europe. Lord Mountbatten, commander of Combined Operations, ordered the doomed plan to press ahead.

With no air support, no heavy naval bombardment, the disaster pressed on. Monty refused to have anything to do with it. The first landing craft crossing the Channel ran into a German convoy. The fight at sea alerted Dieppe's German defenders. The commandos landing in the dark on the flanks of the town had success—though the German divisional headquarters they were to capture had been vacated four months before. Lieutenant-Colonel Cecil Merritt, later a Tory MP and still practising law in Vancouver, won a Victoria Cross for his courage in leading the South Saskatchewan Regiment.

Elsewhere, it was carnage that could have been (and was, in military circles) predicted. Just at daylight, so the German machine-gunners could see them clearly, the main assault troops landed on the open beach in front of the town promenade. The tanks due to land simultaneously with them were 15 minutes late. For those first crucial 15 minutes, the Essex Scottish Regiment and the Royal Hamilton Light Infantry had no support of any kind and were mowed down "in shoals," as they tried to run across the beach. (Insane with rage at the slaughter, Canadian troops in the town shot many of their German prisoners.)

In one landing craft, some 30 soldiers refused to land when they saw the carpet of dead laid out on the beaches. An inquiry later in England was told of some troops being forced by Canadian officers to land at revolver point. Lamb has written: "The wonder was not that a tiny few cracked, but that so many went courageously to certain death."

Incredibly, the Canadian command ordered Les Fusiliers Mont-Royals and the Royal Marine Commandos to make a second frontal assault on the beach. A wall of machine-gun bullets laced through the wooden landing craft of Les

Fusiliers (there were no steel ones left). When Lieutenant-Colonel J.P. Phillips landed his Royal Marines in bright sunlight and saw what was happening, he raised his hands and waved his boats back, shouting, "For God's sake, go back." Then he fell dead.

There has never been, to repeat, any serious examination in this country of an event that was supposed to be the proudest moment of Canada in the Second World War. There was nothing proud about it at all. Cannon fodder for political ends.

September 19, 1977

Blessed are the Bwanas, for theirs is the kingdom of heaven-on-earth. For now

Tell me, trivia experts, what is the area of the world that provides the highest standard of living—the highest index of pure material comfort? The usual reflex answer would be California or Texas, but a serious case can be made for South Africa and Rhodesia.

This is the factor that is overlooked in the wake of Ian Smith, that refugee from common sense, receiving a heavy mandate from his cornered voters, and John Vorster's South Africa retreating into another stubborn defense of him. It is the fact that the outnumbered white residents of those doomed lands are fighting desperately to protect a standard of living that is denied, elsewhere in the world, to all but the rich.

Only southern California can compare with the bounties of South Africa. The country may indeed have the finest climate on the globe. There are no heating bills. Businessmen wear shorts and open-necked safari shirts to work. There are beautiful beaches, fine, wholesome food, superb wines. The sparse traffic on the roads is heavily speckled with the Mercedes Benz, the Jaguar. It is a healthy, outdoor life, filled with sport and parties. Johannesburg may be Toronto with an overlay of Sudbury but Capetown is a lovely city with the sophistication and maturity of Montreal. (It has the second most spectacular setting of any city in the world, topped only by Rio de Janeiro and followed in order, if you must know, by Hong Kong, Vancouver, San Francisco and Sydney.)

In Rhodesia, that sunny land high on the veldt, the same blessings apply. Salisbury is a pleasant city with gracious suburbs worthy of Bel Air winding through such thoroughfares as Orange Grove Drive and Kipling Road. It is entirely possible, as goes the local boast, that the city has more swimming pools per capita than Los Angeles.

In the Meikles Hotel, each pat of butter is formed into the shape of a cob of corn and the black waiters, in white running shoes, white coats and long red sashes, suggest the cast out of a Turhan Bey movie. Across the street, the wild splash of flowers and fountains and trees in Cecil Square is quite up to the standard of San Francisco's celebrated Union Square. Most important, in both Rhodesia and South Africa—which is why those strange lands compete with southern California for affluence—the ordinary housewife has her niggling household chores done by cheap black labor and can graduate to tennis, while the husband has his gardening and handyman duties done by servants as well. The garage mechanic leaps into the upper middle class. They live, those people in 1977, in a manner our grandparents long ago abandoned.

As someone who has been to Africa four times, this is the single biggest thing that impresses: the insane belief that the clock can be turned back. British journalist Colin Legum calls Rhodesia "Cloud-Cuckoo-Land." In Salisbury, the businessmen move about in dark, heavy suits, stubbornly refusing to acknowledge their habitat. They are closer to the equator than either Tahiti or Hawaii and yet dress as their colonial idols did when they arrived from Manchester and Liverpool. Ian Smith and his ministers were offended when they arrived in Geneva for peace talks with black African leaders and astounded reporters broke into laughter at their garb; the narrow lapels and peg-leg pants of a country that has been a world outcast for 13 years branding the Rhodesian outlaws as recognizable as Rip Van Winkle. In the country's radio network, Glenn Miller is very strong. Next year: a rookie called Milton Berle. One has the sense of viewing a corner of the world where values have been turned upside down, as in Orwell. In the real world, the accepted view is that a reporter should be kept free of intimidation. In Johannesburg the *Rand Daily Mail*, a fine newspaper that fights the government, must print the address of the reporter at the end of each political story.

There are all the references in our press about the trouble in Soweto, always referred to as "a Johannesburg ghetto." Soweto in fact is not a ghetto. It is the proudest boast of the Southern African government, the most modern compound for blacks. Critical visitors to South Africa are always taken to Soweto. It is held forth as an example of how well "the Bantu" are treated. It is, in truth, quite the most depressing sight on the globe. It is the compound, 10 miles outside Johannesburg, where the blacks who provide the cheap labor for the city's gold mines and industry and shops and who must, by law, be clear of the city boundaries by sunset, are kept. In reality, it is the fourth largest city in South Africa: 34 square miles of identical $600 huts with tin roofs and outside plumbing. There are four swimming pools for one million people, but 17 funeral homes. Throughout Soweto are huge billboards for Lexington cigarettes, displaying handsome, bounding white tennis players. The point is that the government is not ashamed of Soweto. It is proud of Soweto. It is the finest compound it has and it resents criticism of it.

It is an Upside-Down World, the Vorster government trying to consign 70 per cent of the land to just 13 per cent of the population. But if South Africa, where whites are outnumbered five to one, is upside-down, it is Topsy-Turvey World in Rhodesia, where whites are outnumbered 25 to one. Most depressing, the young and enlightened leave, to be replaced by the original Archie Bunkers of Britain, losers in their low station, who see a chance of having servants in the grand manner. In this reverse flow of bigotry, tolerance, in fact, is being diluted, prejudice reinforced. It's downhill all the way.

To anyone who has been in Vietnam there is an eerie replay—black Africans being moved into "protected villages" to keep them away from any contaminating contact with the guerrillas. The "Liberation Armies" are moving in ever-increasing numbers across the Zambezi from Zambia, in from Mozambique, leaving frightened, encircled Rhodesia with its only secure border that one tiny stretch adjoining South Africa.

The tragedy is the spectacle of the settlers married to the land (the Dutch arrived in southern Africa about the same time the Puritans landed in America) that they have tamed and feel they own. The reality is that they are also trying to protect a standard of comfort that even the ulcer-ridden southern Cal executive, helping his wife with the dishes while they complain about the dearth of household help, would envy.

February 26, 1990

The lessons of Nelson Mandela

So, we are standing around waiting outside the Victor Verster Prison. Waiting for Mandela. Waiting for Godot. This is amidst the lush vineyards of the Paarl country an hour outside Cape Town. Purple peaks rise above us. A restaurant called Le Paris is across the road. A helicopter whirrs overhead, revealing a TV cameraman who is busily shooting film of all the TV cameramen on the ground who are filming the helicopter. Nelson Mandela is more than an hour past his highly publicized release time, and we wonder what the problem is. A *New York Times* reporter muses about the processing ritual going on inside: "Mr. Mandela, you were issued three pairs of socks when you were admitted here 27 years ago. You are returning only two pairs of socks. Where is that other pair of socks, Mr. Mandela?"

We contemplate how much macramé must be piled up after 27 years. How many thousand *Times* of London crossword puzzles filled out? It's daunting to think of what 27 years in prison—27 years in a South African prison—could do to a man, but the remarkable man/myth that is Mandela somehow survived it. He is trim and erect at 71 as he walks through the gate, he is smiling, his voice is clear and strong and authoritative. He beat the system.

Because of his patience and his strength, Mandela became a more powerful figure—not a lesser one—the longer he was in jail. The South Africans finally learned what the British were taught painfully long ago by Gandhi: the martyr in jail can become more influential than the government that jails him. Eventually, they have to release him since the government's legitimacy decreases and the martyr's increases.

Nelson Mandela looked like a young Joe Louis when he went into prison (he used to be a good amateur boxer) and when he emerged, looked like George Armstrong, the old Maple Leaf. Mandela was born to the royalty of the Xhosa tribe. He was given the name Nelson by a white teacher who couldn't wrap her tongue around his given name—Rolihlahla. Later, he became just a number: Prisoner 0221141011.

He opted out of a tribal marriage and, after university, articled with a Johannesburg law firm. He loves to tell the story of one of the firm's typists, a white, embarrassed that a white client had seen her taking dictation from him, demanding, "Nelson, here's a sixpence, please get me some shampoo."

The young lawyer eventually turned from peaceful protest to armed struggle. Charged with treason in 1956, he was acquitted—five years later. He went underground as the "Black Pimpernel," dodged around Africa, took sabotage training and slipped back and forth into South Africa, giving clandestine news conferences to reporters from phone booths. He was 40 when he married 24-year-old social worker Nomzamo Zaniewe Winifred Madikizela. In 31 years, they have spent just a few months together. Disguised as a chauffeur, he was arrested by police in 1962 (supposedly turned in by the CIA) and jailed for five years for leaving the country without a passport.

When security police swooped down on the African National Congress underground hideout in 1963, they found a fanciful guerrilla-warfare document that would have terrorists from Russia and Algeria landing by submarine. Mandela was brought from prison to stand trial for treason along with seven comrades. Defending himself, Mandela gave his now-famous "black man in a white man's court" speech that lasted 4¾ hours. He never denied anything he had done, but explained in a moving address how he had progressed from Gandhi-like nonviolence to violence because he did not feel bound by the laws of the country that would not allow him a vote in formulating those laws. Excerpts from the speech became a sensational long-playing record in London, now a collector's item. The judge, because of his eloquence, backed off on the death penalty for treason and sentenced them all to life.

In prison, they were put to work smashing rocks and, on the first day, were ordered by guards to trot the one-mile on-the-double. Mandela said, "Let's walk as slowly as possible." They did, the guards could do nothing about it and when they arrived at the quarry, an officer was sent to speak to Mandela. That meant, to both sides, that they had already acknowledged his leadership.

One of the ANC leaders just released tells of how, in the early days in the crowded cells, the crickets at night used to drive them crazy and they would try to kill them. Mandela instead would take each cricket, cup it in his hands and release it through the window. He asked for Afrikaans poetry to read, so he could understand the minds of the architects of apartheid. Two of his children are in university in South Africa, and a daughter is taking a PhD in anthropology at the University of Massachusetts. One of his favorite readings in prison was *Ring* magazine, the bible of boxing.

As the years have passed, the myth has grown. Practically every city in Britain has honored him in some way. Over 100 artists from Harry Belafonte to Sting to Whoopi Goldberg honored him with a massive concert in Wembley Stadium on his 70th birthday. A nuclear particle discovered at the University of Leeds was named the Mandela particle.

Nelson Mandela has now outlasted five South African leaders. The present one, President F.W. (Frederik) de Klerk, says, "He is an elderly man, a dignified man, an interesting man." That is the understatement of the decade. If he lives, and is not assassinated, he could be the next president—and not only through black votes.

July 7, 1980

Seeing and being seen: just fake Venetian glass

There was this beautiful tableau, you see, the press held back by cattle barriers on the stone dock on San Giorgio Maggiore island in the Venetian lagoon, Jimmy Carter bearing down on his fancy white admiral's launch, which rather resembles a John Kennedy PT boat. The other six world leaders at the Venice summit are transported across the sickly grey waters by standard Venetian motor launch, but the white looks better—and more presidential—on color TV. Long before the launch approaches the dock, Carter kick-starts his wave and his grin to the non-existent public on the security-ringed isle. The world press stares at this strange man waving to nothing. The bulky U.S. Navy craft, of course, is ill-fitted for these close quarters, misses the dock, and drifts sideways. Jimmy, his fixed grin and wave still operating, stands with frozen feet like a mannequin, not adjusting to the empty sea. One does not know whether to laugh or weep.

The connection between world statesmanship and the suction cup of vanity is most intriguing to behold. With a leadership vacuum at the top, we go to programmed automatons, plastic smiles with plastic thoughts, conditioned response, Pavlov's proof. As Jimmy Carter, leader of the most powerful and prosperous country in history, emerges from a ceremonial ceremony, he reaches in reflex, his grin to the cameras, for the supporting hand that is always beside him, that of wife Rosalynn. West German Chancellor Helmut Schmidt looks down in some surprise, since the president of the United States is holding his hand. A hand in need is a friend indeed.

There is the icy Zbigniew Brzezinski purposely perching on top of the cabin of a motor launch so the lurking TV cameras can pursue his image with a zoom lens. Pierre Trudeau tries it, but slips and has to settle for a standing pose into the waves while his ministers, second-string on the marquee, huddle below. Washington on the Delaware, Caesar on the Rubicon. Margaret Thatcher, resembling more and more a preserved film star of the Anna Neagle era, sweeps imperiously along, a train of thin-lipped and nondescriptly tailored British aristocrats in her wake. Giscard d'Estaing is impeccably groomed, haughty, almost vice-regal in attitude (the reason, insiders claim, why the similarly equipped Trudeau and the French president do not get along). The Venice communiqué, supposedly conceived in two days, in fact was being worked over by bureaucrats as early as March.

In an atmosphere where fewer and fewer men (and finally a woman) spend more and more time arrogating to themselves more and more power while becoming more and more secretive—while coveting and cosseting the appearance of openness by exploiting the zoom lens—what takes the place of the world personalities who hide on a Venetian island? It is natural: those who polish and refine and chip at the image. The image is all. Those who can shatter it or conceal it take on important powers. Here is Barbara Walters one night in the lobby of her hotel which once was a Venetian palace, fussing about flying back to London in the ABC executive jet because this trip it has only one pilot. Lesley

Stahl, one of the teeth-and-hair generational aspirants to the crown of Queen Bawbwa, throws a junior tantrum in a journalists' queue, fearful that a bored stranger is recording her self-important barkings through her walkie-talkie.

Pierre Salinger, once the mouthpiece of Kennedy's Camelot and now with the good life of a Paris resident on his face, waves a begging microphone toward the presidents and prime ministers just like any other reporter—except that $100,000 plus compensates for the humility. Carl Bernstein, the other twin from Watergate, enjoys the fame of a Redford or a Burt Reynolds as he moves his way through the herd of 2,000 reporters with R.W. Apple Jr., the flamboyant young star of *New York Times* foreign correspondents. John Chancellor has trouble with his chair stability in Harry's Bar, the Venice saloon immortalized by Hemingway. Oriana Fallaci, the most famous (and feared) journalist in the world for her devastating dissections of such as Kissinger, wriggles her 100 pounds to the cattle barrier to apprize the showmen-cum-politicians as they climb into their boats (and television masks).

It is delightful theatre. A staged event, purposely placed on an isolated island for fear terrorists (or the public) might intrude, in a city that is probably more grounded in the arts than any other; electronic fabrication reaches its peak. At the wrap-up announcement of the long-mouldy communiqué, with the seven leaders on world television, all sit with plastic earphones leading to the simultaneous translation. They look faintly ludicrous, these persons who can press the nuclear button resembling students in Berlitz—all but one.

Pierre Trudeau sits alone, shunning earphones, that icon visage overtaking his face, indicating to all watching that *he* understands all and does not need to stoop to translation. Brilliant theatre. In a world of artifice, the man who can keep a straight face the longest without giggling is king.

As a man who believes that the glass of life is half full, not half empty, there is always hope. The hope is that in my lifetime, somehow, my country will grow up.

The hope is that the common garden variety of voters—since we don't hold out much hope for our leaders—will take the lead and announce that we have finally grown up.

Grown-up nations do not need, as head of state, a woman—however nice—who lives across a large ocean in a castle in a foreign country. Grown-up nations, such as the United States, realized this long ago.

Australia, though younger than Canada, has realized it. Knowing that the world would be watching on television when the Olympic Games of 2000 are opened in Sydney, Australia has known that it would be demeaning for a woman who lives far across the ocean in a foreign country to officially open the Olympics next September.

The proper diplomatic channels have made that clear to the nice lady— while the preparations for a vote of becoming a republic progress—and the nice lady will travel Down Under earlier, and harmlessly, earlier in the year. And a real, live Australian will open the Games. As is only fit for a grown-up country.

One day Canada, with its usual forelock-tugging mush-mouth attitude about servitudes to toffs who live far away, will take the same action.

It is insane, of course, that Good Queen Bess on her occasional, now rather tentative forays into her largest colony, can only dare take a bridge from Ottawa across to Hull for a brief, fleeting event. She does not dare, naturally, a full-blown tour of Quebec, for fear of empty streets and demonstrations. Ottawa tells her that.

I ask my monarchist friends what would be the reaction in anglophone Canada if the Head-of-State of Canada were French and lived in a castle in Paris. They sputter, of course, and mumble.

That's the whole point. Look at it through Quebec eyes. The silly non-sense of this increasingly multilingual country—try Hongcouver out in B.C. —having an English queen on our currency simply reinforces the angst among the Quebec youngsters the desperate separatists are trying to recruit.

Let's grow up.

April 14, 1980

God save us from our gracious Queen

My fading life, you see, is filled with a recurring nightmare. It is bad enough, those horrors in one's past—Moral Re-Armament, Elvis Presley, Stafford Smythe, puberty, Ronald Reagan at Saturday matinees, Trudeau flow charts, Sen-Sen—but what is depressing is the contemplation of what one perceives on the horizon of one's future. What fills my plaintive little spine with chills is the prospect, as demonstrated once again last week, of plowing through future mounds of newsprint about yet another chinless wonder of the unemployed British royalty snipping ribbons and cowing acne-ridden schoolgirls and dispensing 1938 witticisms to compliant, adoring Canadians. Neither an Olympic boycott, Nelson Bunker Hunt, nor the prospect of Tom Snyder or Francis Fox being regarded as serious thinkers depresses me as much. I have many objections to Canadians as a breed, but acting as obsequious sycophants to outdated toffs who live across a long ocean is probably the least attractive of their traits.

If you must know, I am bored. The surfeit of the Royals, desperate for make-work projects so as to justify their teen-age allowance, drives me into eyeball-rolling paroxysms of ennui. What newsprint that could be usefully taken up by accounts of traffic accidents is consumed by slavering details of yet another clean-jawed prince, displaying clone-like replicas of Prince Philip's arch wit, dazzling factory maidens who know no better. Really, in 1980, do we need this stale titillation?

The reason this pinged upon my forehead is that we just have had—dear déjà vu Queen, save us—another spell of Prince Charles, the thoroughly piti-ful young man consigned to a wretched life of saying nice things to people he doesn't really know and undoubtedly would not like. He has—before depart-ing on a private jet for a "private" visit to Florida which will include a polo tournament, well-known pastime of the privates—been doing this stale, tired ritual in Ottawa and British Columbia, the restricted functions of the Royals in the colonies, dispensing beads and platitudes upon the masses.

Now constant readers of this space will know that I have no dispute with the philosophical concept of the monarchy. It serves, granted, a useful purpose to a state: a buffer one step above saving us from the Nixons and the jumped-up politicians who may be more honest but are equally arrogant. All I ask is that we provide, as a supposedly independent country, our own card-carrying monarchy: Iona Campagnolo, Lily Schreyer, Heward Grafftey, whatever.

Myth is a precious commodity, to be treated tenderly. There was a time when a royal visit, *vide* 1939, was a national trauma. These were gods. We all palpi-tated on the curbs of Moose Jaw and treasured the photos for grandchildren for-ever after. Today? The problem, sorry to mention, is that even the Royals breed too much. Such is the product of their loins, such is the shrinking of the Empire, that the poor kids have time to kill, and Canada—simp-faced Canada—is bored to the gills with the progeny who have good manners, no zits and nothing to do.

When the Good Queen Bess Mark II dropped in on us in 1978, the year after the 25th anniversary of her ascension to the Crown, it was her third visit in three years. Fair enough. There was appropriate affection and nostalgia—mainly in the up-scale age bracket. Since then? Sorry, but it's become the blahs. Mark Phillips, that horsey salesman for British Leyland, dropped in twice that year. After Princes Andy and Eddy dazzled the pubescent set, Prince Philip himself was back in Winnipeg later in the year to complain that politicians didn't have "a significantly higher integrity rating than their constituents." Nice to hear from a democrat.

In 1979 Prince Charles flew to the first of his visits to the Lester B. Pearson College of the Pacific outside Victoria. Later in the year the Queen Mother spent a week wetting eyes. Three months later Prince Philip does a tour. A month later Princess Anne, with her ineffable charm, did Ontario. Now, we've just had, once again, poor Prince Charles, the 31-year-old heartthrob who, in an interview with highly competent reporter Mary Trueman, was protected by Private Secretary Sir Edward Adeane, who asked that part of his replies be struck from the record, and Canadian Press Secretary Vic Chapman, who cut short a question that was not deemed appropriate. The natives, you see, must bow and tuck.

What is so intriguing here is the battle of wills—and bluff. The Royals, running out of countries, have desperate need of make-work projects to justify their existence. John Diefenbaker complained in 1978 that the Trudeau government had stalled for a year a University of Western Ontario request to give Prince Charles an honorary degree. In reply, acting Prime Minister Jean Chrétien riposted that the Queen had visited Canada more under Trudeau than under Diefenbaker.

Of course, Trudeau, the sly republican, knows there is more than one way to skin a cat. Familiarity breeds contempt. Nothing exceeds like excess.

March 2, 1992

Will Elizabeth II yield the throne?

There are two myths floating out there in the void, in all the recent fuss over the 40th anniversary of Queen Elizabeth on the throne of a foreign country. The one is that Dr. Foth, who thinks that the Brits should stick with their royalty and that Canada should grow up, knows nothing about the royals. This is not true.

The second is the misconception that Good Queen Bess is stubbornly sticking to her crown and selfishly won't give it up to the resolutely underemployed Prince Charles. Both beliefs are mistaken. We are here to disabuse you of them. In 1981, your agent, for his sins, was ordered to cover the Cinderella wedding of the Virgin Di and the chap with the large ears. I sat some 50 feet from the fairy-tale ceremonies in St. Paul's Cathedral and was struck most of all by one overriding image. It was the glum and sorrowful look on the face of the mother of the bridegroom.

One would have thought—all London aflame with a party passion understandable in a people who lead such dreary lives—that the Queen would have

been beaming with pride. She wasn't. She looked unhappy. We have shared a glass or two at off-the-record press receptions on the royal yacht and, at the time, your blushing republican was struck by (a) her daintiness; (b) the fact she is more attractive in person than in pictures; (c) her understated wit that borders on withering.

Implicit in that was a good humor. The good humor had disappeared by the time of St. Paul's Cathedral. She has never smiled since. The reason she has never smiled since is because, as she gazed at the altar and the fairy-tale wedding, she knew within herself that her son probably would be an old and tired and discouraged man before he ever acceded to the throne she would like to give up.

She would like to, but she's decided she can't. Because of the past, and because of the present conduct of her offspring, she's been advised by her Buckingham Palace advisers that she has to stay, for the survival of the monarchy.

The past of course was her selfish uncle, the Prince of Wales, who abandoned the throne for the conniving and much-married Wallis Simpson—and spent the rest of his life wandering in exile, a pitiful figure. Good Queen Bess can never forgive her uncle Edward for that: the abdication forced her shy father, who didn't want the job, to become king, a task that killed him—and therefore ruined the youth of a 25-year-old young bride who had to accept a heavy crown.

If King Edward can junk the job for love, can Elizabeth now do it because she's old? And wants her long-impatient son to have it? Nope. The dangerous precedent cannot be repeated. It's too fragile a myth as it is. The crown is not something you can abandon, willy-nilly, as the coinage would be debased. It's not a job, it's a calling—a lifetime calling.

Little wonder the moody Prince Charles is reduced to talking to flowers and wandering the Scottish woods in his kilt while the wife who has upstaged him flits off to the disco with Fergie. He's 43 and could hit retirement age before his coronation. His mother is 65 and certainly not infirm. The genes are in the family. The Queen Mum is 114 or something and still going strong, with the pearls, the corgis and the gin.

The Brits are used to longevity. George III stuck it out for 59 years on the throne. Queen Victoria did better, lasting almost 64. The incumbent may beat that. No wonder she looks so glum. No wonder Prince Charles is reduced to complaining about architecture.

There is the additional problem of the progeny. The royals were once a tight little family unit. Now there are so many of them that some, inevitably one supposes, fall off the back of the truck. Divorce has entered the fairy tale, through Princess Margaret, and is impending through Princess Anne, with her husband, Mark Phillips, in a paternity suit in New Zealand with some horsey lady.

Fleet Street warns that some of the juvenile antics threaten to bring the Windsors down to the level of the partying Eurotrash aristocrats. There was Randy Andy with his porn star, Koo Stark. Fergie, with her aggressive bad taste in clothes, seems a grenade about to explode in the tabloids any week. The young brother Edward, who enraged his father by abandoning the military, seems fey and uncertain about life. There is always some stray cousin up for speeding or drugs or both.

Lady Di, who vies with Madonna for most magazine covers of the year, has become a fashion industry on her own, is bored with Scottish woods and kilts. Do the Brits want a queen in a bikini? Not yet they don't.

Does anyone deserve to be stuck with one job beyond 40 years? Nope. But them's the breaks. It's not a job, it's an inheritance. Duty calls. In order to fulfil the duty—and keep the myth alive—she must watch her one reliable son grow old from misuse and broody from inactivity.

She knows the secret to his morose nature and how to lift it: hand him the crown. But she can't, won't, because it would destroy the myth. It's all high-class soap opera, and the British public loves to watch (while Canada is trying to grow up without it).

Prince Charles has fallen off a polo pony once too often and has been advised to give up the sport. What to do? Perhaps he could try reading the encyclopedia from front to back, as a bored Ed Schreyer once tried in Rideau Hall. Or write down what flowers say when they talk back. We're only offering advice. It's going to be a long wait.

There is one advantage in being late for church. You often get a better seat.

London streets were deathly still the morning I set out for St. Paul's Cathedral and Di's wedding. The reason they were still and empty, of course, was because the entire population—aside from those lining the blocked-off marriage route—was indoors with the telly.

The cabbie, in one of London's famous black taxis, had never had such a speedy and effortless drive in his life. Slipped in the side door by security guards who shook their heads at my tardiness, I found myself in a press seat above the altar, about 25 feet from the Queen herself.

Since I hadn't seen her since the time we once sipped sherry on the Britannia in Victoria's harbor, she didn't nod—to my tremendous surprise—in my direction. What did strike me throughout the entire wonderful and moving ceremony, pomp and circumstance as only the Brits can mount, was her doleful expression.

Never once, during what one would think of a joyous wedding of her eldest child to a beautiful, Cinderella-like girl, did she smile or emit pleasantness of appearance.

That struck me as odd at the time; only in later years did it appear understandable. In retrospect—hindsight being everything—as the doomed marriage became soap opera, then farce, perhaps a wise mother knew on that happy/sad day that it was all a mistake?

On the last day of August 1997, your humble agent was celebrating his usual world-famous birthday party on Bowen Island off Vancouver, the number of guests equal—as it did each year—to the age of the birthday boy.

The denizens of the summer retreat at Hood Point finish off the season before Labour Day each year with a goofy costume dance in a rough hall-with-no-walls beside the tennis courts. Late in the evening, daughter Francesca rushed in, pulled me from the dance floor and announced that Di and Dodi had just been killed in a car crash somewhere in France.

The next morning, as the Fothlets rushed to catch the first ferry so as to leave the holiday detritus and mess to Daddy, my future bride, Anne Libby, said, "You should be in London. It will be the biggest news story in the world for the next week. Every top journalist from anywhere will be there. Besides, you were at her wedding. You should be at her funeral."

"Who'll clean up the cottage?" I protested. "I don't have any money."

"Get in the shower. Get your ass in gear. I'll pack for you."

We raced to a bank machine, raced to the ferry, I caught a Vancouver flight over the Pole to London within two hours and, at Heathrow, phoned Maclean's *editor Bob Lewis and asked him what he thought of my possibly going to Lady Di's funeral.*

He thought that might be a reasonable idea but what was going to be the cost? I said, "I'm at Heathrow now." Bob said, "Oh." That's all. That's why he's a good editor.

September 6, 1997

Diana changed the monarchy forever

My digs, The Stafford, is the best small hotel in the world. It is like a boardinghouse—where they take plastic. The lone elevator breaks down every day. One morning, there is no hot breakfast—"the gas" has disappeared. The unbuttered toast, as always, is stone cold even when there is gas.

Outside the door, there is a narrow paved shortcut that opens on Green Park, one of the three lovely linked hunks of grass—in between St. James's Park and Hyde Park—that are "the lungs of London."

Turn left down Queen's Walk and about 10 m along, intercepted only by a punker with green spiked hair flogging a magazine, is the wonderfully named lane, Milkmaids Passage. At the end is an ugly pile of yellow brick: St. James's Palace, built in 1532 by Henry VIII, home last week to the shattered corpse of the young lady who even in death has changed the monarchy forever.

Out front was the perfect image of a country that can't decide when it will enter the modern world. A lone redcoat, wearing a busby before a sentry box, carrying erect a submachine-gun that was topped by—what's this?—a bayonet. A bayonet! To counter nuclear missiles, no doubt. There is the great confusion of Britain, a faded empire now desperate not to give up the tourist trade.

A stroll to the right reveals the mob around Buckingham Palace's locked gates and the endless mound of flowers with a child's crayoned tribute to her "Queen of Harts." The main objects of attraction, perhaps not so strangely, were banks of TV anchor ladies in coiffed blond hair emoting to cameras—the very media mob the bottom-feeders of which are accused of driving the princess into her grave.

London has never seen a week like it. Winston Churchill, who saved the world for democracy, attracted 300,000 to his funeral cortege when he died in 1965. This untutored girl draws millions, and so shakes the royals that they are forced by public outrage to abandon their beloved protocol and bow to their subjects' wishes that they get a life and get involved.

George Will, the American commentator, has noted that "the monarchy is a residue of the infancy of the British people." Alone among European democracies—almost all of them republics—the Brits persist in turning their royals into movie stars (unlike the Yanks, who turn their movie stars into royalty).

The dead princess may have changed all that, in death perhaps more than when she was alive. Those with sharp memories may know that she died at 36 at the same age as another doomed sex symbol, Marilyn Monroe, and in the same manner as the equally gracious Grace Kelly left this earth.

The spontaneous outpouring of feeling from what is supposed to be the stiff-upper-lip isle left the royals, bunkered in Balmoral up in Scotland, absolutely bewildered and in slight panic—gulping and recalling that they had stripped a bitter "Di the Difficult" of the "Her Royal Highness" label.

Columnist Polly Toynbee, descendant of a rather well-known historian, says "the Windsors are behaving as if a revolution is taking place outside the gates of Buckingham Palace. And they may be right." Every morning, as I went out

Queen's Walk to buy my 10 newspapers, little men in proper blue business suits were headed, a posey of red roses in hand, down to Buck House to lay another wreath—on the dead hand of the monarchy.

There are all the comments on how Prince Charles, in the last year, spent exactly 30 days with those two crushed, pitiful boys. Instead of the world's most-photographed woman taking them to McDonald's and dressing them in baseball caps, will they spend their youth grouse shooting in Scotland?

Someone has noted that getting hooked up with the monarchy these days is like marrying into the Addams family. At the "fairy-tale marriage" in 1981, feminists showed up with lapel buttons shouting "Don't do it Di!" According to the Queen Mum's gene pool, by the time Queen Liz dies Charles will be past 70 and poor Prince Wills will be in his 40s.

It is infantile. It has resulted in *Monty Python* come to life. It is so bizarre that Mohammed Al Fayed (who added the "Al" to his name to appear a Saudi prince and has been denied British citizenship for lying even about his birth certificate) mounts a huge picture display in Harrods' window of Diana and his dead playboy son who could not control a drunk driver—and then sends food vans to feed the drenched mourners standing 11 hours in the drizzle to sign a book for the princess in St. James's Palace.

And the Royal National Institute for Deaf People, saying it is "saddened," turns down a request by journalists to provide professional lip-readers to note down the Royal Family's private conversations during the Westminster Abbey funeral.

Tony Blair, who popularized "the people's princess" description, has emerged as a more powerful influence than the bewildered royals who can't read their people any more.

The princess who once confessed she was "thick as a plank" has revealed, even more in death than in life, the desiccated, bloodless family she left behind.

If I could give only one piece of advice to an aspiring journalist, it would be to travel. (It's why I tell all the kids in journalism classes never to get married until they're 30.)

Otherwise, you get trapped in kids, a mortgage, payment on the fridge and the car. I know more than one journalist in this country—very good and must remain anonymous—who would be far better if they had spent a coupla years kicking around the globe.

They would be better because the one thing travel does is to give you per-spective—on your own country. Only after seeing Canada from the distance of the rest of the world can a Canadian writer understand and observe and appreciate it. Only then can you realize how good it is. You can't write if you don't travel.

There are only two ways to travel. One is when you're young and on the hitch-hike, backpack, youth-hostel gig. The other is when you've finally become a successful reporter, columnist, commentator, TV personality and can do it on someone else's expense account.

The first way is best. If you want to be a useful scribbler, travel is better than any university.

The world has been speckled with scribblers who have never been tainted and spoiled by a university education. Dickens's father was sent to debtors' prison, and Charles as a boy started off in a blacking factory. The elegant stylist and literary critic V.S. Pritchett started off in the leather trade.

The dean of Canadian journalism, Bruce Hutchison, who never got out of high school, ran the editorial page of the major force Winnipeg Free Press *and then the* Vancouver Sun, *while never stirring from his beloved garden in Victoria.*

All he did, once a year, was to take a tour of his listening spots in Ottawa —Jack Pickersgill mostly—then on to Washington for sessions with the Bundy brothers, who had unwisely advised Jack Kennedy to get into Vietnam, and then on to his prestigious London contacts.

He's the only person I've ever met who—well, perhaps, Stephen Lewis is the other one—talked in actual sentences, in actual paragraphs. You could hear, as they spoke, where the commas go, where the period ends—in fact where the semicolons are.

One day, arriving back on the plane from his annual Ottawa–Washington– London stint, he was asked by Vancouver Sun *publisher Stuart Keate if he could come in from the airport and give the editorial board the gist and wisdom of what he had discovered in the three capitals.*

Exhausted from the over-the-Pole flight from London, Hutch came—he never took his hat off, indoors or out—leaned back in his chair, gazed at the ceiling and gave a tour de force *of his view of the perilous state of the world, illuminated all the way by his heavyweight contacts.*

We sat there enthralled, hearing every sentence ending. Every paragraph starting. Every semicolon exactly in line.

Two days later, I picked up his column in our paper. There it was, word for word, not a syllable missing, phrase-perfect as he had described it to us.

It occurs to me now that there is a third orator who can do the same thing—talk as if you can see the words, all parsed, appearing on the page. It is Conrad Black. And, if you have a spare hour and one-half on any weekday afternoon, he will demonstrate it to you.

September 6, 1976

A little travelling music please ... a nice dirge would be appropriate

It was the bee-stung lips and bouffant hairdos that brought it to my attention. Twenty years ago I was rattling about Europe, attempting to avoid work on a meandering route that wandered from Sweden to Morocco. As a Canadian raised in the storybook image of quaint Europeans who differed in wooden-shoe stereotype, I was struck by one astounding fact: every 19-year-old female in Europe looked and dressed alike. It was the era of Brigitte Bardot and somehow, by osmosis, every steno on the continent walked the streets with pouting, half-open lips, back-combed hair and a kittenish stare. The ability of an instant fashion trend to leap mountains and cross seas where statesmen fear to tread has fascinated me ever since.

It was visible once again at the Montreal Olympics, where the once cosmopolitan spectacle of the athletes' village was blurred by a sea of blue jeans. At last the world had a united cause—the ability of the unisex uniform of teenyboppers to disguise genders on all five continents. In this shapeless cloth of conformity, it was almost impossible to distinguish a Bulgarian weightlifter from a Romanian lady gymnast. The horizon filled with blue jeans in Montreal revived the celebrated Fotheringham Law of Travel. It postulates that the more the world begins to look the same, the more it disagrees. The only thing travel broadens is the clothing budget. You can now find young men walking Gorki Street in Moscow who look like the Fonz right out of *Happy Days* fame.

The standard theory we were raised on, of course, was that increased travel would spread understanding. Once we got to know one another, peace and goodwill would flourish like crabgrass. The global village would burst into smiles. The reverse, in fact, has happened. The English don't like the French any more than they did before they started flooding across France on the way to package tours on the Costa Brava in Spain (where they demand, and get, English breakfasts and warm beer). Canadian-U.S. relations aren't any better now that 30 million Americans visit Canada each year. In fact, they are worse. Ask Mel Hurtig. Familiarity does breed contempt.

The leaders of the nations of Black Africa, more travelled than ever before, have now decided to put little New Zealand into an international deep freeze. It is, naturally, an imitative ploy picked up from the Arab world vendetta against Israel. It's interesting to read, in William Stevenson's fascinating book on the Israeli rescue mission in Uganda, *90 Minutes At Entebbe*, the transcript of the ensuing United Nations debate. The tiresome Uganda rhetoric on Israel and Zionism is a replica of the Arab speeches that turned the Habitat Conference in Vancouver into an anti-Israel exercise. It's a simple fact that large hunks of the globe are hiving themselves off into hostile camps, increased travel statistics notwithstanding.

I used to be a travel writer. It was a great life but I eventually gave it up for one reason: I loved travel but I learned to hate people who travel. They are called tourists. Tourism, claim the commercial entities that benefit from tourism, is a boon to world understanding. I'm not so sure it is. There does come a saturation point when the number of spavined, varicose-veined matrons waddling off jumbo jets into some hapless country that is in need of exchange currency does more harm than any potential good. I have seen the island of Bali, which is indeed as exquisite and beautiful as anything you've read on it, and I never want to see it again. It is because when I was leaving they were preparing to expand the airstrip to accommodate the big jets and build new tourist hotels, a move of greedy tourism that would ensure the ruination of the delicate culture and priceless privacy of that fragile little island. Bali has about as much chance of surviving tourism as Coney Island has. It's not Bali's fault. It's the greed of the Indonesian government in Djakarta, seeking more and more tourist dollars.

This is being written from Maui, one of the islands in the Hawaiian chain. I have been coming to Hawaii for 15 years (one of the sinners in the crime) and have watched the transition of the islands and the growing—and understandable—resentment of the Hawaiians. There is no way dignity and pride can be retained when an entire population is transformed into waitresses, bartenders and taxi drivers. The resentment has not yet reached the level of some of the West Indies islands, where violence has erupted, but it will. The slowly gathering resentment of Hawaiians over the past few years reminds me of the silent hostility now directed by the Québécois against unilingual English Canadians who visit that proud province. Condescension is longer abided in the Pacific or on the St. Lawrence.

As one who has experienced it, I am never terribly upset when I hear of tourists who have been robbed in southern Europe or Asia. Whenever wealth is flaunted in front of those in poverty, the flaunters, be they ever so humble package tour zombies, should expect the consequences. As long as a tiny minority of the world travels in order to use the host either for amusement or servitude, it will only manage to rub salt in the wound.

Bob Lewis, the editor of Maclean's *with whom I have a fight only twice a year, received earlier this year a fax from one S. Boyd Anderson of Moncton, New Brunswick. To wit:*

"I have noticed that Mr. Fotheringham's column (and another of your writers based on the West Coast) of late has turned into a travelogue, and a not very interesting one at that. Does anyone care what a rich, elderly, snobbish, semi-retired columnist observes while sitting around exotic locations that most of your readers cannot afford or would not want to visit anyway while he craps on all he sees around him as well as the folks back home. Mr. Fotheringham has turned into a spoiled brat in his old age."

I don't happen to agree, since I think that it's a disgraceful thing to pick on Peter C. Newman as "rich, elderly, snobbish, semi-retired." (I confess only to "spoiled brat," since I've been called that ever since kindergarten, even by my best friends—and children—to this day and certainly do not plan to change now.)

I do not agree, because I think readers, whoever they are out there in the vast wilderness, like to follow their favorite columnists through life's travails —as they progress, get better, get worse, fall down, disappoint, become irrelevant or whatever and if so quite obviously disappear, drool running down their chins in the nursing home.

I'm a reader, obviously, and I love to read columnists who—quel surprise! —obviously get better over time or get worse over time and, as we all do, eventually die. Hopefully, before their typewriters do.

I loved Richard J. Needham in the Globe and Mail, worshipped Red Smith in the New York Herald–Tribune, marvelled at Pierre Berton's inventiveness in the Toronto Star, thought Jack Scott at the Vancouver Sun was the finest stylist in Canadian journalism, as Dalton Camp now is in the Star. (Mainly because, within days of death, he got—through a transplant—a new heart from a 20-ish female killed in a car crash.)

I don't happen to agree with the guy from Moncton who hates my prose, because I think readers like to watch—from afar through print—the evolution over time of someone who for instance, in this case, has been writing in the same space on the same page for 24 years.

Scott Young, in his fine column in the Globe, used to confess—in my mind, with amazing candour—about why his marriages had failed. I'm not into that gig, but different strokes for different folks, and it was fascinating to be *a voyeur who just picked up his column, and his life therefore, over the years.*

I'm so naïve as to actually believe that Maclean's *readers are interested in their back-page scribbler getting to Hong Kong for the handover, or Lady Di's funeral or Hemingway's old hotel room in Cuba or Mexico's reaction to the first grandchild. At least that's what the mail and the phone calls and the faxes indicate.*

Better, surely, than one more endless and boring assessment of Joe Clark's charisma, Jean Chrétien's difficulties with either language, and Sheila Copps's new hairtint.

I was surprised, and delighted, when last year I read Bob Lewis's response to a young inexperienced woman who was writing a profile for Saturday Night. *"People assume that old Foth is here because he's my buddy," he explained in some exasperation. "But that's not the way this works. This is a business and we're selling magazines and he helps sell magazines. When that stops, he's gone."*

It was the same thing I had tried to impress on the innocent young lady previously, but she obviously couldn't grasp the point. I told her I was just like one of the 14 different boxes of cornflakes on the supermarket shelf. When one brand doesn't sell, it's gone.

But I'm obviously delighted that S. Boyd Anderson of Moncton quite clearly reads the column all the way through to the end, before he gets angry. That's all that counts. Keep reading, S. Boyd.

September 3, 1990

Red sand and not a cloud in the sky

O ne afternoon in the 18th century, I believe it was a Sunday, there was an accident to the Count of Arcos in a bull ring. It is suspected that a bull was involved. Ever since, thanks to a ruling by the Marquis of Pombal, there has never been a bull killed in the ring in Portugal. There are bullfights, of course. But the Portuguese tourada is quite different from the Spanish corrida. The bull is never dispatched. It signals the difference between beautiful and poor little Portugal and its proud and large neighbor, Spain.

There can be no more arresting sight on earth than the spectacle on red sand when a horseman, mounted on a caparisoned stallion, takes on a bull. That's the Portuguese way. They refuse to see, in the fight, a mere contest of intelligence against instinct. To them, it is a display of skill, of elegance and of courage. The bull is only the instrument.

The area of research is the Algarve, the flower-drenched strip of beaches that hang below the cliffs facing south on the Atlantic. When I am about to die, my debtors are instructed to take the body and drop it off one of those cliffs. It is heaven on earth and, since I'm headed that direction anyway, this would seem a suitable shortcut.

Portugal, once the poorest of the European Community's 12 members, has now struggled past Greece and is only number 11. Its car sales have risen to record levels, which is ominous, since the country has the worst fatality record levels this year on the roads of any motorized jurisdiction. What the Portuguese refuse to do in the sands of the bull ring they do on the asphalt.

The second best thing in Portugal are the grilled sardines. When you do get to heaven, they will serve grilled sardines for breakfast. Those who are deprived of Portugal think of sardines as those tiny, cocktail-party-size things that sit on a Ritz cracker. No way. On the Algarve, where we're talking serious sardines, the specimens are the size of a small Fraser River salmon. Full of salt and oil, they stoke a man for half a day.

The first best thing in Portugal is the sight of the dancing horse, as swift on his feet as Fred Astaire, charging and sidestepping away from the black bull. His rider, in an embroidered coat of silk and velvet, with shining knee boots and silver spurs, is something to behold—shaming by his shimmery the grounded Spanish chap in his suit of light.

The locale on this coast is the proper place for reflection at the moment, since the Algarve takes its name from the Arabic "El-Gharv" "the west." It was the most westerly region on the Iberian peninsula conquered by the Arabs. One reads the current headlines with interest—washed down with wine.

The horseman, at full gallop towards the charging bull, stabs the *bander-illas* into the nape of the neck, provoking and exhausting the beast. The Americans in the audience yell, "Go, go, go!" to demonstrate their democratic nature. It does not help his frustration, since the hoof-clad Astaire cannot be caught. When the bull is suitably winded, he is faced with the *mocos-de-forcado*—eight dour-looking daredevils who appear (save one) as if they might run the town pharmacy as a regular job. They are lined astern as the bull charges, their leader attempting to seize the bull by the horns while the others overwhelm him with their weight. Their leader, a young man whose near skin-head look contrasts with the thick Portuguese locks of his comrades, at first charge buries his face in the gore pouring down the bull's shoulders. It is a rite of passage, succeeding valiance gashed and bruised with each successive charge. Tourists with their cameras love it. The bull does not and, like his predecessors, is slaughtered the next day.

The rolling Atlantic has carved tiny coves out of the limestone cliffs, like bite-size chunks out of the coastline. The coves are lined with golden sand the color of Michelle Pfeiffer's bank account. They have not invented clouds in Portugal in August. They are clearly against the law.

There are only two minor problems on the Algarve. One involves the Germans. The other involves the Brits. The reason the Germans are so popular at any beach from Portugal to Greece is that they commandeer all the lounge chairs and confiscate all the beach umbrellas. Commando squads creak from their rooms at dawn to stake out the prime territory by the pool: warning encampments of towels and books and suntan lotion mark their areas of conquest. The future peace and tranquility of the European Community may not survive this habit.

It is offensive, indeed almost as offensive as the way the Brits dress. The Brits, you see, are not made for casual garb. Their weather at home does not make them familiar with the sun, and they do not know what to do with it. They emerge into it blinking and confused, as if just landing on Saturn.

The current popular dress code is knee-length surfers' trunks of wild hues and patterns. At least this is what the Brits think California surfers wear. In fact, the look went out in California about a decade ago, worn then only by acne-ridden 13-year-olds. To view a portly British businessman in this ludicrous outfit is enough to blind one temporarily and to make one feel queasy when gazing down at the sardines.

These are really major detriments, as can be realized, and if it weren't for the sunshine and the beaches and the grapes and the bulls and the lack of news about the Arabs it would hardly be worthwhile coming here.

August 6, 1990

The world unfolding by a divine plan

Piccadilly Circus is probably the most vulgar spot, at the moment, in the world. The stench of cheap fries mixes with the odor of bad imitation hamburgers, and pizza that Napoli would never recognize—zapping the olfactory openings of the theatre crowd emerging on Shaftesbury Avenue. The dregs of the punk-haircut and backpack set, extremely redolent downwind, lounge on the sidewalk and festoon the steps leading up to the famous Statue of Eros at the centre of this mess.

London is newly filthy, is noisier, is more insanely crowded than ever. The Mother Country has adopted, from its two colonies across the Atlantic, that

famous reverse-export—the two-finger salute at intersections. The most fictitious
newspapers in existence proliferate in wild popularity alongside fellow journals
that read as if they were penned by graduates of masters' programs in *Beowulf*.

In all, we're saying, Britain seems a disaster at first glance. Maggie Thatcher,
Atilla the Hen, has been so draconian in her slashing of spending in the public sector that the schools (for the masses) are tired and torn, the hospitals a
disgrace, the transportation system still in a Dickensian mode and the beaches,
as everywhere, fouled.

'Tis true, all true, until one ventures into the countryside. England, in its genius, has contrived to construct the ugliest cities in Christendom and the most beautiful countryside ever invented. London, inside the central core so beloved by tourists—not to mention Birmingham, Manchester, Liverpool and the seamier sections of Newcastle, Leeds and Bradford—is a horror to the soul without ever bringing into play the eyeballs.

One angles out of London to the southeast, vaguely on the way to Vera Lynn's white cliffs of Dover. Canterbury is off to the left. In Kent, outside the little village of Westwell, are Jeff and Joan. Their huge old house was built in 1440. That would make it before Columbus set out. (Puts Meech Lake into proper perspective.) You can walk into the fireplace. On a patio over lunch, one gazes across the fence at the sheep scattered in the pasture, a scene out of a postcard.

A neighbor on a sideboard takes for granted the huge bowl that contains "a moving Stilton" slowly bubbling and fermenting away for years as new fuel is added. At The Wheel, the pub in Westwell, they still remember the brash journalist who upset the town years back by violating building restrictions through erecting ugly stone balls on his front wall. No one can recall whatever happened to him.

Driving west, through Tenterden, Biddenden, Holvenden, Benenden, Newenden and Dingleden, we cross into Sussex. There are Beth and Martin. They live on the delightfully named Merriments Lane. The pitchers of Pimm's, the most civilized drink on the globe, await. There is a wishing well and a pond full of frogs.

Martin flies off to Thailand on deals and has never heard of Donald Trump. Beth has her magnificent 17-year-old horse and is into dressage. In his field, sheep cluster at his feet. Overhead in a tree that stretches forever is a fort for the eight-year-old. The English summer goes on endlessly. The English cricket captain, the aptly named Graham Gooch, hits 333 against India at Lords.

Continuing west through Hampshire (where hurricanes hardly happen), through Hinton Ampner, Newton Valence, Hartley Mauditt and Stoke Charity. On into lovely Wiltshire, below the Salisbury Plain. At the Cross Keys pub, just outside Compton-Chamberlayne, a ceremonial plate from British Columbia hangs on the wall. At the Manor House Farm are Andrew and Di. Pimm's is in the garden (beneath the tree house).

Andrew was an anti-submarine helicopter pilot in the British navy. He now runs the 1,800-acre family farm, bouncing through the downs in his Land Rover, braking suddenly and leaning a rifle on the side-view mirror to shoot one of the rabbits that are such a nuisance to the crops. Di drives the small boys to tennis lessons. All English boy-children are named either Simon, Peter, Andrew, Matthew or Oliver.

Along with the cows and the sheep and the grain, Andrew grows low cover to attract the pheasants that he and his father love to shoot. In the village, where his farm workers are provided with low-rent housing, Cecil Beaton lived until his recent death. At Lainston's, a stately home, the wine list puts California, Australia and New Zealand wines in a category titled "New World."

Just behind the dairy barn, Andrew has an uphill, 500-yard grass airstrip for his four-seater plane. On a hillside are still-intact, lime-encrusted regimental emblems of First World War troops stationed here. It is in these Wiltshire grainfields that the mysterious circles are found, caused by either flying saucers, fungal infections, giant hailstones, rutting stags or mass movements of hedgehogs. Mass movements of holidaying university students are a better bet.

The blissful neatness of the English country is best seen from a leisurely light plane. There is nothing wasted, the geometric patterns of the multicolored crops with harvest ripeness broken by the green copses and neat hedges and guarded-by-law splashes of dark forest.

We swirl around the spire of Salisbury Cathedral, glide over stone castles with their sculpted gardens. It is clear, from Andrew's plane, that God indeed had a plan, that an architect laid all this out with a painter's palette. It's almost enough to believe that there is an order in things. All's right with the world when you are above Wiltshire—as opposed to Piccadilly.

August 19, 1985

Wisdom from the islands in the sun

Your faithful scribe, sensitive to the core, has noted with chagrin a recent letter to this here magazine from a world-weary reader in Winnipeg who, filled with ennui, pleads with the editor to save him from the good doctor Foth's "postcards" from his summer holiday. This, I must tell you, is a low blow—and deeply wounding. It has always been my impression, mistaken perhaps (though desperately hard to believe), that my few faithful fans appreciate the random straying from the dutiful detailing of the political and sexual peccadillos of the high and mighty. When you get down to it, what they are doing is not much different from what happens in the slurbs—though admittedly at a higher level. Rosie O'Grady and the Colonel's Lady are sisters under the skin, just as Willy Loman is not that far from the deputy minister of trade and commerce.

It has always been my contention that one learns more on holidays than in months sitting around listening to the artfully crafted lies and bluffing that make up so much of the life of politics and business. As an instance, your agent is ensconced at the moment on an island off the coast of British Columbia where bare feet and insults are the order of the day. When the days are not idyllic, they are merely poetic. The bottle-green mountains rise steeply across the sound. One of the familiar local sites is a formation of peaks that look exactly like Charles de Gaulle deep in sleep. The deer, none bigger than Bambi, come down and nibble in the garden. It is a pleasant sight at breakfast.

One of the first things noticed in paradise is that there is nowhere near the usual number of GMPs on the water this summer. GMPs are Glossy Magazine People, the middle-aged versions of the tiresome Yuppies. In past summers the blue waters have been speckled with a loathsome number of white sails and cabin cruisers that would keep OPEC giggling in happiness.

The dock that handles the wild water-skiers is relatively lonely. The whole scene reveals that the B.C. recession is still alive and well, the stockbrokers and high rollers still sulking in their tents, their yachts in drydock. It's hell, this research, but someone has to do it.

High on a cliff, a proud and defiant original cottager—someone says he is such a gentleman that he would rather be caught without his pants than his tie—flies the White Ensign on this particular day. Once you had to have a certain high rank in the navy to fly it. This day it is in honor of the fact that this happens to be the anniversary of the start of the First World War—and the Queen Mum's 85th birthday.

Everyone noticed, one trusts, that the Queen Mum just visited Saskatchewan, which was celebrating its 80th birthday. She is 85. A Queen older than a province. Love it.

On our island there is a great fuss because someone has a cocktail party for a British lord who arrives bearing someone he calls a "mistress," an expression one hasn't heard in polite society since the 1950s. She seems like a manicurist from Liverpool, says one sniffy wife. Not so, says another sniffy wife, she had a good accent; she obviously was a manicurist from Southhampton.

The island scene, off the coast of British Columbia, where resides the alleged recession, is a movable feast. The fat white ferries, cruising through the waters with the serenity of Queen Victoria, are more numerous than the Canadian navy's vessels—which ain't hard—and drop brisk bicyclists, pastel pensioners and the ubiquitous camper trucks like detritus as they glide into dock after dock.

On one island a hobby farmer, an expansive and generous host with a satellite dish that hauls in 110 channels from around the world, plays videos of himself while healing his wounds, suffered when he overturned a bulldozer into a ravine; his adoring grandchildren hanging from him like grapes.

On this particular island there is a shrewd and knowing woman, aged 82, who sits and writes lyrical prose. She was a missionary in China and has published a book on the experience. One son is a film-maker who works in Africa and travels the Third World. One daughter is a powerful cabinet minister who travels the world. The youthful 82-year-old is writing a book about her early days in Toronto, where the opera had to start late because the orchestra players had come from the pitband in the silent movie theatres. She is writing a collection of poems for entry in the CBC poetry contest. Best of all, she has done small essays for a Victoria paper, observations from her window overlooking her cove, describing the cormorants and the herons swooping down over the pewter-colored water. She is very good.

There is the ritual grass-hockey game, played with hockey sticks and tennis balls, but the standard of violence is generally of the same level as that of Australian Rules football. There is the standard roughrider ride up the side of a mountain in a jeep, through streams and over logs, teetering on bluffs and frightening the sheep, a journey that would terrify Rambo.

Best of all is the juxtaposition of water against mountain, sunlight against tree, the forest primeval with green fern and dark moss, a soothing balm for a man who has listened to too much bafflegab over a year and yearns to see deer that are, each November, plucked off occasionally by a chap with a large beard and biceps like thighs who—as required by law—can use only a bow and arrow. His wife has made him a Viking helmet with horns, and tourists who have come across the sight are still fleeing to Iowa.

No postcards, indeed.

August 6, 1979

Travels with three men, a Beetle and Big Brother's dancing den mother

It was exactly 20 years ago. It was balmy summer and I was travelling endlessly through Russia in a Volkswagen with a blonde. The salvation—as it turned out—was that it was a slightly crowded Beetle, also encompassing two other males, one a lawyer now practising in Vancouver, the other a journalist long ensconced with the *San Francisco Chronicle*. The blonde was our

22-year-old den mother, the Big Sister provided by Big Brother. Ella Dmitrieva was what, in unliberated 1959, we could still call a dish. She was a member of the Young Communist League and loved the tunes from *My Fair Lady*. She had a lawyer boy-friend, spoke impeccable Oxford English and didn't want to read Boris Pasternak, our hot smuggled item.

This was the first year when the Soviet Union felt confident enough to allow foreigners to drive their own cars into that tremulous empire. It sounds insane now, but the project was to drive Russia from top to bottom, exit through the Balkans, wriggling our way through Romania and Bulgaria to emerge in Greece. In those days, one had unlimited faith in a Volks, an automotive Excalibur, to carry one anywhere. That was the plan and you know what happens to plans.

When we crossed the border from Finland into Russia—fully aware that we would be met by a guide-interpreter from Intourist, the state tourist agency—there was mute resignation at the prospect of sharing our rear-engined steed with some earnest dullard who quoted Marx, or perhaps a hefty lady in buttoned shoes and basic black. Instead: Ella. For her part, she confessed later that beforehand she had dolefully concluded she was stuck with three bay-windowed businessmen. Neither side could believe its good fortune. There was justice after all. Lenin indeed had a sense of humor.

Down through the thin birches on the way to Leningrad. One of the saddest sights these eyes have witnessed: a holiday camp for factory workers, the men sodden in their pyjamas, gazing listlessly at the water; the factory women, in their print dresses, solemnly dancing with one another beneath the trees to the haunting melody of *Moscow Nights*. Leningrad, that most beautiful of faded cities, the Bolshoi and the street spivs outside pleading for Dave Brubeck records and red lipstick.

There was the relentless ugliness of Moscow as we forged south, plotting the journey via the infrequent gas pumps, as a voyageur would navigate toward each cache of pemmican. Ella's eye makeup increased. With three men at her disposal on the restaurant dance floors, when the bands broke into a daring Glenn Miller rhythm, she was mistaken for an American tourist. She loved the mistake.

Across the dance floor there they were, our alter egos: those anticipated lardy businessmen from the Midwest, accompanied by sour-looking young academicians or lady weight lifters. We had, indeed, hit the jackpot.

We argued. The Russian topography, mile for mile, will never rival Banff. The mind lusts for stimulation. Canadian men, she concluded, were not serious enough. Little wonder, as she listened to our playful mind-games, requiring each of us to invent spontaneous fiction as we rolled on kilometre after boring kilometre, zany scenarios that often featured the fake-American town that the Russians had created in Siberia and had outfitted its denizens—prospective spies to be parachuted into Kansas at night—with saddle shoes, cashmeres and crew cuts. She thought us insane—and may have been correct. (Have *you* ever tried to count the steppes?)

It was the best education possible, slicing through that surly, sombre land from top to bottom, as useful for understanding as driving Canada from Montreal to Vancouver. From the log cabins north of Leningrad to the sod huts deep in the dry heat of the Ukraine, Ella could not understand our basic interest in photographing the shifts in lifestyle.

She remembered other things. In the siege of Leningrad, when the Germans surrounded the city for 900 days but could not take it, she, as a small girl, was so weak from lack of food she could not get out of bed: her ration was one potato a day. We plowed on south, to rough, industrial Kharkov. The daily out-pouring of demented movie scripts increased as the claustrophobia of the Bug closed in. Delightful Kiev, heart of the Ukraine, full of warmth and color. The plan began to founder on the shoals of mindless bureaucracy. Bulgaria would grant a visa for car travel. But Romania would not. To reach Bulgaria one had to cross Romania. An automotive Catch-22.

Den mother did not fail. There was, to the south, the Black Sea port of Odessa, the famed wartime port, next door to the Crimea and Yalta and the ailing FDR and all that. A ship that could take the now-hated Volkswagen—via Romania and Bulgarian ports—to exotic Istanbul on the Bosporus would soon be available. We made for Odessa.

A most pleasant city, actually, sloping to the water. A most emotional farewell dinner in a hotel courtyard overlooking the harbor—especially as the owner of the despicable little car, once we reached our destination of Athens, would turn left in an attempt to drive to Hong Kong leaving two of us to limp back to London. Many toasts, much wine, good brandy, vows of undying friendship with den mother. We taxied down to the dock, kissed fondly farewell and Ella promptly turned me over to the police, who arrested me and seized all my photographs. Ella and I don't correspond much anymore.

The best food I have ever tasted—or seen, the eye being connected to the taste bud—has been, not in France, but in China. In August 1972. This would appear to be logical, since the French cuisine, based on delicate sauces, was all derived from the Chinese, who have been around a bit longer.

There being a British Columbia election at the time—another boring win for Wacky Bennett—it seemed more interesting to accompany External Affairs minister Mitchell Sharp and 200 Canadian businessmen to a Canada Business Fair in what is now called Beijing.

Sharp's mission, of course, was simply precursor foreplay for Pierre Trudeau's brave venture in recognizing Red China. Years before Richard Nixon supposedly astounded the world by proffering the same recognition.

When I reached Hong Kong, after the endless delicious meals devised by a culture that went back 4,000 years, a phone call revealed that I had missed the real revolution: Wacky Bennett, after 20 years in power in Victoria, had been whacked by Dave Barrett's NDP, Lotusland's first socialist government.

January 10, 1983

A land of scrutable nitpickers

The most droll facts are those concealed within the most formal pronouncements. The mask of protocol disguises the giggles behind the stiff facade. Those with a fey sense of the world recognized such a gem last week in China sending a congratulatory message to Moscow on the 60th anniversary of the founding of the Soviet state. *China.* Congratulating someone on the occasion of a *60th* anniversary? Diplomats around the globe must have been rolling in their canapés, recognizing the sly dig, the condescending nod to the heathen peasants. One can imagine the bland smugness behind the message, the Middle Kingdom that reaches back some 4,000 years patting on the head the vulgar Soviets who struggle on their way to something approaching civilization. It reminds me of the smooth-faced Chinese man, enduring the ridicule from an Occidental who taunted him about not being able to grow a beard, who replied with a quiet smile, "Just that much further away from the ape, my friend."

Anyone who has been to the Soviet Union and to China is struck by the differences that make the congratulatory message so arresting. The insecure Soviets inhabit a land of suspicion, roughness and brusque rudeness. A visitor never feels comfortable, the brooding unhappiness of the atmosphere weighing down like a cloak of fog. It's depressing, humiliating, soul-destroying. China, on the other hand, in its calm blandness, is soothing. One does not feel watched, harried, harassed. Some of the same forces are at work on the visitor, but the essential *gentle* nature of the surroundings, both human and otherwise, softens the suspicion. A land that has endured so long regards foreigners as curiosity items, not threatening, and polite smiles at strangers replace the Soviet scowl. Time and confidence is all.

Chinese cuisine, as presented to foreigners at formal banquets, is not surpassed in the world. The Chinese regard the French (who learned their cooking from the Chinese) as fairly promising apprentices who are coming along and will probably improve in the future. In mythology, in their religion, the Chinese believe the Earth revolves around the Middle Kingdom. In the kitchen, it does. Marco Polo took back from China the idea of noodles, and Italy has based its entire worldwide reputation for pasta on what in China is a side dish. This, too, has not escaped the Chinese.

I once took a train the length of China, from Peking down to the escape hatch of Canton near Hong Kong. It was roughly equivalent to travelling by train from Montreal to Vancouver and revealed to the visitor the most remarkable fact of the most populous country on earth: one can travel for days and never be out of sight, out of the window, of a human being. Imagine travelling the Prairies by train, from Kenora to Calgary, and, every waking minute, being able to spot humans somewhere on the landscape, bent over their toil. That's China. It was a steam train, and we were soon coated with coal dust; anyone who left his window open in the steamy heat resembled an Al Jolson look-alike. The meandering procession looked like a set from a Buster Keaton movie, and each day the train would puff into a station and the grimy kitchen crew in soiled clothes would lift aboard the decrepit buckets filled with still-swimming fish and other vitals. The kitchen, viewed vaguely ahead past the rough dining car, looked primitive beyond belief. Yet every meal there emerged exquisite courses—served by waiters who looked as if they had been shanghaied out of the Barbary Coast—that left us groaning beneath the coal dust. It was a journey of railway agony and culinary delight. First things first.

The Chinese have a sense of time that escapes us. It has been explained that, while the Americans, who have no sense of time, blocked the most populous nation on earth from the United Nations for the decades after our latest major war, Peking was not concerned. Ten years, 20 years, 25 years made no difference. They knew the world would eventually have to come to the Middle Kingdom, and, eventually, Richard Nixon did—years after Pierre Trudeau went in.

The sense of time—rather the lack of it—plagues our own country. The panic-stricken fuss and bother about the place breaking up. The place is not yet 116 years old. Me and thee have been thrown out of pubs in London twice that age. Most of the world looks upon us, if seldom, as a self-indulgent band of nitpickers, squandering our patrimony. The babyness of most of the country, particularly the new rich half, makes it impatient and leads to such goofies as the Western Cowardly Canadians, who rise and fall with the snowflakes. Marc Lalonde, the toughest and most capable of Mr. Trudeau's thin list of competent cabinet ministers, comes from a family that has farmed the same land on an island in the St. Lawrence for eight generations. He has roots in this country stronger than any skyscraper in Western Canada and so does not understand it—any more than that section of the land understands him. Peter Lougheed epitomizes the Western Canada–Central Canada resentments arising out of the Depression, which happened a decade after the struggling Soviet Union was born.

We are a mewling and puking babe among nations. And China, secure in its confidence, can send "warm congratulations and good wishes" to a Soviet people just 60 years into legitimacy. One can only smile.

Your scribbler has been most lucky in his choice of children. Number One Son, on a mountain bike, travelled from Beijing—along Marco Polo's Silk Road past K2—all the way to Afghanistan.

One and Only Daughter, back-packing, made it from a Greek isle through troubled Yugoslavia all the way around the Mediterranean down to Morocco.

Number Two Son, winning, as a door prize, an Air Canada trip to any-where, said he had no interest in the London, Paris or Rome where he had never been—"everyone goes there"—and instead hopped a small sailboat from Athens across the Med to Cairo. And then his hitch-hiking thumb.

His father, by happenstance, was going to Cape Town, to free Nelson Mandela after his 27 years in jail. And walked, on the day of his release, five miles to the prison with the New York Times*'s Christopher Wren—yes, the direct descendant of the chap who finished St. Paul's Cathedral in 1716 and built 52 other London churches.*

Father and son, by wild luck, meet right on the equator.

April 9, 1990

A son's progress to Dad's comforts

This father I know, as a tad, was fascinated with Richard Halliburton and his derring-do. Halliburton was an American explorer and writer who dazzled small boys with his dashing adventures. In 1922, he made an expedition to mysterious Tibet. He traced on foot Cortes's route in the con-quest of Mexico. He travelled around the world in his own plane in 1931–1932.

He traced the route of the first Crusade and the travels of Alexander the Great in the conquest of Asia. He followed the trail of Hannibal from Carthage to Italy. He swam the locks of the Panama Canal. When this father was young, he wanted to be Richard Halliburton—who was lost at sea in a typhoon while trying to sail in a Chinese junk from Hong Kong to San Francisco in 1939.

While Halliburton was a voyeur, Cecil Rhodes was a doer. The old colonial bully hit it rich in the diamond fields around Kimberley in what is now South Africa. Before he was 30, he personally controlled at one point some 90 per cent of the world's diamond output. The Rhodes Scholarships of course still bear his name and Rhodesia used to. He had a grandiose vision of "a map red [i.e., British] from Cape to Cairo." He set out to build the Cape-to-Cairo railway, which didn't quite make it, Cecil being busy with the Boer War among other things.

So, father has this son. Son, with his usual luck, wins as a door prize at a dance an Air Canada ticket that can take him as far as Athens. Father and son hatch this idea. While father goes to Cape Town to free Nelson Mandela and then head north, son will go to Cairo and head south. They will attempt to do what Cecil Rhodes failed to do: link the Cape and Cairo.

Son arrives in the cradle of democracy and immediately hikes up the Acropolis to view the Parthenon. It is covered with scaffolding from a Japanese construction crew. Father, at the rally celebrating Mandela's release, eager to be a reporter again, rushes in where only fools tread and finds himself caught between police bullets and rioters' hurled bottles. Father decides to go back immediately to being a thumb-sucking columnist in an office.

Son finds a Greek who wants to sail across the Mediterranean in a small boat. They need a third body to help in manning the 24-hour watch and find a young Tokyo lawyer who testifies as to his sailing skills. Once afloat, it turns out he has never been on water before. He throws up steadily for four days. When they reach Egypt, he has lost 11 pounds.

Father, with the aid of a cable car, marches to the top of Table Mountain. It is 3,763 miles west to Rio de Janeiro, 7,927 miles to Montreal, 6,009 miles north to London, 6,837 south to Sydney and 8,044 to Beijing. The memorial to Cecil Rhodes overlooks the University of Cape Town, whose students now use it as a trysting spot. It faces north, to Cairo.

There is a communications problem on the Dark Continent. Because of the political situation, African states allow no telephone links with boycotted South Africa. Son cannot find father. Father has no idea where son is. Son phones a lady in Vancouver who phones father in South Africa, at considerable cost to the treasury. It is a shaky source of information, only one step up from jungle drums.

Son apparently is on the Sinai peninsula, south of Israel. In return for room and board, he is teaching English to camel drivers huddled at his feet in the dust. He stops short of Shakespeare. Father, having freed Mandela, spends his time arguing with telephone operators that there must be some way, in the year 1990, to reach a hotel, any hotel, in far-off Kenya.

Son, travelling up the Nile, reaches the fabled ruins of Luxor and finds the ineffable taste sensations of eating deep-fried pigeon, which is apparently short on drumsticks. Father notices, on the way to Cape Town airport, an overpass decorated with new spray painted graffiti: PREPARE AND PLAN NOW—TO GOVERN.

Son is 36 hours on an Egyptian train, in third class, with chickens and the lot. Some of the passengers are sleeping in the luggage racks. Unfortunately, the chickens with them are awake. And doing what chickens do. Son alights after 36 hours, his hair full of delightful chicken droppings. Character-building. It's good for a son. Father, meanwhile, has made it north to Zimbabwe, tracing Cecil's railway all the way to the hardship surroundings of the Victoria Falls Hotel.

With the Vancouver telephone exchange now the hub (and profit centre) of the world, it is determined that Nairobi in Kenya shall be the rendezvous. Son, on arrival to his usual $2.50-a-night hostelry, feels it only proper to get spruced up to meet father—and a hotel with the first hot shower in a month. A haircut would be wise. "We have a little problem here," says the lady barber. Dandruff? "No, lice." It costs son 50 cents for the trim, $20 for the hospital visit.

And so, as the sun sets over yet another country that used to be British red on the map, son looks longingly at father's modern hot shower, the pot at the end of the rainbow. But he can't touch it, since the delousing powder must do its fearsome work for two days. It's character-building, I tell you.

Father and son, the one foraging south on stout shoe leather and street smarts, the other struggling north on an expense account, meet in the middle of Africa, right on the equator. Father meets son. Stanley finds Livingstone. Rest easy, Cecil Rhodes. We have finally done Cape to Cairo.

The "grieving" business is the American growth industry of our time. Death now involves not just funeral directors and a suitably dignified minister of the cloth.

It now comes with "grief counsellors" and social workers and psychologists and shrinks—all a new brand of camp-follower.

The flower phenomenon attending Lady Di's funeral has crossed the ocean, a trendy spectacle that keeps the florist business happy and profitable. No headline figure, however remote, can die without the treatment.

The orgy of complete strangers arriving en masse *to "help" in the mourning of course was most apparent this spring with the school massacre in Littleton, Colorado. As do all American exports, it naturally crossed the Canadian border shortly after, with the school shooting in Taber, Alberta.*

Such was the contagion that the latter shooting became a contentious issue in the Ontario election, and the disgusted and irritated families of Taber finally told the grieving industry to leave town and leave them alone.

August 20, 1979

Thurman Munson and the American thirst for further maudlin heights of mourning

I can tell you, as a matter of fact, when it first started. It began, I can tell you with great certitude, on a January day in 1965 when they buried Winston Churchill with proper ceremony and circumstance. I used to live, by the way, about a block away from the Grand Old Man and could glimpse, on special days, the pale, fading face at the window as he made occasional feeble attempts to satisfy gawking tourist cameras. This was in Knightsbridge, just off the south edge of Hyde Park, where the dignified Lady Churchill went for her daily walk and one day had her hip broken when knocked over by the soccer ball of a couple of careless roistering louts ... but I digress.

The day they buried Sir Winston, with the whole world watching via TV, was a very special day. The Brits do funerals very well. Since they have so little to do these days, it is one of the things they do superbly well. That may seem unkind or macabre, but it is true. All America watched and that is the day that the United States, in its immaturity and insecurity, became obsessed with the rites of the dead. On each appropriate and inappropriate occasion since, the Americans appear in unconscious envy of the elaborate dignity and calm tradition of the way the British—on very carefully chosen episodes—say good-bye to their dead.

These morbid thoughts rise to the surface because of the death, in recent days, of a baseball player. His name was Thurman Munson, he was the thick-legged catcher (and captain) of the New York Yankees and he died—because he was a good family man who liked to renew himself in his family roots in Canton,

Ohio, on any spare day off—when his own small plane crashed and burned. It would be hard to exist on the North American continent in the past 10 days without being aware of the death and funeral and the eulogies pertaining to Thurman Munson.

Now, this has to be done delicately. Thurman Munson, who previously was not known to the general public but only to more discerning sports fans (he was not a star of the very first rank, but a quite acceptable occupant of the upper reaches of the second rank), was given in death the amount of media coverage reserved in other times for esteemed statesmen and public figures. Not to put the man down, but there has to be a fence of priorities somewhere. Something has got out of control. There's a galloping sense of exaggeration here that is in danger of bordering on parody.

It goes back, I contend, to the occasion when the entire American public (thanks to the advances of the multi-camera approach perfected at major golf tournaments) could witness the elaborate ceremony and national respect displayed at the state funeral for Sir Winston. The English, who have been doing it for a few centuries, are unsurpassed in their capacity for quiet spectacle in such affairs as coronations and burying their carefully selected heroes. They do it magnificently—and then wait a long time before they do it again.

The problem is that the nation that can hardly wait to enshrine roller skates before it has barely finished enshrining skateboards suffers from an equal thirst for sensation when it comes to grief. The Americans, God knows, had more than their fill with history's most public and well-recorded murder (John Kennedy) and the subsequent assassinations of Martin Luther King and Bobby Kennedy. One would think a nation that has endured such genuine tragedy would be more selective in meting out heartfelt compassion and acres of newsprint. To the surprise of a foreigner with supposedly some perspective, the opposite is true. Each occasion, each rock star, each baseball player elevated to deity on his death, demands further maudlin heights of mourning.

We will even leave aside, for the purpose of arguing on this particular scene, the obvious attraction of the cult of the dead—James Dean, Marilyn Monroe, now Montgomery Clift, most recently the Elvis Presley phenomenon that borders on necrophilia. What is pertinent is that it reveals a lack of purpose in life for the most vigorous nation in history to devote so much attention to the demise of an athlete who, for all his merits, was no Ruth, no Gehrig, no Willie Mays or Stan Musial, no Ted Williams, Ty Cobb or Hank Aaron. The accidental death of a back catcher unknown four years ago is hardly the event that should obsess a mature nation.

It demonstrates, among other things, the spurious sentimentality of the sports pages. An action freak (being one who feels sports writing is designed for the description of muscular people doing their thing, just as ballet columns are designed for the description of how dancers perform) finds it difficult these days to discover actual sporting events. What is not devoted to the boring legalese of Alan Eagleson is dedicated to the latter-day soap sisters of pseudo-drama. The late (and lamented) Thurman Munson falls into the latter category. If death were not so serious, it would be almost laughable to observe the instant boom to thrust Munson into baseball's Hall of Fame (an institution that long denied the legendary Hack Wilson, because he was a drunk, and Satchel Paige, because he was black).

Thurman Munson in death, in the dog days of summer, suddenly became the victim of a bored society in search of titillation. There is a sickness when even grief is made a trivial affair.

Lawyer jokes immediately come to mind when reviewing this column in the light of Bill Clinton's problems and the death of his own credibility.

Nixon of course was a lawyer and, as noted here, so were all his guys who went to the slammer. Mitchell. Haldeman. Ehrlichman. Magruder. The whole gang.

Young men who want to get ahead, as we know, go into law school. Because it teaches them how to talk and how the use of precise language can be profitable.

Eisenhower was famous for his mangled prose, but he was a soldier and not a lawyer. And he was a good president, just right for those 1950s times— "the bland leading the bland," as they used to say. Hoover was an engineer, and I guess it wasn't really his fault he was in office when the Depression hit.

Washington was a surveyor who married a rich widow and became a country gentleman (with wooden teeth) and died childless. Thomas Jefferson was an aristocrat who lived in Paris, was an expert on wine and designed his own famous house at Monticello.

And William Jefferson Clinton, named after the third president, became a lawyer and a Rhodes Scholar who smoked pot but didn't inhale and at his own impeachment trial argued that it depended on what the definition of "is" is.

The legal profession really hasn't progressed that far from Nixon in 1974 to Clinton in 1999.

August 20, 1984

Nixon's footnote salute to history

A man who spends the 10th anniversary of Watergate in Washington marvels, in retrospect, at Richard Nixon's supreme contempt for his country. The power and dignity of the capital meant nothing to him; he placed above it a "second-rate burglary" and lied and corrupted the highest office in the land for two years while slipping and sliding in grime. He cared nothing for America when you think about it. He cared only for Richard Milhous Nixon.

Well, he ain't done bad. The man who had less than $500 in his chequing account on the day of his resignation is now a millionaire. He lives in a 15-room, $1-million mansion among other millionaires in a plush retreat in New Jersey, across the Hudson from Manhattan. He still gets $119,000 in pensions and $300,000 in government expenses. He still has his Secret Service guards, who drive him to his Wall Street office every day. CBS paid him $500,000 for the privilege of an interview. He made a $1.5-million profit on his last real estate move. His books are best sellers, the books that are always self-serving, telling some of the truth about the press, some of the truth about government but never the truth about Richard Nixon.

He was Tricky Dicky when he started out in politics in California, smearing an opponent with allegations about being a Red, and he never changed. That unctuous smile reeked of insincerity, and his insensitivity, on leaving the White House by helicopter that August day in 1974, had him holding his fingers aloft in the "victory" salute. In effect, it was his own version of the uplifted index finger; he was telling the American people that he was still right, that all these charges were unfair and unjust. He has never apologized to this day, never admitted that he was wrong. Instead, he is taken by limousine to lunch each day at exclusive restaurants such as the 21 Club or Le Cirque, to dine with bank presidents, the furtive Henry Kissinger, the furtive Alexander Haig. He has visited 18 countries since his disgrace and has been welcomed by the heads of state of all but two of them. How soon we forget.

Nixon believes in the maxim quoted by Talleyrand, that "it is worse than a crime, it is a blunder." He maintains Watergate will be a mere "footnote" in the history books. He regards it as just an error in tactics. If he had destroyed the tapes, everything would have been all right. What he chooses to ignore is that Watergate was simply the logical extension of the Nixon personality, the belief that once in power anything is permissible—as long as you don't get caught. The secret bombings of Cambodia were okay as long as you didn't have to admit them. The wiretaps, initiated by the devious Kissinger, were okay, as were the break-ins, because the boys in charge were smart enough and arrogant enough to know they'd never be caught. The vile comments about Jews and Italians in the privacy of the Oval Office were okay because only the boys—and the tapes—were listening. As syndicated columnist Joseph Kraft says, "He was a crook through and through, a complete cheat."

The feckless Gerald Ford, his head pressed firmly against his Peter Principle, pardoned him after Kissinger used the blackmail that Nixon was contemplating suicide. His partners in crime, after tarrying briefly in jail, are now respectable and well fixed. John Mitchell, who as the highest law officer of the land, attorney general, lied and cheated like any car thief, still wears expensive suits and meets with Nixon regularly. Charles Colson is a born-again Christian and can be seen on television regularly, his pink face emanating sincerity of the same calibre that protested his Watergate innocence. Gordon Liddy, the man who used to hold his hand over a flame to prove how tough he was, still justifies the conclusion the group made that Washington columnist Jack Anderson would have to be killed because of the leaks appearing in his column.

Jeb Magruder is out of jail and he too has discovered God. Ehrlichman writes books about mystery and intrigue, for which he is eminently qualified. Haldeman is back in California as a hotel president and at last account hadn't missed a meal. The slimy John Dean, who ratted on his boss and therefore earned only a short time in the slammer, is still on the college lecture circuit, clean of collar and still tacky around the edges. Dwight Chapin, Nixon's appointments secretary who supervised the "dirty tricks" sabotage projects, has been publisher of a Chicago magazine, *Success*. Beautiful!

The fact that they were practically all lawyers, Nixon included, was the most outrageous of all. If they had been grasping businessmen—or piano movers or chiropractors—it would all have been so much more understandable. But the men trained in the law, appointed to uphold it, descended to the level of grafters and petty thugs in their desperation to save their own reputations after they had used the White House as a home for crime. That is the ultimate insult, why Nixon and Watergate will always be more than a footnote in the books. The man who was given the greatest majority in U.S. political history did not take inspiration from that victory; it moved him to further contempt for those who elected him. He had even more power, so he could abuse it even more. He was a crook and remains one.

And Frank Wills, the security guard who discovered the break-in at the Watergate complex and triggered the whole thing? He was caught shoplifting a pair of running shoes in a Georgia department store two years ago, spent 14 months in jail and now lives with his mother. The banal continues to the end.

November 26, 1984

Our blandness is the best defence

*Z*owee, Dr. Foth, am I ever glad to bump into you after all this while! Delineate precisely the specificities of your ineluctable ignorance.

Well, gee, is the rumor true that you have become a Yank?

Never. The moon will turn into blue cheese and Erik Nielsen will develop charm before that ever happens.

Well, like, why have you moved to Washington?

Simple. The inequality of nations. One must spread one's talents around. Now that the main task of later life, the eradication and removal of the detested Liberals, has taken place, one must move on and save another country. It's only fair to the Americans. They need salvation too.

Do they realize haw lucky they are?

Considering the fact the Good Doctor can't get White House security clearance or a parking spot, apparently they do.

Could you tell us, in a few words, how you plan to save America?

The same formula. Constructive advice. Moral guidance. Supportive praise. Selected niggling. In general, anything that will lead to the uplifting of society's finest dreams and aspirations. I think they'll appreciate it. After all, they are a generous people.

Do you plan to have any help in this project?

Indubitably. My friend Paul Robinson, the U.S. ambassador to Canada, who as they say is the only bull who carries his own china shop around with him, is my guiding force. I will pattern my activities after his.

Is it true that Nancy Reagan is the secret power behind her husband?

Behind those adoring eyes, cast upward at his podium pose, is Edgar Bergen. At the podium is Charlie McCarthy. What we have here is something more powerful than Geraldine Ferraro. The feminists don't know this, but this lady is in the closet. A card-carrying member. Some day the truth will be told.

Do you find any difference between Washington and Ottawa, one of your favorite cities?

Yes. In Washington the men's trousers end around their ankles, and all parties end abruptly at 10 p.m., namely because the heavy hitters have to get up early for an 8 a.m. business breakfast that opens with a prayer.

Do you mean Ottawa parties last past 10 p.m.?

No. No one in Ennui-on-the-Rideau goes out after dark, because they're sitting indoors, watching old reruns of *Gunsmoke*. Besides, the gas stations close at dusk.

Why do Ottawa gas stations close at dusk?

It is a mystery that has always escaped me. Otherwise, I suppose, they'd go broke. Whatever Ottawa people do when the sun goes down, they do it behind their curtains. Ask Mackenzie King.

Get serious. What do you find to be the significant differences between Americans and Canadians?

Americans really believe that anyone can make a million. Those who do have a lot of fun. Those who don't, they go on green stamps. In Canada people have the modest belief that one should not try too hard. Both having fun and green stamps, among Canadians, are considered not a good idea.

Is this a metaphysical insight into Brian Mulroney's soul?

Mulroney is a freak, if you really want to know, in that he thinks politics can be fun. At the moment, he's like a cocker spaniel pup chewing on a slipper. He believes all things are possible.

Are all things possible?

It depends on whether Ronnie Reagan's hearing aid throws a piston in the next few years. Mulroney has an Irish friend in the White House and a valuable bullpen with Allan and Sondra Gotlieb at the Canadian Embassy in Washington.

Are the Gotliebs' cocktail parties really as glittering as the social pages claim?

All I know is that whenever Reagan finds someone missing from a cabinet meeting, he phones Gotlieb's chef to check the table setting. It's rumored the invasion of Nicaragua was cancelled in the Gotliebs' men's room.

But, really, what's it like being so close to the red button that could blow us all up?

That's not the real problem that consumes the town, not the crucial matter.

Pray tell, what's that?

Well, Art Buchwald and Henry Kissinger and their pushy friends commandeer all the tennis courts. The second most important thing in Washington, next to the business breakfasts that open with a prayer, is the fight for tennis courts. Nicaragua comes rather down the list.

You're saying, then, that Washington is rather obsessed with itself?

Was Athens? Was Rome? The chaps know that this is where it is happening and, after the power breakfast and tennis is disposed of, we'll blow up Central America. Everything in its proper perspective.

How do you then see, sir, the future relationship between the Great White North and the Excited States of America?

Hopefully, nebulous. Ignorance is our best hope. Invisibility is our best guide. The more they forget we exist, the less chance they will send in the marines. Our blandness is the best defence we will ever have. Smother them with boredom. Let's keep that ennui flying.

Gee, thanks, Dr. Foth, Your fuzzification of the situation certainly muddifies things for me.

No probs.

February 18, 1985

Reagan recruits the Lord

Slowly the fog of the mind lifts and the truth emerges, creeping in on its tiny feet. We can see now, quite clearly, why Ronald Reagan is such a tremendous success. Unemployment in his land is down, the inflation rate is down, the dollar is soaring, the military have all the death weapons they want and the American public is exuberant in its home-again self-confidence. The reason? The President has recruited God as a member of his cabinet. An extra chair has been placed at the table and God is in there voting faithfully the Republican ticket—and especially approving any new appropriations for the military.

God never strays very far from Reagan's speeches, and in fact manages to make an appearance in almost every one of them. Then, last week God came right out and joined those who want more nuclear arms. In a speech to a group of leading businessmen the President reached into St. Luke and plucked forth a passage about a king who plans to make war, finds out he is under-armed and has to back away from his plan. Mr. Reagan, having proven the Bible is on the side of the Pentagon, said, "Well, I don't think we ever want to be in a position of only being half as strong, and having to send a delegation to negotiate, under those circumstances, peace terms with the Soviet Union." Jesus, as we can see, is into the nuclear arms race and we know whose side he's on, now don't we?

Later, on the same day, he addressed a gathering of the National Religious Broadcasters, a sect of electronic fundamentalists who believe in the verities of the Bible and cited the same distorted passage, stating that "Divine Providence" was into the stressful arms debate. The President, naturally, did not go into the whole parable in St. Luke, which is about the folly of wanting to make war. It

doesn't matter, since God is clearly planning to vote the right way at the nego-
tiations in Geneva. The feminists say that, contrary to suspicion, God is not a
woman because if She were, She would have treated females far better than
they are treated now. God, in fact, turns out not only to be an American, but
a Republican. Every coin in America bears the inscription "In God We Trust"
(all others pay cash). Now the deity has left the world of finance to get into
global politics.

That's the trouble with God. He's always changing sides. You can't rely on
Him. In our last big war, every German soldier went into battle with *Gott mit
uns*—God is with us—inscribed on his belt-buckle. Now the rascal has switched
camps and is working for the Americans.

To make sure God doesn't change countries again and go to a new suitor,
President Reagan is heavily into prayer breakfasts, where the MX mixes with
the Bible and the cruise missile gets entangled in St. Luke. There was one in
Washington the other day, attended by some 3,000 at the fearful hour of 7:30
(does God never sleep in?). There were supposed to be some 60 Canadian MPs
present, even including one NDPer, whose identity is still being chased. Friends
of mine attended and found themselves seated beside The Galloping Gourmet,
Graham Kerr, who has given up the sauce, is born-again and wolfed down the
congealed eggs benedict with a passion only a true believer could have. (How

does one make enough eggs benedict for 3,000 people? You start last Tuesday.) Prayer breakfasts were started under Eisenhower back in the 1950s, and people come from as far away as San Diego to gaze upon concrete eggs benedict and make sure that God's American citizenship has not lapsed.

If Luke is on the side of nuclear madness, how about Matthew, Mark and John? Surely, now that the Bible has been revealed to be on the side of the Star Wars defence system, surely we can find some gospel urging that plowshares be turned into swords? It's always been said that you can find anything you want in the Bible, and President Reagan is proving it.

Canadian politics is full of saints such as J.S. Woodsworth and preachers such as Tommy Douglas. Lester Pearson was a son of the Manse. Mackenzie King was the expert on the after-death, though it seems he was more into the occult and the ouija board than straight religion. John Turner is a deeply religious man. But essentially God doesn't get too interested in, or intrude upon, Canadian politics. Perhaps He thinks it's too dull.

This corner has another theory. God can't spread himself too thin. When He has to get up early for prayer breakfasts, it makes for a tiring day. When He has to spend all those hours poring over Caspar Weinberger's requests for increases in the Pentagon budget and approving George Shultz's plans for the withdrawal from Lebanon, you don't have too much time left to worry about the baby seal problem. Give a guy a break.

The one thing Ronald Reagan is famous for in Washington is demanding complete loyalty from his underlings. He supports, without nitpicking, some rather dubious companions, including his new attorney general, Edwin Meese III, who gave government jobs to those who helped him out of his financial problems and fudged on expense accounts and seems puzzled, as the number 1 law enforcement officer of the nation, about the definition of the word "ethics."

In return for this loyalty, Reagan demands the same thing. It is thought that God knows this. He is going to stick with this administration as long as required. Four more years.

June 3, 1985

The trouble with democracy

T hese are rapidly moving times, the speed of events dazzling and confusing the mind. Each little event whirls and tumbles over the next, causing the memory to go on fast-forward. Perhaps that is why the silly season, which normally does not arrive until the dog-days of summer, has arrived so early this year. The goofies can't even wait for their proper seasonal cue: they want to get into the act early.

Leading the pack is the strange politician called Ronald Wilson Reagan, master of all he surveys, owner of the greatest landslide in U.S. electoral history. As such, he grows angry and frustrated when he can't get his way. He is irritated because Congress won't go along with his plan to ship more military aid to the contra guerrillas in Nicaragua; so irritated that in a meeting with Republican leaders he banged the table with his fist and proclaimed, "We've got to get to where we can run a foreign policy without a committee of 535 telling us what to do."

The 535, of course, just happen to be the 435 members of the House of Representatives and the 100 members of the Senate. In other words, the voters, in their rumblings toward wisdom, elected last fall to keep a check on the President. This thing called democracy is a very cumbersome, inefficient thing. The United States, the most democratic country in the world, purposefully set up counterbalances to the President because the people didn't like the way an English king was treating his colonials. There is no way the Americans would put up with a system that makes Brian Mulroney, in effect, an elected dictator for the next $4^1/2$ years. Reagan, now into his fifth year in office and often ridiculed for his rudimentary grasp of what politics is all about, has suddenly come across the amazing discovery of what democracy and his country are all about. That bothersome "committee of 535" is doing exactly what it was elected by the citizenry to do: refusing to let him have his way when he tries to do something dumb, which is the perfect description of his infantile approach to Nicaragua.

It's a bothersome thing, this beast called democracy. Ask Frank Miller, another man who can't count. For all his success as a car salesman, he doesn't seem too swift with mathematics. He can't seem to comprehend that the voters of Ontario gave more votes to the Liberals than they did to his Regressive Convertibles. He can't even figure out that the voters piled up 73 seats opposing him, between the Liberals and the NDP, while leaving him only 52. With the verdict clearly against him, he still tries to cling to power when the public wants change and wants him out on his duff. It's tough to face reality, as both Reagan and Miller are demonstrating.

There is the problem of poor General Dynamics, the Pentagon's largest defence contractor. Some of the chaps in that busybody committee of 535 have rooted out the fact that the Pentagon was being charged $434 each for hammers it had ordered. It was discovered it was paying $600 for toilet seats. Plus $2,500 for a coffee maker. General Dynamics chairman David Lewis suddenly announced he was retiring, explaining that he had been planning to do that this year anyhow. Sure.

Moving right along, we have the most inane spectacle of the year with an alleged rapist and his alleged victim becoming a travelling minstrel show. The bizarre farce involving Gary Dotson, who either did or did not rape the dippy born-again Cathleen Crowell Webb some eight years ago, has become a media event, with competing networks smuggling them into New York, hiding them in taxis that are then pursued around Manhattan by cars from the other networks, a telegenic Keystone Kops caper. To top it off, former Miss America Phyllis George, who flounders every morning as the gilded hope of CBS Morning News, blithely asked the publicity-hungry duo—during her interview—to shake hands and hug. Millions of North Americans looked into their corn flakes and wondered what they were going to do with the rest of their day. Gloria Steinem went back to bed and cried.

As it happens, the elongated heroes of the winter sport of basketball are racing the wool-underwear heroes of the winter sport of hockey as to which can extend their playoff seasons well into the merry month of June and compete with baseball, where the millionaires of the diamond are about to vote to go on strike, thereby moving any ordinary sensible person to give up on the sport pages entirely.

There is, when you think about it, a thread leading from Reagan's puzzlement about democracy to the $434 hammers and Frank Miller who can't count and Phyllis George who can't quit smiling. The thread leads to Philadelphia, where all the best brains in the City of Brotherly Love decided to bring Beirut to America. The surprise of the mayor, the police chief and the fire chief that dropping a bomb on a rowhouse often causes fires ranked right up there with the prize moments of our premature silly season. You might expect the chairman of General Dynamics or some colonel at the Pentagon, or even Phyllis George, to have made such a decision. Instead, it was made by authorities who, we're now told, have been practising with the bomb for a year. If you have a bomb, you want to use it. Right? Right.

In all the premature goofiness, the only sanity comes from Samuel Frustaci, the helpless chap in Orange, Calif., who found himself the father of six babies and, on being asked if he would have any financial problems, replied, "You never have any financial problems when you don't have any money." There sits a wise man.

Not much changes, really, in the world of sex, when it comes to politics.
We all remember the unforgettable Wilbur Mills, chairman of the House Ways and Means Committee, who was found in the Potomac Basin, somewhat

soaked, late at night, with Fanne Foxe, the celebrated Washington stripper known as the Argentine Firecracker.

We recall the unfortunate Senator Gary Hart. There he was, six inches from the White House. Gary, as we know, went to Bimini with Donna Rice on the craft unluckily called Monkey Business. Gary claimed he and Donna slept on different boats. Which is true. Gary slept on his yacht and Donna slept on his dinghy.

And then there was Fawn Hall and Col. Ollie North, Fawn testifying that she slipped incriminating Nicaraguan documents out of the White House hidden in her underwear.

And so 1999 brings Monica Lewinsky, and all her goofiness. It's not much different. Your scribbler does not claim to be omniscient. But the insanity simply goes on. Andy Warhol, with his 15-minutes-of-fame prediction, just smiles in his Campbell Soup crypt.

May 18, 1987

A truly Hart-stopping chickadee

It is standard wisdom, as we know, that it is the supposedly staid Brits who specialize in sex scandals. Their politicians lurch from bedroom to boudoir. John Profumo was brought down by Christine Keeler and Mandy Rice-Davies, and Harold Macmillan's government nearly came down with him. Maggie Thatcher's favorite and would-be heir, Cecil Parkinson, was brought down by the secretary he impregnated and lied to. There are all those fairies at the bottom of the garden, and the tabloids simply wait for the next juicy item to break in Westminster or Buckingham Palace.

In American politics, however, the custom has been that it is money—not the mistress—that talks. Their scandals are financial. From Teapot Dome all the way to the current Wall Street lawbreaking, it has been greed, not lust, that ruled. The nation went all the way through the long, drawn-out Watergate drama—high lawyers sent to the slammer, a president deposed—and rarely did sex, let alone women, enter the scenario. The only prominent female in the whole thing was Richard Nixon's secretary, Rose Mary Woods, who had that nervous foot on the dictaphone machine. There are no females involved as major players in Ronald Reagan's own Watergate, the Iranamok scandal.

How welcome, then, to see that Britain's former colony is finally catching up to the motherland. In quick succession, Fawn Hall, Jessica Hahn, Tammy Bakker and Donna Rice have become household names, ladies of stunning obscurity just months ago and now traffic stoppers everywhere they go. They require police escorts. Squads of lawyers and bodyguards precede them at every public appearance. Andy Warhol (who would be amused at his own news-making ability even while dead) is as famous for his aphorism that everyone will be famous for 15 minutes as he is for his art. Fawn, Jessica, Tammy and Donna prove his point.

Nothing is so awaited in Washington in the marathon televised hearings on the Gippergap caper as the inevitable appearance of Fawn Hall at the witness table. Fawn, with a name only a press agent or a mother could invent, in fact looks like one, a dewy-lipped long-limbed secretary who, her boss used to boast, was the best-looking steno in the White House. Her boss was the crazed cowboy, Col. Ollie North, who was conducting his own one-man foreign policy in the White House basement while The Gipper dozed in the Ovaltine Office.

At the recent White House Correspondents' Association annual black-tie dinner, veteran journalists elbowed Caspar Weinberger and George Shultz out of the way for a chance to ogle Fawn, making her first public appearance since revealing that she shredded key documents on North's orders when the whistle was blown on him. She has the type of hairdo achieved when you sit in the bathtub in the morning and stick your finger in the light socket, and she wore a lollypop dress at the formal affair that came down to here and came up to there and almost met in the middle. (David Letterman had a contest on Fawn's 10 biggest thrills and decided the winner was when she sat on Ollie's shredder and turned the control knob up to high.)

We get even more saintly when we get to Jessica, the virgin church secretary who on her first try in the sheets destroyed the million-dollar empire of electronic evangelist Jimmy Bakker and almost cracked the mascara of Tammy Faye. Jimmy says it took only 15 minutes, but Jessica's affidavit takes two hours to describe it, which would indicate she is better with the language than he is with the action.

At any rate, it proved to be the most expensive roll in the hay Jimmy has ever had, since it has cost him his ministry and his Praise The Lord money-making machine—that being stripped away from him by Rev. Jerry Falwell, who loves the Lord, but doesn't fool around with girls. As impressive as Jessica's toll was, it pales beside Donna's, who has destroyed a trip to the White House with just one picnic and one yacht trip. Jimmy at least got his 15 minutes' worth; Gary Hart says he got nothing—while committing public suicide.

Donna Rice was a Phi Beta Kappa honor student at the University of South Carolina, which doesn't quite explain why she once took her shirt off for a photographer's fee and had to ask Hart if he was married or not. But Donna is

29 and Gary is 50, and you know how these things are. She wasn't half as dumb, however, as the front-running Democratic candidate, who is a graduate of Bethany Nazarene College as well as Yale law school but seems to have been hiding behind the door when the common sense was passed out. Mrs. O'Leary's cow burned down Chicago, and Donna—than whom there is nothing finer in Caroliner—barbecued Gary's presidential chances.

Hart, even after the cruise on the yacht aptly named *Monkey Business* and after repeated phone calls to the model, had the audacity to dare reporters to tail him since it would be "boring." You should never dare reporters anything. They are quite curious enough without that taunt.

Why would a man who seemed to have the Democratic presidential nomination cinched, at a time when everyone agrees the next man in the White House will be a Democrat, even give the appearance of playing around by sailing to Bimini and picnicking beside the Potomac with a wealthy married friend and two young chickadees from Florida? Ask John Profumo. Ask Jimmy Bakker. Ask Cecil Parkinson. Women, in their own way, still run the world.

March 1, 1999

Why Bill and Monica made such a lovely couple

As I told my buddy Pam Wallin on one of her TV gigs, the acquittal was the greatest miscarriage of justice since Jesus Christ was nailed to the cross.

This was simply the case of a middle-aged man, most often emerging from church with wife and daughter, carrying a Bible in his hand, who then reverted that afternoon to the Oval Office to be serviced by a silly infatuated twit. In effect, it was hiring a prostitute without having to pay for her.

The story of Bill Clinton, as the story of all of us, can be found in his roots. He was born William Jefferson Blythe III, one month ahead of schedule by caesarean section. In Hope, Ark. His mother, daughter of the town iceman, smoked two packs of Pall Malls a day, bathed in a sunken tub, was an irrepressible flirt who spent most of her days at the racetrack. Her father would give her swigs of whisky at age 12.

When she married travelling salesman Bill Blythe six weeks after meeting him, she didn't know that he had been married to a 17-year-old (sent her clothes home in a suitcase), then to a 20-year-old, then to the first bride's sister, then had a girl born to a Missouri waitress to whom he also might have been married.

He almost immediately went off to war and then, trying to drive from Chicago to Hope overnight, died in a ditch when his Buick overturned. Billy, whose mother was with his father less than six months, was born three months later.

When he was 1, his mother left for New Orleans for two years to train as a nurse anesthetist. He was raised by his grandmother, who worshipped him. While he was in his high chair, she taught him with homemade flash cards containing letters and numbers. He could read at 3.

Mother then married car dealer Roger Clinton, who came from the fleshpot gambling town of Hot Springs, Ark., where Al Capone had a corner suite and kept a machine-gun in the closet. He was a drunk and beat her, until the 14-year-old future president, towering over him, warned his stepfather never to do it again.

He drove a four-door finned Buick to Hot Springs High School. At 16 he was already six-foot-three and over 200 pounds. Clumsy and awkward, he could never make a sports team and so took up saxophone in the school band. *Washington Post* reporter David Maraniss, who wrote in 1995 a wonderful book on Clinton, *First in His Class*, notes that he practised every night, filling up the lonely hours of childhood: "He had always hated to be alone, and playing the sax was one of the few ways he could tolerate it."

He was so bright no one in high school can ever remember him studying. Sent to Washington with an elite group of boy leaders, he shoved his way with his bulk to the front of the line in the Rose Garden to get the now-famous photo of him shaking hands with his idol (in the sexual mode also?), JFK. It was the only photo taken. Moving on to the prestigious Georgetown University in Washington, the hillbilly kid from the hick state easily became president of the freshman class over all those Ivy League preppies, and sophomore president. A favoured professor told him that great men in history slept no more than five hours. Clinton returned to his dorm and set the alarm clock to begin sleeping five hours a night.

While on campus, his drunken stepfather died. As Maraniss notes, it was "two fathers dead—and in a sense he knew neither of them." He had been raised, in reality, by two mothers who competed for his love and attention.

Even his closest friends at Georgetown laughed when he applied for a Rhodes Scholarship—founded by Empire fanatic Cecil Rhodes for bright boys who demonstrated "fondness and success in sports." Clinton simply stick-handled his way into chairman of the Student Athletic Commission and dazzled the Rhodes interviewers with his charm.

At Oxford, one of 32 American elite, half of them thought him "a classic southern glad-handing politician." Brits were astounded that, within 45 minutes of meeting, he convinced them he was going back to Arkansas to be governor or senator or a national leader.

As the astute Maraniss figured out, even then these contradictions co-existed in Clinton: "considerate and calculating, easygoing and ambitious, mediator and predator."

His prescient book, which ends in 1991, when Clinton announces his run for the presidency, predicts everything that follows. The detail of his sidestepping and prevarication at Oxford while trying to avoid the Vietnam draft is sickening. While his fellow Rhodes Scholar Frank Fuller, honestly not draft-dodging, goes home to Spokane and takes a pistol and kills himself.

Mom, in the meantime, has married her third husband, Jeff Dwire, a divorced handyman who ran a beauty parlour and had been convicted in a stock-swindling case and spent nine months in the slammer.

Monica Lewinsky has confessed: "I have lied my entire life." They make a perfect pair.

The insanity of the American fascination with guns supposedly goes back to their constitutional right to bear arms. Because the local militia had to arm itself to throw out the Brits. The Boston Tea Party and all that.

As the insanity reached Columbine High School in a suburb of Denver in Colorado this spring, we learn that the exceedingly comfortable middle-class family of four that produced the main killer had eight cars and the nutcase kid drove a BMW to school.

Seems a far cry from the local militia.

Within the week, the National Rifle Association held its annual convention in Denver, and its president, Charlton Heston (Moses must be tossing in his grave), defiantly announced that the real answer was that if there were even more guns around there wouldn't be so many felons. 'Cause then we'd catch 'em all. Take that.

The slopover effect on Canada is that the worry about guns is what keeps the Reform Party from building itself into a national force.

The worry from Reform diehards is that smart-ass, pinstripe types in Toronto who wouldn't recognize a gopher if it fell in their soup are behind the gun-control legislation in Ottawa that would make them register an itsy-bitsy .22 rifle even it was used only to knock tin cans off the fence on Sunday afternoons.

The worry in the urban class of Toronto is that Alberta, birthplace of Reform, is a bit too much like being an offshoot of America. And Charlton. The Wild West. All that.

The stats tell it all. According to figures from the Department of Justice in Ottawa, some 39 per cent of homes in Alberta contain a gun. That's half again as many as the Canadian average of 26 per cent.

Most telling, Alberta is closest of any province to the appalling situation in the United States. According to a 1997 Gallup poll, attests Michael Rand, chief of victimization statistics for the Bureau of Justice Statistics, 42 per cent of American homes have guns therein.

As any twerp (but Charlton) knows, the more guns there are, the bigger is the problem with guns.

Strangely enough, we can look at the rate of child deaths by firearms in Alberta. From 1991 to 1995, the rate of children under the age of 15 killed by guns in the province was more than twice the national average: 0.9 per 1,000, compared with 0.4 per 1,000 for the country as a whole.

Wendy Cukier, who is a professor of justice studies at Ryerson Polytechnic University in Toronto, says that you would have to add together the rates of both Israel and Northern Ireland to reach the rates of child deaths by gun that Alberta reaches.

One of the problems, as any journalist who has roamed around Alberta knows, is that it was settled in measurable hunks by American ranchers who moved north across the border from Montana and Idaho at the sight of all those empty grasslands.

(As opposed to neighboring British Columbia, which was settled mainly by Fabian socialists and Scottish shop-stewards.)

The second injection of American mindset came after the famous Leduc oil strike south of Edmonton that set off Alberta's first oil-and-gas boom and brought in all the promoters and technicians who knew about the industry, from Oklahoma and Texas.

Alberta has a very American "feel" to anyone even geographically close to it, as to this scribbler who was born in Saskatchewan, on one border, and raised in British California, on the other.

An Alberta sociologist has suggested—accurately—that his province's love of guns has its roots in Alberta's pervasive free-enterprise model of behavior, the whole idea of which is that the individual is more important than the collective. Which is very American.

Example? Alberta's vigorous gun lobby is led by the very noisy, Edmonton-based, National Firearms Association. Its lobbying is one of the reasons why the Alberta government of Ralph Klein has spear-headed the constitutional challenge to Ottawa's gun-registration laws.

Which gets us back to the Reform frustration in attempting to cross the Rubicon, which would be the Manitoba–Ontario border.

Gun ownership in Canadian homes ranges from Alberta's 39 per cent down through (surprisingly) 35 per cent in New Brunswick to 32 per cent in both Saskatchewan (understandable) and Newfoundland (I thought they only clubbed those seals?).

But it's down to 24 per cent in mellow-yellow British Columbia, where everyone is either smoking pot instead or playing tennis.

Most significantly, however, is Ontario, which records the lowest statistic of all—15 per cent.

Ontario voters see Reform as cowboys, a little too trigger-happy, the Taber copycat nonsense after Columbine the latest example. There have been seven incidents in Alberta since 1996 when kids from age 11 to the 17-year-old in the Taber high school, son of a preacher, have been killed— mostly accidentally while playing with guns at home.

Preston Manning had no answer to the culture he inherited.

April 13, 1981

Living the Hollywood dream

Violence, after all, has more variety than sex

In the opening minutes of a current hit movie, *Fort Apache, The Bronx*, starring box-office king Paul Newman, a drug-crazed black prostitute shoots two policemen square in the face with a pistol she carries in her purse. Moving right along, she later picks up a middle-aged motorist, begins to neck with him and then slits his throat with a razor held between her teeth. Newman, a cop, watches as two of his colleagues throw a Puerto Rican boy to his death off the roof of a tenement. His girl-friend dies of a heroin overdose arranged by two drug dealers who, along the way, sink a knife into the abdomen of the black hooker and, wrapping her in the carpet where she fell, leave her on a garbage dump before they are filled with bullets in the middle of a hospital by Newman and helpers. And so it goes. It's a smash.

In another new release, *Thief*, James Caan is a professional jewel thief. He is beaten unmercifully by four detectives attempting a shakedown. Not a mark shows on his rugged face. In the final minutes of the movie, he watches as a friend is machine-gunned—in lovingly detailed photography—in a car dealer's lot. No one in this large American city apparently hears the noise. Friend's body is dumped in a vat of acid. Caan calmly blows up a million-dollar home (his own). No neighbors appear. He blows up a nightclub. He leisurely sets fire to the automobiles in the car dealer's lot. No one intrudes. He then proceeds to a mobster's home, shoots him with the cameras carefully following the blood sprayed on the walls, kills two more on the lawn in a prolonged shootout, then walks away down the sidewalk—presumably to more jewel thefts—as the screen fades to black. No neighbors appear, no police, no ambulances. That would spoil the fun. Sure to be a hit.

The love of violence, as a form of entertainment, is the underlying theme of the American society that makes a practice of shooting at presidents. There is, after all, such opportunity for variety. Sex is okay as a staple, but the variations are rather limited and have been basically covered by now—as most any moviegoer knows. Violence, by contrast, has unlimited possibilities and 20-minute car chases, children being thrown off the roof and ladies who carry a razor as well as a gat in their handbag are the breadwinner for those artists armed with the latest in sophisticated photography. Americans have grown so accustomed to crime and violence that they have become used to it, almost, one could say, cosy with it. The ride from the airport in a New York cab is now rather like a trip in a marine tank—to an innocent Canadian. It is not just the filth and decay in yet another shoddy product of Detroit's famed technology. There is the heavy metal and glass barrier between passenger and driver, a tiny slot where money can be exchanged between the customer and the man who warily transports the customer, the intimidating signs, warnings, regulations that the drivers do not carry more than $5 in change. One escapes the armored vehicle—for the "freedom" of the streets where you grow nervous after dark.

There are 60 million handguns loose in America: one for every five citizens. In 1978, there were more killings with handguns by children aged 10 and under in the United States than the British managed to total with killers of all ages. It is not for us to lecture the Americans who elect a man from the Sun Belt, where the proud right to pack a dispenser of self-defence is so established, who has a First Lady who owns "a tiny gun," who then must watch in televised horror with the rest of us as yet another of the madmen on the fringe acts out his bizarre imitations of the James Caans and the Paul Newmans of the screen. We watch the drama of someone else's lives. *Fort Apache, The Bronx* and *Thief* are just as popular in Canadian movie houses as they are south of the border. We dine on leftovers, even other people's violence.

The television screen, surely the most sadly used invention in man's reach for perfection, dispenses bullets as regularly as deodorants. Violence is the currency of a television age that ended a war in Vietnam by the simple fact that it grew *bored* with it. A new TV season approached and some variation was required. It is why Alexander Haig, that warrior in mufti, has come into trouble so quickly with the jelly bean ambience of the Reagan administration. He bristles with antagonisms and affronts—a Patton let off the leash among diplomats—at a time when Americans wanted a horseback version of Ike in the White House, gently paternal, promising a return to the *Saturday Evening Post* version of life. Haig clashes with the jelly beans. He doesn't fit.

The events of last week have a similar meeting of opposites. Ronald Reagan was elected because he seemed, in his certainty that he has been preaching from platforms for a decade, to embody values that were simple and understandable and down-home. Government must not intrude on Americans' lives. The individual can handle himself. If we get back to basics, society will sort itself out. It's not quite that simple. There are two warring factions within America: those who feel comfortable and contented with what they've got—and another slice that feels disaffected. The violence that the nation condones (and uses for quick bucks as entertainment) comes out through the John Hinckleys.

The
Scurrilous
Scribe

The problem with journalists is that they censor themselves. My old joke— which isn't really a joke—is that I just printed in my column what the reporters in the beer parlor after work talked about, but never wrote.

The problem with newspaper owners is that they never turn loose on the world an eager and aggressive kid columnist who will attract 26 libel cases —but will win 24 of them.

The reason newspaper circulation, over-all, is going down is because they don't have enough interesting newspaper writers who write the way people talk. I have editors, very intelligent, who don't understand this.

Read Damon Runyon. Read Mark Twain. Read Dickens. It's not a complicated formula. It's the simplest formula. Write the way people talk.

The problem with most journalists is that they never get out of the office. Essentially shy people, they fall in love with the most wicked mistress of all— the computer.

Newspapers were actually better before the telephone was invented. You had to get out to the coffee house and talk to real, live people. It is so easy to lie over the phone; that's why they have public relations people. It's much harder to lie when you're looking someone in the eye.

The fax and e-mail have simply encouraged people to lie to some inanimate object at the other end of cyberspace.

The computer has destroyed all human conduct. When this scribbler was at the Vancouver Sun *and first started in the column-writing dodge, my wonderful secretary, Miss Framsham, quietly mentioned one day that the complaining newsroom gossip was that I was never in the building.*

That's what good secretaries are for. They should always transmit the bad news.

I took her gently by the hand and led her out to the edge of the news-room. I told her I could figure out, by inverse ratio, the annual income of everybody in that room because of how little time they spent out of the office.

The problem with most journalists is that they go to lunch every day with other journalists—which will yield you nothing but inter-office gossip, bile, bitterness and—eventually—oblivion.

The Brits on what used to be Fleet Street say, accurately, that American (and Canadian) journalists know how to start an article, but don't know how to finish it. So true. The Brits know how to start and how—and when— to finish.

One day in 1952, Douglas Leiterman, a very good reporter for the Southam newspaper chain, wrote a story about yet another Royal Tour, this one featuring Princess Elizabeth.

"There arrives in Canada today," he wrote, "a young lady who, had her last name been anything else, could very well have ended up a barmaid."

There was more than one fusty Southam publisher who could not abide such blasphemy and Mr. Leiterman departed soon after for the world of television—eventually with Patrick Watson and Laurier LaPierre setting the country on edge with the brilliant This Hour Has Seven Days.

Everyone knows that television has cut into the power of the printed word in informing the public, but Leiterman was an early example of another problem: TV *stealing away so many of the good print journalists.*

Joe Schlesinger was as good a print reporter as he is as a CBC *analyst and commentator. So was Don Newman, now so perceptive from Parliament Hill for the Mother Corp., when he was with the* Globe and Mail.

Pam Wallin was a terrific terrier of a reporter for the Toronto Star *in Ottawa before the bright lights of the studio beckoned her away. Jack Webster was the toughest reporter in Vancouver before he submitted to the fame—and money—of television. Pierre Berton was one who moved effortlessly back and forth between the two media—not to mention his third, radio.*

The problem is that you need a whole newsroom to put out a newspaper or magazine. You need only a few stars with good hair to speckle out a TV *station.*

One is always amused, when the newspapers go on strike, how sparse and spare are the TV *and radio newscasts. Since, as camp-followers in the real world of journalism, they of course rip all their "news" out of the newspapers who do their work for them.*

What has one learned after a quarter-century on the back page of Maclean's? *Forty-five years in all in professional journalism? Aside from the fact that I couldn't get another job? Not much, really.*

Politicians still lie as much as they used to do. Jean Chrétien is as arrogant, in his own way, as Pierre Trudeau was. The only difference is that Trudeau's arrogance was stylish—expected from a rich man. Chrétien's is cloddish, and thinly disguised.

One of the things the public still does not understand is the vast mismatch between press and politicians. The Ottawa Press Gallery is bigger than ever, 300-some members now. There is a picture in the Gallery lounge of John Diefenbaker, walking down Parliament Hill trailed respectfully by a dozen reporters, all middle-aged men in hats.

The Prime Minister knew everyone of them by name, probably their wives too, and on some Friday nights—despite his fake teetotaler reputation—used to share a bottle of rye whisky with some of them.

Today of course it is a mob scene of pack journalism, cabinet ministers in danger of having their front teeth removed by the extension mikes jabbed at them in the "scrums" by TV cameramen hired mainly for their bulk and height by the networks.

Andrew Morton, the author of the lachrymose biographies of Lady Di and the ditzoid Monica Lewinsky, has confessed that the reason he established contact with the princess in the first place was that he was so tall, in the press mob in London, as opposed to the bandy-legged Cockney scribblers from the tabs, that she could notice him every day.

And as the pack journalism of Ottawa pursues the poor politicians, like the wolves pursuing Little Eva on the ice floes, still obscured from the public is the truth about the pitiful pols.

There is, despite the ever-expanding bloated numbers of the press gallery —every two-bit radio station in Otter Haunch now wanting a representative there—still an over-match.

For every high school graduate with a portable mike in the press gallery, there are a gaggle of flacks, flunkies, PR men and spin-artists in the office of every cabinet minister, all apprentices in defensive bafflegab—and all paid by the taxpayer.

It is no different in Ottawa, of course, than it is in Washington (and now in Clinton-copycat Blairdom in London), but it is disgusting, deplorable and such that it would make a truthseeker fwow up his cookies.

What has happened in this scribbler's lifetime in the trade is that the government's investment in concealing the truth now exceeds the media's expenses in trying to unveil the same truth.

This scribbler, over time, has watched too many talented journalists— frustrated at being passed over for advancement, or bitter, or tired, or turned cynical—give in to government blandishments and "go over the wall" for more money than free enterprise will pay them.

There is something basically wrong when the taxpayer is subsidizing good people who were once honest to hide the truth in open contest against those who are trying to reveal it.

Ottawa is a cesspool of cynicism. As Washington was long before. Harry Truman said it best: "If you want a friend in Washington, buy a dog."

Everyone knows the Earnscliffe Group of consultants in the town that fun forgot has been working for years, at high fees, to ensure that Paul Martin will be the next prime minister. Jean Chrétien, who is not quite as stupid as we all think, knows that.

(If Martin doesn't get it, and returns to lucrative private life, Earnscliffe will turn to Allan Rock, Brian Tobin or Joe Bloggs, whoever is available and knows which fork to pick up.)

That's the way Ottawa works. Don't pity the poor politician. Pity the poor scribe, who's actually in the game because he had an ideal, and doesn't get paid as much.

December 26, 1977

Hey, man, have you read Hansard? No ... but I saw the show.

There is a new spot of honor for the big console television set in the National Press Club on the second floor of the Norlite Building at 150 Wellington Street in Ottawa. It sits in pride of place on a table in the corner of the lounge and there is now a daily coterie of shrewd observers—the veteran Mark McClung, the elegant former diplomat Charles Ritchie and a few others—at strange afternoon hours usually reserved for the electronic versions of Ma Perkins and the bathos-sphere. The occasion now is the daily live televising of the House of Commons question period and the fascination around Ottawa at how much it is changing journalistic practices as well as political.

The evidence is there on each floor stretching above the Press Club in this building where the offices of the country's important papers, magazines, TV reporters and wire agencies are stacked one atop the other. Reporters have long grown used to the habit, when checking the time, of merely raising their heads and glancing out the window of this building to the clock in the Peace Tower on Parliament Hill across the street. But now there is something even more convenient: the ability to keep on bashing one's typewriter, or contemplating one's navel, while keeping one eye and one ear keyed to the large color set in each office, where the Commons business is unfolding, in close-up.

It is not just that it now makes unnecessary the trek of some 150 yards across to Parliament Hill and a jostling for a seat in the overcrowded Press Gallery. The view on the boob tube in fact is better—just as the best seat in the football stadium is now in your den. Who has the telltale quivering of the hands? Spot that shifty, ill-confident eye, undoubtedly indiscernible from the removed precincts of the Press Gallery itself. The only thing missing is the instant replay of each burp, each example of tangled syntax and mangled grammar. The serious columnists and investigative reporters can stick close to their phones and their files across the street while leaving the "hot room" off the Press Gallery itself to those in need of filing for deadlines. It may not be an aid to the democratic process, but it's a boon to anyone wanting to save shoe leather.

More important is what the square eye has done to the public perception of political figures. Here, suddenly, is a new Pierre Trudeau—bereft of the structured, controlled TV studio background where Liberal Party strategists can select the set to suit the national moment and the makeup girl has oodles of time. Here, instead, is a Pierre Trudeau continually on the defensive, carrying his painfully lacklustre cabinet on his back, bobbing and weaving verbally in semantic desperation over the RCMP farce. The accidental lighting is all wrong for him. The tired pouches under the eyes are naked in the cruel lights. All those intriguing facets of his sculpted face are emphasized, exaggerated. He appears stiff and humorless. For once, Pierre Trudeau appears vulnerable.

Equally, the public has been astonished to discover a Joe Clark unlike the caricature they have grown accustomed to read about. The press (this corner contributing its share) has painted a picture of an amiable young bungler who cannot jump a mud puddle, tie a reef knot or control his nervous tic. The electorate, therefore, came to the obvious conclusion that the Tory leader also could not put four sentences together. In fact, Joe Clark is a good university debater—which is all question period is about. The first principle of war is attack and Joe Clark—since he doesn't have to provide solutions in question period—has looked on TV to be a decisive, well-controlled critic. The Gallup poll proves it.

Years ago Marshall McLuhan predicted that color TV would create a need for hotter, spicier foods, more exotic furniture, and wilder clothing in men. As usual, he was correct, as witness the trend-setting uniforms of the Oakland Athletics and the standard fixture now around any convention, men dressed in what is known as "the Full Winnipeg": white shoes, white belt, white tie. The Liberals as yet have not realized what they have loosed on the nation by allowing cameras into the Commons. Sartorial anarchy is about to burst upon us.

As anyone who has been on TV discovers, content matters little, appearance is all. The MP from Kicking Horse Pass has learned, to his wonderment, that the only thing that interests his TV-watching constituents is his tired, bulletproof blue serge suit with last year's egg stains. It has been, for decades, the standard uniform for an Ottawa pol, as recognizable in an airline terminal as the short pants of a private school tad.

Now, thanks in part to the heat of the TV cameras and aided by the comments of their wives and girl friends, MPs (especially on the opposition benches) are discovering the Peacock Revolution two decades behind the rest of the world. Bette Midler, the Queen of Raunch, says her personal definition of bad taste is "double-knit polyester trousers." The Tories may yet be X-rated.

It is a measure of the forward progress of democracy that the next election may hinge on which party learns, like third-base coaches in the World Series, that one can no longer shift one's underwear with impunity. If you're one of those who have managed to defy McLuhan and have not yet succumbed to junk foods that give you heartburn, do not fear. The full-frontal MP, with a Hawaiian tie and window-check sports jacket, may provide your life with more color than it really needs.

April 28, 1980

There's nothing like a Deep Throat now and then

One of my heroes is Scott Young, a man I have never met (though we practise the same black art, letting thoughts run out of our fingertips). I prefer to keep my heroes at a distance, finding things less messy that way. I like Scott Young, perhaps because of that dreadful, flat Henry Fonda–like prairie drawl, one of the *Guinness Book of World Records* slow-talking champions. Perhaps because he was once banned from the *Hockey Night in Canada* broadcast by the boors who run the Toronto Maple Leafs because he said something honest rather than hokey. Perhaps because, in his column in the *Globe and Mail*, he used to write years ago about a rather awkward, mixed-up, dropout son who insisted on struggling through the tank towns of Northern Ontario (in an old hearse, if I recall correctly) in the early days of 1960s counterculture music. That awkward son eventually emerged as part of Crosby, Stills, Nash and Young, one of the big groups in the folk/rock explosion. People still talk about the column Scott Young wrote when he went to New York and walked around and around Carnegie Hall, savoring the marquee that told the world a boy called Neil Young was in solo concert that evening.

This troublesome Scott Young has just resigned from the *Globe and Mail* in a celebrated and supposedly minor fuss which actually is most intriguing to larger life. He quit because he disagrees strongly with the habit of younger *Globe* sportswriters of quoting unnamed Leaf players in critical comments on the coaches and Harold Ballard, the clown who has turned the once-deified Maple Leafs into the *Gong Show* of hockey.

Now, we have a very interesting issue here that should consume half a hundred journalism school seminars. Mr. Young's idealism is admirable—if you want to take a potshot at your boss you should put your name to your quote—

but I wonder a bit. What would happen to journalism, to politics (to Fothering-gay's income) if that rule were applied outside the sports page and throughout the newspaper?

Political journalism, as she is practised, is essentially a game of contacts, some to be rewarded, some to be punished for lies and deceits, some to be stroked and courted for another day. I suppose you could make a point that if the Scott Young rule were applied universally, Richard Nixon might have survived in the White House. Bob Woodward and Carl Bernstein, the two young *Washington Post* reporters who have become rich and famous because they broke the Watergate scandal, got their material from Deep Throat, the still-unidentified Washington bureaucrat who passed on information in an underground parking garage and then disappeared back into his job. There is still a minor cottage industry in Washington—the guessing game as to the real identity of Deep Throat. Because someone who couldn't be quoted was willing to talk, they got rid of a president who had to go on television claiming he wasn't a crook, thereby (as Dalton Camp said) becoming the first man in history to issue a denial and tell a lie in the same sentence.

There is, one suggests, another and more useful aspect to this can of worms. The art (and it's growing, which is a good thing) of getting secrets out of government by guile and stealth is a necessary trade, aided by insiders. Governments by their nature like to keep hidden that which doesn't have to be hidden, but it's much more efficient to proceed along the God-given Liberal path to righteousness if there is no one peeking. One of the reasons why a greatly disappointed Bryce Mackasey did not make the new Trudeau cabinet is that he had a reputation as being the leakiest minister of an old one. Every reporter in Ottawa, a matter of his trade as much as his notebook, romances his cabinet sources in return for the usual favors: not calling him a blaggard, knave or poltroon—at least not until next week.

It is useful, in vain hope of keeping secretive bureaucrats and politicians on the alert, to have the threat of some minor Deep Throats lurking near the Xerox machine. The duplicating machine has changed government, just as it has changed journalism, school and libraries. No document is safe (few really have to be), and the constant suspicion that an underling who disagrees with a policy has access to the outside has made officials paranoid (as well as marginally more honest). It is, to be blunt, a form of institutional blackmail. Leaks have been used for years by governments to test public opinion, fly kites (and reward favored journalists). Now, those within government who feel a point of principle is involved are using the same weapon. Would anyone argue against the value of the Pentagon Papers, leaked to the *New York Times*? Unspoken blackmail, wielded by those within who can't be named, will help to keep the Trudeau rats nervous.

The other day Manitoba Premier Sterling Lyon spoke at the National Press Club and delivered a small rebuke to the press, saying that it's the easiest thing in the world to simply be agin government. He's wrong. There's one thing easier, too much practised. It's to simply be for, and agree with, sacred government and all its holy works.

April 18, 1983

Sweating all the way to Peking

The best news we have had for some time is that the *Globe and Mail* is sending its clever and astringent sports columnist, Allen Abel, to Peking as its next China correspondent. By "we" I mean those of us who are in the privileged enclave known as geriatric jocks. We know it's an inspired assignment because all the great ones come from the sporting section. The good, grey *Globe*, of course, has rather a reputation for eccentricity in its picking of fresh-faced tyros sent off to decipher the inscrutable face of the Middle Kingdom. The editor a few years back boggled his colleagues by shipping to China the paper's ballet critic, John Fraser. All that resulted was a torrent of delightful copy and a best-selling book. (Fraser, for his sins, has now disappeared into the bureaucracy of the newsdesk, a terrible fate for a man who, thanks to his university days in St. John's, is the only deliciously bitchy Newf I have ever met.)

It's a little-known fact, privy only to those of us who type, but the cream of journalism is populated by types who got their start sitting around lacrosse dressing rooms, listening to the beer caps pop. Before the accountants and computer boffins took over, most managing editors and publishers came into their stations with the whiff of old sweat sock still lingering on their new three-piece suits. Cast a glance at the curriculum vitae of most any scribbler of note and you will find that he started it all at space rates, covering the local midget hockey tournament. From Paul Gallico to Mr. Hemingway to Scott Young (Robert Fulford, if you can believe it, started in sports), the lists are sprinkled with graduates of the press box. Scotty Reston, arguably the single most influential political columnist in the world from his platform at the *New York Times*, was once the press agent for the Cincinnati Reds. You can look it up.

The reason why sportswriters rise to the top is quite simple. They are born enthusiastic. The reason they go into the scribbling trade in the first place is because they lust to be close to the action, their heroes and the game that fascinates them. It doesn't really matter if they are failed athletes themselves (hello there, mother) or are just slobbering acolytes. Their passion pushes them. They would cover the jocks for nothing, the mere proximity to the demigods reward enough. They *care*. Compare this with your average young reporter going into straight (i.e., boring) reporting. One cannot really convince me that one is *born* with an innate desire to learn more about sewer bylaws at city hall or lies awake at night atingle with the next development in the Law of the Sea conferences.

Eventually, sportswriters grow bored with their calling (hello there, boss) and drift upward, levitated by the smarm they have learned by consorting with millionaire club owners and low-IQ plutocrats who have been made rich by their ability to discern a curve ball. There is a logical reason why so many graduates of jockdom wander into political reporting. It is the only other game in town where there is *suspense*. Sportswriters are essentially curious types, with low attention spans, and so much of life is so, when you get down to it, wretchedly dull, so predictable. The only thing that makes sports and politics so attractive is that they are two of the few areas in life where the result is unpredictable. It's why bread and circuses were the opiates of the Romans: there was always a faint chance that the Christians might win. It's why the working slob likes his hockey or football game. For 2½ hours of his life the result is in suspension, frozen in aspic, one portion of a dull, predictable existence held aloof from certainty.

It's why an interesting politician is usually a sports trivia freak; he recognizes the drama and essential ludicrous toss-of-the-dice mutuality of interests. (It's why Pierre Trudeau, bored with the trivia of sports, is not an interesting politician. He's an interesting person but not an interesting politician.)

The other reason sportswriters rise to the top of their dubious trade is that they use their eyes. The reason newspapers are dying (if you really want to know) is that a picture is not really worth a thousand words. Newspapers have abdicated to television by raising a generation of reporters who act as if they were equipped with only ears and no eyes. The worst thing that ever happened to newspapering was the tape recorder. Reporters go to press conferences and mentally go to lunch, leaving the rest to Sony. Newspapers were actually better (if you really want to know) before the telephone was invented. The ink-stained wretches were then forced to go outside the office and meet real people, a heresy in the current newsroom where Mother Bell is the real city editor.

Most reporters, being shy egomaniacs, tend to shun the social hustle and use the phone as their security blanket. It is their own version of aural sex. The scribe who is going to succeed is the one who is never in the office, the one who is out on the rumble talking to nonnewspapermen.

Sportswriters have the advantage of meeting, early on, the scam artists of the playground, whose only gift is quick reflexes, and the scam artists of the countinghouse, who play Scrabble with sports franchises. This equips them admirably for introduction in later life to both types to be found in politics, the silver locks and silver voice concealing a vacuous brain on the one hand, the artful grifter on the other, who survives by working the scams and perfecting the bump-and-run. Stick with the jocks, I say. Peking had better be prepared.

The lesson endeth.

December 5, 1983

Ducking an explosive press issue

The two best examples of the cozy Old Boys' clubs that defile and insult our society are the House of Commons and the banks. The best example we have had in a long time of the way they operate is in the Bryce Mackasey case. It is essentially protect your own, cover your ass, the hell with the public and scratch each other's back. It is hard to judge who was the most hypocritical in this astounding caper: the lily-livered MP or the unctuous, three-piece world of banking. It is easy to understand why the public has every right to be cynical about both.

Members of the Commons privileges and elections committee grunted nervously and came forth with an opinion that the Montreal *Gazette* damaged the Liberal MP's reputation and the privileges of the Commons by reporting allegations that Mackasey was a paid lobbyist. What a load of codswallop. What a terrible indictment of the sleazy practices of the Bank of Montreal—which the committee failed to mention in its embarrassingly short report. The question remains: why cannot me and thee, when we trot into the local branch of the Bank of Montreal, get the lenient financial treatment that was granted to Mackasey, an MP, a former chairman of Air Canada, a former cabinet minister who has been lobbying for some time to get back into the Trudeau cabinet and just might possibly be in on future banking legislation.

The story has been pounded to death in the newsprints. *The Gazette* (which stumbled upon the story when it was investigating something far bigger) found that by the autumn of 1981, Bryce Mackasey had run up some $625,000 in debts, presumably in bad stock investments. Mackasey, son of a railroader, has never had any real money of his own and, his chances of returning to the cabinet appearing slim, apparently gambled on a stock market that subsequently fell to pieces. The friendly Bank of Montreal, *The Gazette* discovered, loaned $400,000 to a numbered company, 109609 Canada Ltd. The loan was guaranteed by Les Ateliers d'Usinage Hall Ltée., a Montreal machine tooling firm. *The Gazette* reported that Robert Harrison, an accountant who was president of the Montreal Board of Trade, told a bankruptcy court, under oath, that Mackasey was acting as a paid lobbyist for Les Ateliers. It's known that Les Ateliers was paying roughly $7,500 a month to 109609—which was about the monthly payments on the loan. Harrison said Mackasey owned 109609. It's known that on October 27, 1981, Mackasey wrote to his fellow Liberal, Supply and Services Minister Jean-Jacques Blais, on behalf of Les Ateliers, which was seeking federal contracts. On November 27, 1981, the $400,000 was deposited into Mr. Mackasey's account.

Here, clearly, was an MP with serious money problems. The official court record, tape-recorded, has a man, who after all had been president of the Montreal Board of Trade, testify that the MP was a paid lobbyist—which happens to be a criminal offence in Canada. That's what *The Gazette* reported. That's what a good newspaper is supposed to do—tell the public what is said under oath about public servants (just as it reported that formal charges against Mackasey were thrown out in a preliminary hearing).

And how did Mr. Mackasey pay back the $400,000 to the Bank of Montreal, which comes out of this affair looking very gringy? Mr. Harrison gave him a cheque for $400,000 for his faded stock portfolio, which by this time was worth some $178,000. Did the Bank of Montreal clear its throat and suggest naughty naughty? Never. Mr. Mackasey is known throughout politics and journalism for the passionate pleading he can do on his own behalf. The public relations assistant to Bank of Montreal President Bill Mulholland is Dick O'Hagan, a former Lester Pearson and Pierre Trudeau press secretary who is known for his loyalty to old friends.

Mackasey, as time wore on, was some six months in arrears on his repayments. One straightforward chap at the bank recommended that it go after his house, his pension, his salary—as the loving, kind Bank of Montreal would do to me and thee. Instead? A vice-president was put in charge of the delicate situation.

The whole thing defies logic. Why would 109609 (on a guarantee from Les Ateliers) pay $400,000 for a stock portfolio that was worth less than half that? *The Gazette* held back the story for six days, after working on it for three weeks, to give Mackasey and Harrison a chance to explain their side of the affair. They declined. Mackasey has never sued *The Gazette*, relying instead on the belief that the chummy club of MPs would come down on his side. He did not miscalculate. The 10-member committee, after wrestling for seven months with its "investigation," came out with a tortuous and vague on-the-one-hand-on-the-other-hand report that was arrived at, admitted Tory MP Chuck Cook, "by exhaustion as much as anything." Only the NDP's Rod Murphy perceived *The Gazette*'s rights and defended the newspaper's conduct.

Faced with the public right to know, the MPs decided to protect their own first. When in doubt, kill the messenger. *The Gazette* had reported some unpalatable circumstances, so the conclusion is to announce pompously that the newspaper had "adversely affected" the privileges of the House of Commons with its series of articles. It did no such thing. All *The Gazette* did was to confirm in the minds of the Great Unwashed something always suspected: that when confronted with a choice, the Old Boys' club—in politics or in banking—will always take care of the Old Boys.

September 23, 1985

All the news that's fit to forget

T he problem is that there is a large surplus in the world today. The surplus is not of wheat nor of talk about AIDS nor of too many football teams in too many leagues. The problem is that there is too much news. The human brain, not to mention human patience, can absorb only so much. Modern journalism and modern communication and modern transportation thinks it is doing a grand job transmitting into our living rooms and our newspapers and our car radios the up-to-the-minute crisis of the moment. Instead, it induces ennui in the viewer/listener/reader. We become unshockable. Did you know there was a military coup in Uganda the other day? Or an abortive one in Thailand? Or was it the other way around? Do you care anymore? I'm afraid not.

It is called media overkill. (Some media guys were killed in a coup attempt the other day. Quick—tell me which one.) Do you remember Lebanon? Surely you must. That was the crisis before South Africa. Do you recall the Air-India crash? You're allowed a moment to think. That was the one before the Japan Air Lines crash, which preceded the blaze of a jet at the Manchester airport. How many were killed in each? Gotcha. One of the reasons you can't remember is that those of us in the information/communication/titillation trade now treat air crashes as we treat Pete Rose's records up against those of Ty Cobb. Each crash becomes the "largest death toll in a single-aircraft crash"—as opposed of course to the death toll in a two-plane crash. Meaning those two 747s that collided on the runway on that little island where we used to holiday. Quick now—the Spanish Canary Islands, right? Or was it Bermuda? The Bahamas? The Bermuda Triangle? Atlantis? I forget.

You get the picture. You faintly remember Patty Hearst? Was she the one who married her prison guard or was that Lyndon Johnson's daughter? Does it matter? They're all policemen. They're all daughters of famous men. It figures. Who was Squeaky Fromme? Was she the one who tried to kill Gerald Ford? Or George Wallace? Do you confuse the demented young man who shot Ronald Reagan outside the Washington Hilton with the demented young man who killed John Lennon? What are their names again? Welcome to the club.

We get too much news. Just as we get too many calories, too much gossip and too much information about AIDS, more than we really want to know. It has long been the contention of this here scribbler that newspapers were better before the invention of the telephone; those being the days when reporters actually had to leave the office. The chaps who interpret the news really had to leave the office and go out and meet, face to face, the guys they were writing about. They had a cup of coffee or a beer or a martini with the objects of their later derision. It both informs and aids the derision. Long lunches are not only good for journalism (and therefore readers), but they are good for the heart. People who take long lunches will never die of heart attacks (they may die of other things: i.e., shotguns, but they will never die of heart attacks. Long lunches are therapy for the heart).

I digress. The problem is the wretched telephone. And the wretched teletype. And the wretched Video Display Terminal. (You know the old joke. Yuppie male to Yuppie female in a singles bar: "No, I don't have a vasectomy. But I do work on a VDT.") There is too much of what passes for news. You've heard all the latest AIDS jokes? Young man phoning mother. "Mum, I've got good news and bad news. The bad news is that I'm a homosexual." Mum: "Oh, no!" Son: "The good news is that I've got AIDS and I'm going to die." A friend recently covered the war in El Salvador and was dumbfounded to find that all the rage were Ethiopian jokes, the ultimate sick version of what used to be Polish or Newfie jokes. Shirley MacLaine, now hailed for her extraterrestrial visions and an affair with an unnamed parliamentarian, once had to publicly apologize after she joked on television that a bankrupt New York was "the Karen Ann Quinlan" of cities. Now, jokes on Ethiopia are the In thing. Michael Jackson—remember him?—was last year's sensation, a phenom who was supposed to be the greatest thing ever to hit the stratosphere where they fix your nose and straighten your hair. He was replaced by Madonna, who barely had time to get her nude photos in the grown boys' magazines before she was replaced by Bruce Springsteen, who already had his pictures in the magazines too much. You're yawning, aren't you?

The world is too much with us, late and soon. People tune out and worry about crabgrass instead. You can see the reason for the success of Harlequin romances: housewives zonked on trying to remember the difference between Lebanon and Pretoria, the Christian Phalangists from the Druze, the Air-India prang from the JAL, the John Hinckley from the Squeaky Fromme, the contras from the Sandinistas. Who are the good guys and who are the bad guys in the Iran–Iraq War? Does it matter that Pete Rose had more at-bats than Ty Cobb, while playing one less season? Should a Roger Maris asterisk be put beside the record of Gerry Ford, who as president hit more spectators with a golf ball than Ike Eisenhower? Does anyone care?

The answer, ultimately, is no. It is information overload. The human mind, and human patience, can take only so much. Do not worry if you cannot remember what last week's crisis was. Content only in the knowledge that Pete Rose will disappear from your viewing/listening/reading screen. Erase. Rub. Forget. You will be better for it.

October 23, 1978

A word in defence of the Corp: battered, bruised, but still a relief from the alternatives

Would it be permissible to say something in defence of the CBC? Society has its own rules of conduct and what it feels constitutes fair play: bear-baiting is no longer legal in this country, cock-fighting is regarded as cruel and unusual punishment and the spectacle of torturing small animals in public for private amusement is regarded as outside the law. Despite all these humane advancements, the Canadian public insists on getting its sado-masochistic jollies by stripping naked its psyche and flogging the confused old Holy Mother Corporation.

There, before the inquisitors of the CRTC, sits the ever-earnest Al Johnson, president of the CBC, looking as always as if he has accidentally left the coat hanger in his suit jacket. Ever-earnest Al Johnson, the wrong choice for CBC president, a career civil servant attempting to absorb a crash course in communications while wrapped in the marshmallow cocoon of the impenetrable CBC maze.

Now, for perhaps the first public time in his life, Al Johnson is mad and, in support of his network's application for the inevitable renewal of its licence before the CRTC, he turns on his tormentors and surprises his own jaded broadcasters with the vehemence of his response. Johnson, for the first time, seems to realize how venal and cynical his Liberal masters can be with that massive slashing of the CBC budget in their sudden concern for right-wing votes. Re-election—not an endorsement of the CBC mandate to bind the country—is the Liberal priority.

Johnson states quite correctly that our children are in danger of growing up Americans. That by the time they are 11, they have spent twice as much time watching television as they have in the classroom. And that, by inference, they may be doomed to expire of Terminal Howard Cosell. He's right, of course, to be annoyed at having to defend the need for Canadian broadcasting while we are being inundated with Pablum for the mind from our rich neighbors who prosper in the puzzling belief that there is only one use for the airwaves that can transmit electronic images: profit. So we get *Laverne and Shirley*, *Love Boat*, *Three Jiggling Stewardesses*, *Three Jiggling Private Eyes*, *Three Jiggling Sportscasters*. It's the triumph of mammary over mind.

Now, as someone who occasionally allows his winsome visage to be captured by the cameras of the people's network, I am more than well aware of its lumbering, paperwork-encrusted deficiencies. It is, granted, a hidden cave for large clutches of incompetents who would be thrown on the breadlines if ever exposed to daylight or the free-market system.

And yet. And yet. There is—to frighten us—the spectre of the pap that flows unhindered across the border. Even such a rock-ribbed Neanderthal as Herbert Hoover, when he was U.S. secretary of commerce, could see in 1922 that it was "inconceivable that we should allow so great a possibility for service to be drowned in advertising chatter." The Americans did not take his advice and turned the most striking communications device ever invented over to the deodorant manufacturers. By 1958 Edward R. Murrow could say: "If there are any historians a hundred years from now ... they will find recorded, in black and white or color, evidence of decadence, escapism and insulation from the realities of the world in which we live ... If we go on as we are, then history will take its revenge, and tribulation will catch up with us."

Retribution has caught up with us. It is 20 years later and we have *Laverne and Shirley*, *The Love Boat* and screen-to-screen nipples.

In the most under-rated book published in Canada in this decade, Herschel Hardin argues in *A Nation Unaware* that just as much as the Americans have a genius for private enterprise, the Canadian genius is for public enterprise. He points out that "public enterprise is indigenous to the Canadian demography" and makes a very persuasive case that Canada, in its essentials, is a public-enterprise country, always has been and probably always will be. His prize examples, of course, are Air Canada, the CNR and the CBC—forces that were needed at the time to bind the country together and have remained as distinctive services that mark our differences from the Americans.

Can you imagine, for example, a newsreader slightly down the scale from Walter Cronkite standing before the Federal Communications Commission in Washington and complaining about corporate surrender to political pressure in ABC, NBC or CBS—as the gutsy Peter Kent has been contending about his CBC employer before the CRTC hearings? In that irrational way alone—while Kent flies off back to Rhodesia to file reports for the employer he has (accurately) criticized—the CBC justifies itself.

What the CBC needs to fend off the slavering yahoos of the hotlines (the Liberals, in their genius, have made the CRTC an open target by stupidly arranging that six of the nine commissioners are from Quebec) is not fewer powers but more: the confidence to have a sensitive tyrant at the top who will clean house and clobber the career cob-webbers. One thing that is supposed to distinguish us from the Yanks is our modesty and undue respect for authority. One thing that really distinguishes us from them is a more responsible broadcasting system.

May 31, 1999

Out to lunch at the CBC

The idiots who are running the CBC into the ground move on apace, bureaucrats who lunch but never think.

The latest brilliance is in dropping Lister Sinclair, whose evening *Ideas* program was the essence of what the CBC used to stand for: intelligent stuff for intelligent listeners.

These are the same idiots who have killed off Pamela Wallin's highly intelligent evening hour on Newsworld, because they apparently want to appeal to all the teenagers with nose rings and tattoos, all those viewers who move their lips when they read.

As Robert Fulford, the reigning intellectual in Canadian journalism, pointed out in a recent magazine piece, Wallin has evolved into the best interviewer on TV in Canada. She now is (was?) to CBC TV what Peter Gzowski used to be to CBC Radio, a seducer who can extract from a guest stuff that even his mother didn't know.

These would be the same bureaucrats, out to lunch as usual, who let the stars of *Front Page Challenge* know the show was killed by the romantic notion of a conference call. Pierre Berton learned about it when they called his secretary, not Berton, who only was the main personality of the show for every one of its 37 years.

They allowed that, in time, there would be an official lunch where all the usual clichés of thanks would be issued.

As a master of vicious memos, I wrote the Head Idiot of the CBC department in charge of the show. I said the way they handled Berton and Betty Kennedy and Fred Davis was a disgrace. All they needed was a nice champagne lunch, announce the long-in-the-tooth show was to be retired and everybody would be happy.

But to take the aging horse out behind the barn and shoot it in the dark was disgusting, I suggested. And guess what? They cancelled the lunch! To this day, not a single CBC executive has talked to Berton or thanked him.

The corporation of idiots, under Perrin Beatty, has been a disaster. As could have been predicted. The cynical Jean Chrétien hates the CBC because he believes its Quebec equivalent, Radio-Canada, is full of (probably true) separatists.

As an example, we've had the Chrétien puppet, press secretary Peter Donolo, try to bully the CBC into silencing a fine reporter, Terry Milewski, after revealing what really went on in shielding dictators at the APEC conference.

The cynic PM stunned even his own ministers when he anointed Beatty, a defeated Tory minister, as CBC boss—merely to deflect attention from the usual flood of Liberal patronage appointments. Beatty, privately wealthy, is a naïf, an MP at 22 who had done nothing but politics all his adult life. At 40, he was named communications minister and invited a *Globe and Mail* reporter to his office. Describing himself as a "techno-junkie," he said he had just bought a compact disc. "Do we have 59 seconds to spare?" he asked.

He pressed the button on a CD behind his desk. There was a breakneck version of Chopin's *Minute Waltz* with thunks and a scratchy sound quality. As a recording it was terrible but as a document, Beatty pointed out, it was unique: the pianist is Frédéric Chopin himself.

"This is the oldest recording in existence, 143 years old," says Beatty, explaining its origin. It was found in the summer of 1990 by construction workers digging in Nohant, a town in central France.

They found a steel box, containing a glass cylinder and a barely legible letter from an eccentric inventor named Hippolyte Sot, who perfected a primitive method for recording sound, and tried it on his neighbour, Chopin, in 1847 (which would have been 30 years before Edison invented recording).

The proud new minister, who has photocopied an article before the interview, says: "I think there are wonderful ways in which this relates to this department. First, you have the artist performing his work as he wished it.

"Second, the technology affected that artistic choice and the type of piano Chopin was playing on allowed him to play more quickly than we can on modern pianos. Finally, we now have a technology that allows us to optically scan and digitize it. The inventor himself had no way of playing the cylinder to see if it worked, and had to bury it in his garden. He was forced to wait for technology to catch up with him."

Within days, of course, gleeful letters-to-the-editor informed the *Globe* that "sot" in French means fool. The record label was the unknown XOHA, an anagram for HOAX. The British magazine *Classic CD*, revealing the scoop on the buried Chopin, explained the number of the historic CD was 010491 (April 1, 1991).

And when did this goof start as CBC boss? Fittingly, April Fool's Day, 1995. Will this madness never end?

March 4, 1991

Relax, the boss loves the action

Your humble agent finds himself in a most uncomfortable position, most disconcerting. It is a posture that is unnatural to my nature, inimical to the soul and generally discombobulating. It has put me off my feed and caused several restless nights tossing on the pillow. Through reasons no fault of my own, I am forced to be a referee, a peacekeeping force, someone consigned to hold the coats of the combatants.

This is contrary to the whole nature of the beast, someone who loves a battle. Not being able to join in, hip and thigh, is a cruel punishment. The problem arises from the fact that one Philip Mathias, one of the most esteemed writers at the *Financial Post*, penned a small and thoughtful piece suggesting that—amidst the madness in the Gulf—one could admire the courage of the Iraqi soldiers who are being bombed back into the Stone Age. At that, one J.D. Creighton wrote a steamy letter to the *Post*, expressing outrage and puzzlement that such nonsense could be printed in the paper. He had some personal interest, since J.D. Creighton just happens to be the chairman of the board of the corporation that happens to own the *Financial Post*.

There is a problem you must understand here. Both chaps happen to be friends of mine. Phil Mathias has a peculiar gift for always wandering, uninvited, into the broom closet that is laughingly called my office right in the middle of a burst of Shakespearean prose. Doug Creighton, on the other hand, signs the meagre pittance that is my paycheque. You will discern the dichotomy.

As befitting matters of global concern, Mathias immediately became a media star, given his 15 minutes that eventually will come to everyone. Earnest guardians of freedom of the press called and interviewed him and he was famous for at least two or three days. The droll fact was that no one phones and interviews reporters whose brilliant theses never get in the press because publishers won't print them.

Creighton, an eccentric sort, prints what his scribes write and then, if he doesn't like it, writes a letter like any other reader. The *Toronto Star*, for example—the largest and richest paper in the land—never prints anything that hasn't had the imprimatur of Liberal group think, with the result that everything tastes the same, reads the same. Better to have a publisher, this scribbler contends, who complains after the fact than before.

We are dealing here with a columnist, one must realize, who views all editors and other high-muck-a-mucks with suspicion. One must be on constant guard against them—except for the ones who are so high up they sign the paycheque. Chairman Creighton at a booklaunch party once complained publicly that I had written that he always looked as if he had slept in his clothes and combed his hair with a Cuisinart. This was outrageously inaccurate. I wrote that he combed his hair with an eggbeater. Ever gracious, I did not sue.

As a matter of fact, I have had only one column killed during 150 years of column writing—a column that in fact I had not even authored, it being the simple transcript of a court case revealing a judge using bullying and dirty words before a female prosecutor. And it was all the fault of a daughter. Said daughter, some eons ago, was being lovingly steered, in some frozen outpost, through figure skating classes one Saturday morning when a frightened junior editor on a Vancouver paper got on the phone to advise that the column, apparently a threat to the public safety, had been killed.

This particular frightened junior editor, who it seems to me was called MacGillivray, or some such name, suggested to the mother of my children over the phone that perhaps I might hustle down to the office and write another column for the second edition. She replied: "Does Bobby Orr play another game just after he has played one?" Frightened junior editor gurgled and hung up.

Since then, I have stayed away from figure skating rinks on Saturday mornings, feeling no good can come from them. The frightened junior editor—I have since lost track of him—for all I know is in charge of military censoring of the dispatches emanating from the Gulf. He showed the inclination early. It doesn't really matter, since the only taste one should exercise is in the choosing of one's publishers.

A famous departure came at the now-dead *Toronto Telegram* when sportswriter John Robertson, then in his drinking days, came into dispute with publisher John Bassett. History indicates that publishers usually win these battles.

Robertson was so clever as to plot his revenge typographically. In his next dispatch, he arranged the capital letters starting each paragraph to tell Mr. Bassett to attempt the sexually impossible on himself. The author then phoned all his friends, after the presses rolled, to boast—which of course ensured his swift unemployment.

What I'm saying is that one should be honored—you listening, Mathias?— when the only way you learn that the boss thinks you are a twit is through the letters-to-the-editor columns. Better than a memo, carried by an executive secretary in a cleft stick. Better than a pink slip. The *Toronto Star* doesn't care what you write, as long as it has a Liberal party slant. The Thomsons don't care what you write (can they read?) as long as it makes money.

The essential problem in journalism is not in getting spanked in public by publishers who do not agree with you. The serious stuff comes with those publishers who vet your stuff first—and no one ever sees it again. Relax, Mathias.

August 1, 1994

The channel surfer blues

The major problem with the information industry, of which I am an employee, is that it does not really help those who are helpless consumers of information. The nonsense of the vaunted information highway, that would deliver 500 channels into our living-rooms and produce department store shopping, not to mention Chinese food to the doorstep, is here before us.

The reason it is nonsense is that we already have more information than we actually want. The major example is Haiti. Most Canadians, not to mention Americans, could not locate it on a map if given a pointer and a large crayon.

It contains fewer people than New York City and yet rates huge headlines in all the best newsmagazines and your favorite morning newspaper. In reality, it is a piffle, no threat to world security, of no consequence to the average

inhabitant of Omaha or Moose Jaw, and yet it makes it onto every morning's 8 a.m. newscast.

Why? Because modern technology, and TV and satellite transmission, make it possible. Because technology can make it possible, trivial news masquerades as importance.

Haiti has no relevance to the world order. It is about as important as Yellowknife. But the *New York Times*—and therefore the *Globe and Mail*—puts Haiti on the front page. It is a joke.

When the Korean War dragged on, trench by trench, nothing really happening but always reported, the late and great Hal Straight, managing editor of the *Vancouver Sun*, gave an order to his deskmen. Run the same Korean War story, on the front page, three days in a row and wait to see if anyone noticed. Two (2) people phoned in. The same would happen with Haiti today. Trust me. Marshall McLuhan, one of the three Canadians who could be called genius (the two others available by a self-addressed envelope) accurately predicted that we were evolving into a global village.

He was right, of course, as proved by Peter Arnett, sheltering under a table in downtown Baghdad and describing on CNN George Bush's attempt to get re-elected. CNN has spooked the established networks—which is why fading *Time* magazine, in one of its few recent bright ideas, made Ted Turner, author of CNN, its 1991 Man of the Year.

(What's the difference between Bill Clinton, Dan Quayle and Jane Fonda? Jane has been to Vietnam. I digress.)

Thanks to Peter Arnett, now whenever there is yet another world crisis the nervous establishment networks dispatch their anchormen immediately to the hotspot, Peter Jennings in a safari suit, Dan Rather trying to disguise his nervousness, Tom Brokaw in his Midwest twang never really fitting in on the world stage.

Our current example of sad information overkill is Rwanda. Now that we can see, live in color, millions of innocent and ignorant people being chopped up and trampled to death, the mind goes numb. Then satiated. Then bored. Ho hum. Somalia yesterday. Rwanda today. Let's turn to the World Cup. Where's the disaster tomorrow?

McLuhan's genius insight produces—as he probably knew—a First World population inured to the pain of others. We watch the numbing pictures on the tube and wait for the sports scores. The mind can absorb only so much, the conscience can take only so many hits. How about them Blue Jays anyway?

When the history books are written, the man credited with the responsibility for the death of communism and the crumbling of the Berlin Wall will be one of two figures. Either Ronald Reagan, for insisting on an arms race that he figured, accurately as it turned out, would bankrupt the Soviet Union and the bad guys would blink first.

Or Pope John Paul II, who on returning to his native Poland on his first visit purposely supported Lech Walesa's Solidarity movement and thereby encouraged the watching Soviet principalities that you could indeed beat city hall.

The real thing that brought down the Communist empire, if truth be known, was the proliferation of the unstoppable TV satellite dish (hello there, Keith Spicer) and the fax machine, which made Warsaw Pact inmates totally aware of what lay outside their frozen existence. Once you've experienced Oprah Winfrey, how you gonna keep 'em down on the farm?

The television phenomenon that allows peasants in Thailand to watch O.J. Simpson chased down the freeway in a tableau that the Keystone Kops could not have invented also dopes us with tragedy. One year it is Ethiopia. The next it is Chad, or Somalia, or Bosnia, or Rwanda or Burundi or whatever.

Constant exposure to the tragedy of others does not make us more stricken, more grieving, more dumbstruck. Thanks to live television, it makes us accept the worst, knowing that next week there will be more.

Peter Arnett, we see, is now in Haiti, retailing more horror stories to make the evening news to follow up on George Bush burying alive untold thousands of Iraqi soldiers in the mother of all slaughters.

Information overload, it is called. A survey taken 20 years ago asked North American television viewers how many TV channels they felt comfortable with, how many they required. The answer came out to seven. What ho, we are in 1994, the age of the star wars and a recent survey divined that most viewers feel —world scoop!—that about seven channels is all they can, or want to, absorb.

Those of us in the industry of information are killing our consumers with overload. Saturation. Brain dead. What is wanted is quality, not quantity. Switch that channel.

November 18, 1996

Follow these steps to the heights of journalism

In the mailbox is a polite letter from a young man wanting advice. He is wise because he has come to the right place. Advice is the speciality of this department, offered free on almost any subject under the sun, even on subjects of which I know nothing.

In this case, the polite young man wants some tips on how to become a success in journalism. This is simple, because your humble agent is a world authority on how to become a success in journalism, if not in life. To wit:

Always wear shoes that are smartly shined. It is the first thing a female notices when she meets a man. A wise woman never marries a man who is ill-shod.

Stay away from journalism schools. You can't teach journalism any more than you can teach how to make love. You either got it or you ain't. A matron once asked Louis Armstrong what jazz was. He replied that if she had to ask, she'd never know. It's the same as the chap who asked J.P. Morgan what a yacht cost. He was told that if he had to ask, he couldn't afford one. Journalism schools fall into the same category.

Never wear button-down shirts with a suit. Verboten. Most of American malehood doesn't understand this. It's still verboten.

Never accept a present from a politician that can't be consumed at one sitting. The thing to tell the politician is this: if it's a gift, it's too much; if it's a bribe, it's not enough.

Never argue with a woman. No good has ever come from it. You know the definition of an editor. That's a guy who separates the wheat from the chaff. And prints the chaff.

Learn to listen. The greatest shortage in the world is not someone who can explain computers or VCRs; or cheap plumbers; or honest lawyers. The greatest shortage in the world is good listeners. Most people, when you are telling them about the leg you broke on the ski hill, are not really listening. They're just waiting for a break in the conversation so they can tell you about the gall bladder operation they had four years ago.

Most people in the world think they are misunderstood. Especially cabinet ministers and high executives. If you simply sit there—interspersing "Gee" or "Golly" or "I didn't know that!"—it's absolutely amazing what they will blurt out, all in the belief that at last they've found someone who will listen. That's how bartenders make their money, just mumbling "Uh-huh" while swabbing the bar and listening to unhappy husbands. Throw away your tape recorder. Listen.

To quote the immortal Satchel Paige, "Never look back. Someone may be gaining." Never wear cuff links with a sports jacket. Verboten. If a politician asks if he can tell you something off-the-record, excuse yourself and go to the loo and don't come back.

The definition of an editorial writer is someone who comes down out of the hills after the battle and shoots the wounded.

Get a good, broad education—while avoiding journalism school—in history, economics, some psychology might help. You don't need English classes, since you're enamored of literature anyway.

Travel. It's the finest education there is. The reason for travel is not to learn about other countries, but to learn about your own. The more you travel the more you will understand Canada—not an easy country to understand.

Don't get married until you're 30. If you do, you won't have the time to travel, and therefore educate yourself. Never join anything. If you do, sooner or later you will run into the uncomfortable fact that you will have to write something about one of your new friends—stock fraud, faked expense accounts, groping the waitress, whatever—and you will have lost a friend. The only friend a newspaperman can have is another newspaperman.

Read. If you don't read, you can't write. Be suspicious of everyone. If you watch more than four hours of TV a week, you need serious help. Stay out of the office as much as possible. Newspapers were better before the telephone was invented. It meant you actually had to go out and meet people.

Take long lunches. You may die of a shotgun wound inflicted by an irate husband, but you will never die of a heart attack if you have long lunches. Long lunches are good for the heart.

Be wary of journalists at the press club who tell the best stories and can talk very well. Most journalists who can talk very well don't write very well. They leave it all at the bar.

Stay away from people you have never seen laugh. They are dangerous, as well as boring. There are more boring people in the world than there are good listeners.

Never—ever, ever—in your writings use the two most useless words in the English language: "should" and "must." It has the same effect on politicians as when your mother told you that you "should" wash behind your ears and you "must" not go out with that girl who arrives on a motorcycle. "Should" and "must" should be eradicated from the dictionary.

As the wise man said, you have two ears and one mouth. Use them in the same ratio. Pretend that the "I" key on your typewriter/computer doesn't exist. Devour five newspapers a day. Never play poker with a man named Doc. Never order a martini in a town that still has a high-school band. If your mother gives you her age, check it out.

When Jesse Owens, in 1936 at the Berlin Olympics won four gold medals in front of Hitler, he was regarded as the finest track athlete in the world. He returned to the United States as a hero.

Within a year, he was racing horses at gimmick events in order to make a buck.

Canada, too, had a sprint hero. Ben Johnson at the Seoul Olympics. Last year, guess what, he was racing a horse at a gimmick event in Prince Edward Island.

Someday, somewhere, someone will produce a PhD thesis—or, better still, a good book—on who was really responsible for the tragedy of Ben Johnson, an unlettered immigrant kid who was urged by others (would you believe a government?) to get faster than anyone else, no questions asked.

It is one of the remarkable journalistic puzzles of our time that no Toronto sportswriter who covered him regularly on his rise to world class ever wondered where all that muscular development came from. Barbells are one thing. This was an ambulatory drugstore.

As mentioned below, a Liberal government in Ottawa for prestige reasons (meaning electoral appeal) purposefully set out to imitate state-supported sports programs—mainly in communist countries—and quietly hired 27 professional coaches from abroad to boost our jockdom to a world level.

At the end of that food chain, meaning at the top of that food chain, long after this column appeared, was the inevitable result. His name was Ben Johnson. Winning at any costs. Politicians were behind it.

Canada, in the Guinness Book of Records, *leads the world in sanctimony.*

The more obvious one is the holier-than-thou attitude to the United States— which happens to be a more democratic country than this one is.

A less-talked-about one is the disgraceful fact of the statistics on the number of our aboriginal citizens in our jails. Editorial-page lectures about South Africa would be better left in the round filing basket.

The most recent sermonizing has been over the high hypocrisy over Juan-Antonio Sammaranch and his pooh-bahs of the International Olympic Committee, the largest collection of sybarites since the Greeks invented the Olympics in the first place.

Canada, in fact, was part and parcel of making Pierre de Coubertin's idealistic dream into a determined and cynical drive for gold medals as a measure of national worth. Iona Campagnolo, as perhaps an innocent, was the major participant in that little-reported process.

October 10, 1988

The Johnson saga in perspective

In his memorable speech at the Democratic convention at Atlanta in July, Rev. Jesse Jackson had another of his celebrated word pictures. He noted that his ancestors had come to the United States in ships from Africa. Slaves, he meant. And the immigrant ancestors of Michael Dukakis, the man who beat him for his party's presidential nomination, came in boats from Europe. "But now," Jesse concluded, "we're all in the same boat."

It was a nice analogy, a testimony to the racial mix of the United States, a salute to the fact that, once within the shores, everyone is considered an American. That ideal is not quite true in Canada, as the saga of Ben Johnson demonstrates.

The country's shock and horror over his scandal is mixed, beneath the surface, with chagrin—the slow realization that the Ottawa-funded attempt to push the nation's sports profile on the world stage has been done at the expense of imported talent. Canada has a professional track team, almost all of it from the Caribbean, running for the glory of the Maple Leaf. Ben—poor, dumb Ben —has merely been the most exploited.

The Americans of course do the same with their black underclass. Europeans have long pondered how the United States equates its treatment of the mass of blacks at home with its proud display of them abroad at the Olympic Games. The United States has long dominated the track events at the Olympics with black runners. Carl Lewis is now the official winner of the 100 m and the long jump. Black Americans swept the 110-m hurdles and the 400 and dominated the 200.

Canada, meaning Ottawa through Sport Canada, leads the world in import-
ing talent in the attempt to do well on the world scale. The Canadian sprint
coach is from Poland. The basketball coach was brought in from New York.

The guts of the Krazy Kanucks ski squad's technical staff is from the Alps.
Ben Johnson's manager is an American who was bounced as track coach from
his U.S. College because of under-the-table payments.

In the Iona Campagnolo era, which coincided with the real rise of Sport
Canada as a burgeoning entity in Ottawa, there was the official decision made
by the Liberal government that Canadian international athletes had to become,
in a way, government employees—paid to display the flag abroad. The Tories

have followed. In all the sports funded by Sport Canada (i.e., taxpayer) dollars, foreigners have been hired to shore up the sports (unlike the indigenous specialty, hockey) where Canada has lagged behind in international arenas.

That's okay. If a country barely a century old feels ashamed that it can't compete in gymnastics or Greco-Roman wrestling with such countries as tiny Bulgaria and minuscule Romania—let the ebullient bureaucrats of Ottawa unleash the funds to put athletes on full-time salary, as has happened.

What is not okay is the blatant hypocrisy of the bureau-jocks on the Rideau who nervously didn't want to challenge those around poor, dumb Ben because of Ben's growing success. These rheumy eyes, once the eyes of a sprinter, have been around track meets ever since a pigeon-toed John Turner from the University of British California set the Canadian record for the 100, premetric, yards.

Only Olympic champion Bob Hayes (later of the Dallas Cowboys) got by on muscle alone, and those were real muscles—in the days when only the Soviet lady shot-putters owned steroids. It takes a remarkable collective blindness (or patriotic greed?) for all the Sport Canada bureau-jocks over the past few years not to have noticed Johnson's new weight-lifter physique. Can any sensible nit explain how Johnson, the rumors already rampant, was allowed to get through the Canadian Olympic trials this summer without being tested?

Government (bureaujock) greed for international acclaim? Government hypocrisy? For the latter, we have the imitation of Reagan in the swift prime ministerial phone call to the CBC booth in Seoul containing the confused young man, doom almost written in his eyes even then.

Swiftly thereafter, the same government banning him "for life" from the Canadian team (the International Amateur Athletics Federation has banished him for just two years) and the harrumphing announcement of a government inquiry at which he will be invited to appear. Johnson is not a criminal. He's stupid, but he's not a criminal, required to "appear" as if that is something in the law books.

More stupid are those who have used him, doctored him like a race horse with strange substances, hoping to cash in on a $4-million bonanza. One other member of the professional track team centered on one Toronto coach took it on the lam from future Seoul events once the chemists of the IOC unfrocked the once–Gentle Ben, who in the end was not so much a sprinter as a mobile drugstore.

Diane Clement, one of the officials of the Canadian Olympic team in Seoul, said that the Johnson scandal had "set Canadian track and field back 12 years." Well, maybe not. Perhaps it has set ahead, by 12 years, the thinking of the applause-hungry politicians and the bureau-jocks in Ottawa—with the realization that when you hire others to do your work for you, you reap the results.

The Don Cherry–ization of what was once was our national game, hockey, has of course been going on for some time. This example, explained below, of Punch McLean pre-dated the CBC's Hockey Night in Canada *making a Sam Six-Pack icon of the jerk Cherry.*

The author of this tome, a superannuated jock, of course—as is every prairie lad—was going to be a future Toronto Maple Leaf left wing, his early speed and fearlessness being perfected on the curling rink in Hearne, Saskatchebush, when the curlers and their beer bottles could get out of the way.

Said failed jock then watched two sons destroyed by the mindless maniac parents of minor hockey in Vancouver, the nutty mothers and fathers screaming for their NHL-bound darlings resulting—as could be expected—in the fact that the list of the top 10 NHL scoring champions is now dominated by lads from Russia, Sweden, Czechoslovakia and everywhere but Hearne.

September 17, 1979

"This leader of youth sent onto the ice his finest barbarians and bench warmers"

Punch McLean is a teacher of barbarians. He is, by all standards, a most successful teacher of barbarians. The junior hockey team that he coaches and partially owns has won the Memorial Cup the past two years. He has practised his particular brand of barbarism for 18 years, the first nine in the Saskatchewan town of Estevan, the past nine in New Westminster, a tired suburban stepsister just up the Fraser River from Vancouver. The New Westminster Bruins play in a shambling civic rink called the Queen's Park Arena. Mayor Muni Evers is a Bruins fan and likes to watch. Fans from the adjacent sawmills struggle in from the beer parlor and set up rhythmic chants of "bullshit" and more pungent four-letter-isms at the decisions of the referee with which they disagree. It is a scene most educational to anyone who wishes to understand Canada.

As a new hockey season opens to display the skills of the sport we supposedly exported to the world, it is useful to examine what has happened to our game. This is what has happened. On March 22, the New Westminster Bruins met the Portland Winter Hawks in Queen's Park Arena. It was the final regular

season game. A meaningless game, since both teams had qualified for the play-offs. There were only four seconds left and the Bruins had already lost the game 4-1. All that remained was a face-off in the Portland end.

Punch McLean, this leader of youth, sent onto the ice his finest barbarians, heavies and bench warmers playing out of position. As the puck was dropped, the Bruins discarded their gloves and sticks and attacked the Winter Hawks. McLean sent the entire Bruin team over the boards. Portland Coach Ken Hodge held his team back. That made it 16 Bruins on the ice against five Winter Hawks. The Bruins' Boris Fistric made for a Portland player, Blake Wesley, who attempted to skate away. Fistric knocked him to the ice with a blow to his throat. Wesley attempted to cover up. Fistric, who is 18 and the highly penalized "policeman" on the Bruins team, slugged him unmercifully and then kneed him in the head.

Bruins players Bill Hobbins, 19, and Rod Roflick, 17, then pinned Wesley's arms to enable Bruce Howes, 19, to smash him repeatedly on the face and chest. When Wesley finally made it to the dressing room, one sportscaster said he was "almost unrecognizable."

Fistric skated over to the Portland bench where Coach Hodge was restraining his players from going out onto the ice. Fistric slugged him full in the face, sending his glasses flying and causing headaches that lasted for two days. Howes, at the dropping of the puck, knocked Portland's Jim Dobson to the ice with a blow to his head. Terry Kirkham, 20, and Richard Amann, 18, came to assist Howes. The three of them proceeded to administer a beating to Dobson. In the words of a judge who would later try them, "two of the Bruins would hold Dobson's arms while the third would hit him in the face and chest area. They would then switch positions, with one of the three doing the hitting as the other two held Dobson."

Dobson's head was also smashed several times into the Plexiglas above the boards. In a pitiful scene replayed for TV watchers with strong stomachs, a Portland player crawled desperately toward his bench, half-conscious, a crippled animal seeking shelter.

John Paul Kelly, the New Westminster captain, skated to the Portland bench, swung his stick like a scythe and smashed Coach Hodge on his wrist, demolishing his wristwatch. In the dressing room the surviving Portland players were in tears. Their top player, Keith Brown, possibly the best-skating junior defenceman since Bobby Orr, was taken out late in the game because of the obvious intent of the McLean goons to cripple him for the playoffs. Their next best player, Perry Turnbull, was wiped out in the second period when Fistric highsticked him into the boards and Turnbull swallowed his tongue. There were 191 penalty minutes in the game, 156 of them to New Westminster.

It all fits. This is the Punch McLean who boasts that he produced Dave Schultz. The Bruins perfected that ultimate Canadian art form: the brawls during warm-ups *before* the game. McLean was once suspended for 25 games for slugging a referee skating past his bench. When the Bruins, as Memorial Cup champs, were to go to Finland last year to the World Junior Championships, the Jockarina of Sports, Iona Campagnolo, laid on briefings from External Affairs types and as a last resort had Bobby Hull deliver a lecture on deportment abroad.

McLean's barbarism of March 22, significantly, happened just weeks after this country's sluggish skills were cruelly exposed by a 6-0 slaughter by the Soviets. Fistric and Kelly, typically, were the two Bruins selected in the NHL draft. Seven of the Bruins in the gang-beating were charged in B.C. provincial court and, strangely, were given conditional discharges. Judge J.K. Shaw, while barring the players from hockey until December 1, ruled: "These young men are manipulated—apparently happily—by the owners and coaches to do exactly what they are told." Coach McLean responded by saying: "That's his opinion. My style of coaching is going to remain the same."

At a recess during the trial, a smirking Boris Fistric proudly signed autographs for admiring young boys. Hooray for Canada.

December 5, 1994

Laying down the law

Dick the Butcher: The first thing we do, let's kill all the lawyers.

—Henry VI, Part II

T he poor babies. Always being picked upon. Willy Shakespeare in 1590 foresaw (as he foresaw everything) that the legal beagles would forever be in trouble with their public relations. Poor babies. Always misunderstood.

What's the difference between a skunk on the highway and a lawyer? Skid marks.

The Canadian Bar Association's Ontario branch, as you may have heard, is going to do something about this dreadful image, these disgusting jokes. They plan to monitor the way they are portrayed in newspapers and magazines and books and on radio and on television. They are going to mount an organized response to "the media's unfair assault on our collective image." Poor babies.

Question: What do you call 200 Toronto lawyers at the bottom of Lake Ontario? Answer: A start.

This vigorous effort to repair the image of this underprivileged group is sure to garner immense public sympathy. Whenever I argue with my many lawyer friends and they respond with the usual palaver about journalists being lazy, undisciplined, undereducated and downright rotters—all true—I reply that the last time I checked there were more lawyers in jail than journalists.

I would suggest, always trying to help out the poor babies, that they initiate their amazing new PR campaign by publishing a list, province by province, of how many people with a law degree are in jail. Let's be frank, boys.

Not just those thrown in the slammer, as we read with boring regularity month by month, for borrowing widows' trust funds and forgetting to put them back in the safety deposit box. Not just those convicted of fraud and misrepresentation.

We're talking here of every single holder of a law degree who has never practised law but tried to flourish on the Vancouver Stock Exchange by selling moose pasture masqueraded as silver mines, or who got into real estate and got greedy, or who made a million selling passports to eager Hong Kong immigrants. All of them, guys. Fess up.

Passengers on the cruise ship watched in horror as a tipsy lawyer fell overboard into shark-infested waters. To their amazement, the ravenous sharks instead of chowing him down raised him on their snouts and gently lifted him into a lowered lifeboat. "Just professional courtesy," he explained as he arrived back on deck.

One Igor Ellyn, president of the lawyers' association, explains: "If there's greater respect for lawyers, there will be greater respect for the justice system. Respect for the protectors of the justice system—lawyers and judges—goes hand in hand with accepting why the justice system does certain things."

One of the certain things the "justice system" does is allow Mr. Ellyn to charge $295 an hour for his services from his 44th-floor office in downtown Toronto.

He says lawyers should be seen as "caring, reasonable, down-to-earth people, the majority of them family-oriented." Oh, gee. I guess this would be the description of the clutch of celebrity lawyers who are presently presenting the zoo act of the O.J. Simpson trial, which, all the experts estimate, will leave the millionaire bereft and his children deprived of private schools even if he avoids the crowbar hotel.

Voltaire went bankrupt twice. Once when he lost a libel suit. And once when he won a libel suit. He and Willy could commiserate.

The idea of lawyers setting up a monitoring program to pounce on nasty reviews of their performance (Big Brother is not only billing you, he's now watching you) is hilarious. Next? Aluminum-siding salesmen keeping a check on their reputations? Used-car touts whining about what people think about them?

Lawyers have a bad reputation because they have a bad reputation. They might sit down and think about that a bit. Nurses don't have bad reputations. Neither do botanists. The lawyers, the masters of talk and politics, might think about that, too.

You've heard perhaps that scientists are now using lawyers, rather than rats, in laboratory experiments. There are three reasons for this:

1. There are now more lawyers in the world than there are rats.
2. There is no chance you will ever become fond of a lawyer.
3. There are some things rats won't do.

I happen to be an expert on lawyers because, due to the way I make my pitiful living, I have had to spend so much time with them. I know more about libel law than most lawyers in Canada, mainly because it is my job to see how close I can get to escaping it.

They are lonely, unappreciated guardians of our democracy, as we know. Like the clever ads, each succeeding the other, supposedly defending Paul

Bernardo in the Ontario scandal that so far has cost the taxpayer some $400,000 in legal aid fees with no end in sight.

Poor innocent Mr. Ellyn, setting up his monitoring system, trying to track every offending article on his noble craft, transcribing tapes of each hurtful broadcast, trying to trace every miscreant who has ever emitted or emoted a description of his breed.

He might best save his breath. And his money. Better still, he might go back and read *Henry VI*.

On perusal, this is a column I wish I had not written. Perhaps it was a bad-hair day. Perhaps food-poisoning. Perhaps a fight with the boss. Or the mail was lousy. Whatever.

It comes across, too many years later, as anti-female, anti-women, or what moniker we're allowed to call them these days.

The surprising truth is that I actually like those of the female persuasion. My mother, as luck would have it, was a female. So is my daughter. So is my wife.

So is my editor, who, I suspect, included this as one of the 100 columns she selected for this tome just to make her author cringe. She has, it must be admitted, succeeded.

My only problem with the female race, actually, is the complaint that I take too many of them out to lunch. My mother tolerates it. My daughter tolerates it. My wife tolerates it. The complaints come from husbands, who, as we know, are not famous for their sense of humor. And probably have their own views on Adidas-on-the-way-to-work.

September 2, 1991

The revenge of the grannies

Everything, these days, is symbolism. Tokenism. A computer-stained wretch can't put a finger to keyboard without offending some outraged group of litigants. At the moment, the Defenders of Grandmothers are on my neck. Including, of all people, one of my sisters. I feel like Arte Johnson, the little guy on the park bench on Rowan and Martin's *Laugh-In* who was continually smacked over the head by the prim lady with the purse who always kept her knees together.

The DoG are upset by the references here to the fact that the brilliant delegates of the Social Credit leadership convention in Hongcouver chose grandmother Rita Johnston as their champion to fight off the Red Hordes of Mike Harcourt, who is destined to be the head of the next government of Bennett Columbia.

You'd think I'd been caught drowning small kittens. Or stomping on Mother Teresa. There is nothing so enraged as the DoG when aroused and in full cry.

First of all: my credentials. As strange as it may seem, I have had a grandmother. Two, as a matter of fact, as they usually come in matched pairs. My mother, strange as it may seem, is a grandmother—12 times over, as a matter of fact, with 11 great-grandchildren to boot. My daughter, strange as it may seem, someday will be a grandmother. My sister, God save her soul, is a grandmother.

We have thus established that I am generally in favour of grandmothers. I wouldn't be here without one. The reference to Grandmother Rita has nothing to do with grandmothers. It has everything to do with politics.

Until John Kennedy came along, there was the perceived wisdom that leadership of a political party could only be bestowed on chaps (no chapesses). Men who had potbellies, pinstripe suits and liver spots on the back of their hands.

Kennedy changed all that, as can be observed at any political gathering in the world. Bright and ambitious people in politics have discovered that they don't have to wait at the end of the queue: They don't have to sit in smoke-filled rooms till they are 60 before they are allowed to grab the levers of power.

Sister rails, in a letter, about my disgusting, disgraceful, degrading description of the fact that the race for the Socred leadership was between "two grandmothers." Would you, she asked, have written about "two grandfathers" if they had been the contenders?

That's the whole point. Certainly. Sex, or gender as we say, has nothing to do with it. Age does. Mind-set does. A linkage to the modern world does.

Rita Johnson continues the fine B.C. tradition of producing B.C. premiers who've never made it, educationally, past the high-school dance. Her opponent on the final ballot, Grace McCarthy, said she was 63, although the jury is still out on that one. That tells you everything you want to know about the present state of the Social Credit movement, in 1991, as it waits to march into the next century. It can't find someone of another generation in its upper ranks, anyone there capable of challenging the leadership. This is a party with a serious hardening of the arteries of the mind.

Look at Ontario. On the retirement of the charismatic Bill Davis, the intellects of the party chose as his successor one Frank Miller, a grandfatherly type who wore Rotary-style plaid jackets with a philosophy to match. Ontario voters were so appalled they immediately voted in the young David Peterson—

who wore out his yuppiedum eventually and was replaced by an even younger Bob Rae.

Grandmothers are not an endangered species. My kids say (correctly) that they have the two strongest grandmothers in the world. My beef is not with grandmothers (I'm not that dumb). My beef is with the political parties who signify—by their leadership candidates—that they are in Dreamsville, out to lunch with the younger voters that they have to attract to retain power.

All you have to do is take a look around you. The premiers in this country—like the governors in the United States—are getting younger and younger, as witnessed by the energy and resolve that they have to put into the process to achieve reaching the top. There will be, eventually, a female prime minister of Canada—as there have already been in India, Israel, Norway, Sri Lanka, Pakistan and Britain—but she will be a Kim Campbell, not a premier Mom.

As it is symbolism, and tokenism, it is gender-ism, the new buzzword of writers who write to the editor. Grandmothers are suddenly as vulnerable as whales or seal puppies, or elephants slaughtered by African poachers for the aphrodisiac quality of their tusks. In my considerable experience, the grandmothers in my own family ambience would frighten any poacher out of his blunderbuss.

There has been an overreaction here. Grandmothers can take care of themselves very well. Everyone of my children, who can hitchhike through Africa, ski down glaciers and jump out of airplanes with a late-developing parachute, are terrified of sitting down with Granny to discuss, ah, modern hygiene. Sometimes known as condoms. It's the Socreds' own business if they, in 1991, want to choose between two grandmothers to put before the voters, as they must, before a snow falls (as it never does in Hongcouver). They inadvertently put out a signal to the electorate that they have no fresh blood, no zip, no new ideas. That's their business. I'm just a reporter. Sorry, Sis. But you're wrong. (Mother always liked my brother best.)

April 26, 1999

"What's a scribbler to do when a subject hits back?"

Well, you see, we have this dilemma. On balance, your obedient servant would best have faithful readers figure it out, their common sense and wisdom well known.

The dilemma is this. Should an employee be allowed to thrust nasty words at an employer, in a crowded setting, at a social occasion, before the High and

Mighty? It is a confusing question, and what might be the remedy?

The setting is Politics and the Pen, a magnificent evening that is one of the events on the Ottawa calendar. It is put on by the Writers' Trust of Canada. A board of directors of 20 worthies, and a volunteer committee of 18, spend a year trying to outdo last year's event. And usually succeed. Ladies sell their Porsches to finance the right frock for the black-tie bun toss.

Rich Ottawa types, and there are many, fill out the gaggle of some 375 to people-watch.

The idea is to throw together 44 published authors—on this particular evening everyone from former American ambassador James Blanchard to Maureen McTeer to Ben Wicks—and 44 politicians, everyone from Paul Martin to Speaker Gib Parent. There were 17 "The Honorables" spotted. The gossip was X-rated.

The backdrop was stunning. It was wall-to-wall champagne at the cocktail reception in the foyer of the Senate. Under the direction of our own Maurice Chevalier, MC Laurier LaPierre, authors—each festooned with a ribboned award resembling a Victoria Cross—were marched for dinner into the Hall of Honour with its magnificent vaulted stone arches overhead. It made you, for once, proud to be Canadian for dining in such history and symbolism.

And so? And so, your blushing lad, over dessert in the crowded Reading Room, is chewing over a chocolate truffle when a handsome woman, beautifully coiffed and beautifully dressed, approaches. "Mr. Fotheringham?" she sez.

My mother always taught me to be polite to handsome ladies who approach me uninvited. I allow that that would be me. "I am Susan d'Aquino," she calmly announced. "I know," I said. She said: "I think you're a fucking son-of-a-bitch." My mother always taught me to be nice to ladies I have never met. "Thank you very much," I said. She turned on her heel and swept off.

My immediate impression was that Susan d'Aquino reminded me of Mark Twain's wife. Twain was a great scholar of the greatly underestimated gift of cursing. He prided himself on his vocabulary of the genre.

His wife detested his hobby. One morning, while shaving, he cut himself and launched into one of his marathon blue phrases. Thinking to shame him, she repeated his entire words. Twain replied: "You have the words, my dear," while lowering his razor, "but you don't have the tune."

Susan d'Aquino, sad to say, didn't have the tune.

The problem, it seems, is that some time ago—last year, I believe—I twice took on in this space husband Tom d'Aquino, the spokesman for the billion-aires club Business Council of National Issues, for yapping his yap off to Peter C. Newman on how he had actually orchestrated Liberal legislation and had invented everything from penicillin to rock'n'roll. He protested in a vigorous letter to the editor.

The further problem, though—while Mrs. d'Aquino loves her husband as all wives should, she is my employee. I am a Canadian taxpayer (paying a trifle more than I think healthy, especially when some of it goes to help Jean Chrétien's friends in his riding).

But I am Mrs. d'Aquino's employer. She is a very senior assistant deputy minister in Ottawa's Department of Finance. Faithful televiewers will know her well. Whenever there is a federal–provincial conference or national unity windbag, she can be detected in the second row behind the ministers because she is so obviously handsome and intelligent. She could do a cover of *Vogue*.

A day's telephone calls to Mrs. d'Aquino's Finance department only results in the result that no one can, ahem, find her exact salary. (We're only taxpayers.) Senior ADMs in Ottawa are in the $130,000-to-$140,000 range.

But should an employee swear at an employer at a high social event? I ask some of the usual suspects around the dessert table. A woman says, "That would be a BCM." A BCM, in Ottawa speakese, is a "bad career move."

Men swear at me all the time. I get on elevators in Vancouver, Toronto, Montreal, and a muffled voice comes from the back, "Fotheringham, you are a *xpl?z.*" I get off, content that they at least read the guff. The champagne that evening was copious, the single malt quite reasonable, the wine ever-flowing, but Mrs. d'Aquino seemed quite in control of her faculties, as one would expect of an ADM, as one would expect of one of my employees.

What does one do? Ask my MP, Bill Graham, a loyal Liberal, to ask in Question Period of Paul Martin why one of his higher-paid staff can swear at one of her employers, at a nice social occasion? It is, as Yul Brynner said long ago in *The King and I*, a puzzlement.

May 30, 1977

For shame, you filthy perverts! You ought to wash out your mouths with soap!

The funniest magazine article I have ever read is a piece by a woman, some 70 years of age, that deals with a certain way of pleasing the male sex organ. It is in the May *Esquire*, it is by Helen Lawrenson and is entitled "How Now, Fellatio! Why Dost Thou Tarry?" It is the first magazine article ever to deal with that tricky art and Lawrenson somehow, by the ruse of artful innocence, manages to reduce the whole practice to high farce to an extent the reader is left, uh, limp with hilarity. The lesson that can be drawn from this is that there is now no aspect of sex that cannot be made fun of publicly.

I mention all this because of the now famous quote by John Merner, the 59-year-old Canada Customs official who explained why he, in his bureaucratic wisdom, had made the decision to ban the May issue of *Penthouse* from our pristine borders because of 12 pages of naughty pictures. The Canadian public, he explained, speaking for all of us, "is anti oral sex." Just when several million people on this continent are laughing their heads off at Lawrenson's deflation of the oral subject in detailing her experiments with it over 40 years, Merner is taking it all much too seriously.

The whole thing reminds me of what James Thurber said in 1929 in explaining why he and his confrere E.B. White had written a book called *Is Sex Necessary?* Thurber explained that "the experts had got sex down and were twisting its arm, and someone had to restore the subject to the levity it so richly deserves." I don't know where Merner does his deep research into the Canadian public's preference in the bedroom and automobile, but he obviously hasn't been hanging around movie houses and bookstores.

One of the greatest audience reactions in recent filmdom came in *Shampoo* when Julie Christie announced that she'd like to perform that specialized deed on Warren Beatty under the table at a political banquet. The current hit movie is *Slap Shot* and Paul Newman spends what seems like half of it talking about the same supposedly verboten subject, women to women, men to men. The movie is billed, as you'll notice, as the comedy hit of the year.

What poor Merner doesn't realize is that real pornography is boring after 10 minutes and the only way to stretch the interest is with humor. Do the Customs guardians of our morals know that the Governor General's award for fiction in Canada this year was awarded to a book that details a woman's sexual encounter with a bear? (Even more pertinent, when the Governor General presented the prize to Marian Engel, did he read a précis to the august spectators, explaining the book *Bear* is about a female almost getting it on with an animal? Does Canada Customs know about this?)

The English gentleman who said long ago that sex is highly overrated explained that "the pleasure is purely temporary, the price is exorbitant and the position is absolutely ridiculous." The reason *Deep Throat* made $40 million and enabled Linda Lovelace to get into the enclosure at Ascot is that it was the first porno film made with tongue-in-cheek, as it were. The breakthroughs are not being made in technique—since nothing really new, beneath all the whipped cream and black whips, has ever been invented—but in the humorous ways of treating it.

Everybody thought a semi-underground book, Terry Southern's *Candy*, had exhausted all the comedy aspects of eroticism until Gore Vidal gracefully swept the best-seller heights with *Myra Breckenridge*. We assumed that Philip Roth, with *Portnoy's Complaint*, had left nothing more to deal with after making male masturbation funny. Now? He looks old-fashioned and humorless after Erica Jong.

Critic Robert Fulford complains that Jong writes "pornography for people who have gone to college." Perhaps, but doesn't everybody have rights? Why discriminate against the poor deprived PhD? Should he have to buy his own dirty raincoat to get his jollies? Ms. Jong, who taught women about zipless things in *Fear of Flying*, is now soaring to the best-seller lead with *How to Save Your Own Life*, which advances women's liberation yet another hilarious step on the road to somewhere. She is of the school of raunchy old Henry Miller, who thought that sex was delicious but also very funny, and Erica romps through lesbianism, group sex, aids such as champagne bottles and other subjects too droll to dwell upon.

You can't pick up anything these days without finding sex wrestled to earth. A copy of *Toronto Life*, which all the trendy people consult before buying their gold-plated bathtub faucets, deals with "Rape Fantasies" by Margaret Atwood, contraception advice by Germaine Greer and a third piece on the new "Parameters of Porn." *New West*, the California equivalent for the upwardly struggling middle class, has a cover story on Sexual Power—explaining why certain males can get girls into the sack and why certain others flame out on the launching pad. Even the wife of the Prime Minister brought a hint of Krafft-Ebing to Swift Current with her lessons on the turn-on qualities of garter-belts.

In this decade of liberation, when any self-respecting career girl can't make it through coffee break unless she knows all the words from *Slap Shot*, it is even more imperative for the male to have a sense of humor about the most ludicrous sport of all, since there are indications he is going the way of the wombat. Ms. Greer is marching about the lecture halls of the globe advocating that women used a new birth control method—abstinence—until male society is forced to devise a more acceptable contraceptive device than the pill.

Moving right along, the new folk hero of the feminist movement, Shere Hite, says there is a solution to the dearth of female orgasms: do it yourself. In the newest book sensation, *The Hite Report*, she takes the Mr. Fix-it rage of the 1960s, when everyone was taught one could do one's own plumbing, to the ultimate extreme. It's the newest cottage industry. The male animal, with his attachments, is superfluous in the Hite world and any imaginative woman who owns a shower nozzle can get along without him very well. A man reading *The Hite Report* gets the sort of queasy feeling a buggy-whip manufacturer must have felt when he saw the first quarterly sales figures on the Model-T.

If Ottawa is missing all this, it's hard to imagine how it can cope with the nuances of inflation. Just when sex is getting funnier, the government is taking it more seriously. Censorship is not the answer. Laughter is.

January 24, 1994

The sweet mystery of manhood

In a restaurant last week, four women of a certain age, emboldened by the grape over lunch, turned to the table containing this reporter and, in unison, chanted, "Bobbitt! Bobbitt! Bobbitt!" Their glee was uncontained.

New joke: A survey shows that 90 per cent of American men now sleep on their stomachs. The *Toronto Sun* runs a full page on The Penis Primer: urologic surgeon Roger Buckley of North York General Hospital puts the average erect penis at 6$1/2$ inches. (Go to the mirror, chaps.) David Letterman reports that while doctors say John Wayne Bobbitt may be able to function sexually in two years, it will be five years before he will enter a Benihana Japanese steak house. Old joke: Elephant to a naked man, "It's cute. But can it pick up peanuts?"

What's going on here? Why is mutilation such a source of humor? The press and the late-night comedians have never had so much fun. Marilyn Monroe, we're now told, used to tell the story of how actor Errol Flynn, famed for being among the best-endowed men of his era in Hollywood, would play "You Are My Sunshine" on the piano with his penis. Why is all this suddenly funny?

The reason, of course, is that the organ in question is inherently goofy looking. An architect could have done it better. God must have been a woman to achieve such revenge.

Now that the thing is out of the closet thanks to CNN and Lorena and John Bobbitt, the *Toronto Star* helpfully informs us that some 400 men from Saudi Arabia, Poland, England, New Guinea, Australia, Germany, Sweden, the Philippines and the United States have consulted a Toronto plastic surgeon who has become world-famous for his penis-enlargement operations. His name? Unfortunately, it is Dr. Robert Stubbs, who learned the technique from—wait for it—Dr. Long Daochou in China.

CNN, which now rules the world, first brought us the Gulf War live. Then the riveting contest between Anita Hill and Clarence Thomas—Long Dong

Silver and pubic hair on Coke tins—that split the nation on sex lines. The coverage of the William Smith rape trial in Florida signalled the end of the Kennedy family myth. Now? Now work stops and housework is suspended while the TV screen details how Lorena Bobbitt sliced off her husband's weenie with a super knife that, as advertised, can indeed cut through anything.

If John Bobbitt, who by his testimony proves that his IQ is about as long as his equipment, had sliced off the left breast of his wife he would be revealed as a monster. But when the opposite happens, the comedians exult in joy. Manassas, a little Virginia town across the Potomac from Washington, was previously famous for a momentous Civil War battle. Now it's in the joke book, a symbol for all womanhood.

Several years ago, on glancing through the *Globe and Mail*, I noticed a headline—"Turkey Necks and Hat Racks." Thinking it was a cooking or decorating column, I passed it by. Several days later a female-type friend phoned and suggested I take a second look.

It turned out to be a column by June Callwood, the tireless civil libertarian and card-carrying feminist. She explained, with sound scholarship and full documentation from psychologists and other experts, why it is that men start wars and kill one another and get into fistfights in bars.

It is, she explained, because their sexual apparatus hangs outside their bodies, rather than being tucked neatly away as with women. This makes them feel vulnerable, always worried about damage to the said equipment, and so they defend their territory with their fists—or guns.

Her quote came from James Joyce's *Ulysses*—famous for the closing sentence which runs 45 pages without punctuation—in which Molly Bloom contemptuously dismisses the entire male race: "Oh, men. One minute it's a turkey neck and the next minute it's a hat rack."

Aye, there lies the rub. The erratic nature of this erotic organ—as any schoolboy forced to recite in front of the class knows too well—makes it a subject of ridicule. It's hard to respect something that the owner can't control—rather like a large dog when visitors arrive. The Manassas doctor who conducted a 9½-hour operation to reattach Bobbitt's whatzit moved from Ontario to the little town because he wanted a quiet practice.

Summoned from home in the middle of the night for an unknown emergency, he walked into the hospital foyer to find eight policemen "all with their legs crossed." Now the poor doc is world-famous, besieged by Japanese TV crews and German magazines. Everybody thinks it's so interesting because it's so funny. It's funny for women, terrifying for men.

Freud, as it turns out, was wrong. Women do not suffer from penis envy. They only want to see the penis tamed. Lorena Bobbitt, with her knife, did what so many thousands of women have wished metaphorically for centuries. Deprive the guy of his weapon and his dominance will be over. Mrs. Bobbitt may go to jail, but more important she will go down in history and in martyrdom.

One can imagine it already. Midnight vigils of women outside the Manassas slammer, waving candles and rubber dildos in the moonlight. Joan Baez or Joni Mitchell will soon pen a lament that will hit platinum and there will be the made-for-TV movie plus the books.

Molly Bloom would have understood it all.

January 26, 1998

Why sex-free Canada gets no respect

Canada's problem, as with Rodney Dangerfield, is that it just don't get no respect. It is not, as imagined, because with a mere 30 million bodies we don't count on the world population meter. It is not that we have never had a civil war, or that Canadians—the surveys tell us—talk more on the telephone than any citizens on earth.

None are the reasons why we are so impoverished on the global scale. Ottawa has just been pleasured by the visit of British Foreign Secretary Robin Cook, who illustrates the high standards that other countries can brandish when it comes to juicy matters in bed. When it comes to sleaze, Mr. Cook is the early leader in 1998.

Mr. Sleaze, in one fell swoop, has dashed the pristine hopes of Tony Blair's "New Labour" with all its talk of family values, a welcome change from those dreadful Tories who were always leaping into the sack with other ministers' wives. Cookie has done it all.

The foreign secretary is considered the intellectual superior to those two other Scottish-trained boys, Blair and Chancellor of the Exchequer Gordon Brown. He feels he was cheated out of the role of prime minister, however, because he is what is called facially challenged. He has acknowledged he has "all the sexual allure of a garden gnome."

He apparently, however, has other attributes. Last August 1, he was in the VIP lounge at Heathrow with his wife—a highly respected doctor who made more money than he did before he became a cabinet minister—about to fly off for a three-week holiday in the United States. His cell phone rang. It was

Blair's office, warning him that a tabloid the next day was to break the story of his affair with his secretary, one Gaynor Regan. The message from the PM: it's either the wife or the mistress.

Cook, the architect of Cool Britannia's foreign policy, put down the phone and informed his wife that their 28-year-old marriage was over. Now, that's cool. His 24-year-old elder son went to Heathrow to wave his parents off—only to be told things were gonesville.

How can this dull country compete with stuff like that? Especially when the most powerful man in the world, running the most powerful nation on earth, is facing a May court case where a girl with big hair is going to claim that she can identify a peculiar bent to his ying-yang? The competition is not fair.

We haven't had a good giggle since Gerda Munsinger, the good-time Munich girl, rocked the Commons with her affair with the Tories' Pierre Sévigny, who had lost a leg in our Second World War. The RCMP, while investigating, identified him only when their listening device figured out the signature thump was his wooden leg being dropped on the bedroom floor.

The flamboyant George Hees, John Diefenbaker's most handsome minister, allowed during the subsequent hearings that he indeed had lunched with Gerda, but nothing more. The Ottawa press gallery, under the leadership of president

Charlie Lynch, for its annual black-tie dinner had a mural of a naked Munsinger painted on the entire wall of Parliament's Railway Committee Room.

Lynch escorted his guest Hees into the room. The entire gathering, excited, froze. Hees, elegant as ever, gazed at it for a few moments and announced, "I think they've got the eyes wrong."

This, admittedly, is not up to the Kennedys, wherein Teddy, as someone said, is "the only senator who goes to spring break in Florida." We know all about Chappaquiddick and Michael Kennedy, who lost an argument with a tree in Aspen, who destroyed his brother's bid for the governorship of Massachusetts by the revelation that he, Mike, had conducted a long affair with the family babysitter starting when she was 14.

Canada has a tough time matching this. At François Mitterrand's funeral, his wife, his daughter and his mistress stood side by side. All we have is a Reform MP from the Okanagan Valley who shouts about "gonads" and wants to go out in the alley to settle things. It doesn't really scan.

Christine Keeler and Mandy Rice-Davies brought down the Harold Macmillan government when war minister John Profumo lied to the Commons that he did not know Christine in the biblical sense. When Margaret Trudeau ran off with the Rolling Stones, it didn't destroy her husband's government.

Instead, in his 70s he fathered a child by a woman young enough to be his granddaughter and now eats spaghetti, happily, with her, her happy newspaper columnist husband and the kid. Very Canadian. No muss, no fuss.

In Thailand a woman, *à la* Lorena Bobbitt, cuts off her husband's penis, ties it to a helium balloon and sees it fly off to oblivion. In the United States, journalist Seymour Hersh, who offers proof that John Kennedy daily swam in the White House pool with naked aides called Fiddle and Faddle, is pilloried by JFK fans.

In Canada, a publisher still pleads with a divorced wife of one ex-premier to spill the goods. We have to get on the ball. If we want any respect.

June 6, 1983

The tangled web of fabled words

One of the more hilarious aspects of the week was England's Lord Dacre, who used to be (i.e., several weeks ago) that land's most respected historian, explaining to a Montreal panel why he was made to look like a gormless rube over the Hitler diaries hoax. The good lord, perhaps because he was a director of the London *Sunday Times* that bought the phoney diaries, had spent only one short afternoon examining a few documents before attesting to their authenticity. Now he's had to reverse himself, confessing that he forgot the one thing a historian is supposed to be famous for: take your time and be patient. There are a lot of traps out there—Pierre Elliott Himself, as explained therein, being the victim of one of them.

Churchill, the school failure who became one of the great masters of the English language, stirred the world with his famous 1946 Speech in Fulton, Mo., in which he "coined" his celebrated Iron Curtain phrase: "From Stettin in the Baltic to Trieste in the Adriatic an iron curtain has descended across the Continent." As a matter of fact, he first used the phrase a year earlier in a top secret telegram to President Truman. If you must know, I'll have to reveal that the great man was as big a thief as the rest of us. As you learn early in the academic world, if you steal from one person it's plagiarism; if you steal from several it's called research. In 1915 one George W. Crile wrote, in *A Mechanistic View of War and Peace*, page 69: "France ... a nation of 40 millions with a deep-rooted grievance and an iron curtain at its frontier." And on February 23, 1945 (three months before Winnie's wire to Harry), a Reuters dispatch told us that Dr. Joseph Goebbels warned: "If the German people lay down their arms the whole of eastern and southern Europe, together with the Reich, will come under Russian occupation. Behind an iron curtain mass butcheries of people would begin."

That's the way it goes, chaps—Churchill becoming celebrated for a phrase he lifted from Hitler's propaganda chief. It fits right in with the mushy background of so many revered quotations. There ain't that much new under the sun, son.

The Duke of Wellington did not say, if you insist on pressing me, "The battle of Waterloo was won on the playing fields of Eton"—which has become the justification of the jock. Hate to do this to you, but the *seventh* Duke of Wellington, after offering a reward for the historical facts about the saying, found that the first duke on a visit to the *classrooms*—not the playing fields—of Eton, had said, "It is here that the battle of Waterloo was won." Voltaire did not say, "I disapprove of what you say, but I will defend to the death your right to say it." A biographer invented the quote in 1906 in a rather flowery attempt to paraphrase Voltaire's somewhat prosaic advice, "Think for yourselves and let others enjoy the privilege to do so too."

"The only thing we have to fear is fear itself." Everybody credits Franklin Roosevelt, of course, in his 1933 inaugural. FDR, in fact, did a lot of reading. It is suspected that he lifted it from Henry David Thoreau, who in 1851 wrote, "Nothing is so much to be feared as fear," who got it from Francis Bacon, who in 1623 was credited with, "Nothing is to be feared but fear." I don't want to pursue it further.

I happen to know these things because my mind is an absolute gold mine of useless trivia, sort of like a garbage truck full of used bottle caps. Who was Wally Stanowski's defence partner? Who was captain of the *Flying Enterprise*? The name, please, of Lou Boudreau's co-conspirator in that famous Cleveland Indians pickoff play in the 1948 World Serious? What was the Green Hornet's real name? I warn you, don't toy with me late at night when other minds are fuzzy and meandering. I play for money.

There's never any way of stopping these myths once they get galloping, because people believe what they want to believe. C.D. Howe never did say, "What's a million?" What he did say, in the Commons on June 14, 1951, was: "So I hope the Honorable Member will agree that to operate a department with 1,100 people for a year, $3 million is not exorbitant. Will he go that far with me?" Innocuous enough, but John Diefenbaker on a Prairie platform a few days later, with his infamous imagination, improved the quote. It *sounds* like something C.D. Howe would say and so it's in the folklore. Engine Charlie Wilson, head of General Motors, never did say, "What's good for General Motors is good for America," but it doesn't matter now—his ghost is stuck with it. Right-wing Republicans for years circulated a quote attributed to Abe Lincoln: "You cannot strengthen the weak by weakening the strong. You cannot help the poor by destroying the rich." It was exposed in 1954 as a hoax and traced to a 1942 leaflet distributed by Edward R. Rumely, who had served time as a German agent.

One of the funnier phoneys is the much quoted Desiderata, that print of platitudes that hung in the bathroom of every card-carrying female rebel in the 1960s. It was quoted so approvingly on national television by Mr. Trudeau on election night in 1972, "no doubt the universe is unfolding as it should."

The Desiderata became the theme song for the counterculture types, partially because of the fact that its genesis was supposed to be a parchment found in Old Saint Paul's Church in Baltimore in 1692. In fact, it was written in 1927 by Max Ehrmann, an Indiana businessman who was sort of a human version of the Hallmark greeting card. Sorry about that, prime minister. I know you're the forgiving type.

April 10, 1989

The dangerous New Puritans

There was this pitiful scene the other morning. It was the chilly end of March, and the man in a thin sports jacket shivered as he stood in the parking lot outside the large Toronto office building on Bay Street. Inside, there was a spacious mall and an atrium that reached up seven storeys. But a new sign signified it was now that most pristine of areas, a smoke-free zone, and the unhappy-looking man—driven from his office by the regulations and now from the mall—had to stand in the cold to indulge in his disgraceful act: a midmorning fag.

Somebody really should do something about this endangered species who have become the victims of today's bullies. Today's bullies are the New Puritans, vigorous crusaders who would save everyone with their righteousness. They have found a cowering group to whip and they are doing it with a tight smile of glee. It is not pleasant to watch. Someone must come to the defence of the children of nicotine.

Your blushing agent does not partake in the filthy habit, never has, never will. This is not the ranting of a convert (the worst kind), not the pious declamations of someone who has given up the weed. It is merely a declaration from a well-known champion of the downtrodden, the picked-upon wretches of society, the dregs of humanity. In such company has been placed the unhappy chap in the parking lot.

Go in any restaurant and, before waiter Ralph gives you a 15-minute recitation of the specials, you are asked if you require a smoking or nonsmoking table. This is always great when you have no idea of the habits of the stranger you have arranged to meet. The planes are mostly smoke-free. Hotels now ask if you'd like a nonsmoking floor. (What do you do when an uncle drops by for a visit with a son who happens to have a main squeeze on his arm who smokes? Ask her to go out in the parking lot?) Toronto city council, in an act that is draconian, has just banned both drivers and passengers from smoking in taxis. Orwell lives.

Everyone goes to hell by sins of individual choice, and if smokers want to kill themselves, it doesn't worry me. What does worry is the unseemly joy of the New Puritans who have now been given a legalized whip and are utilizing it with glee. When Carry Nation took her axe and started chopping up saloons, her enjoyment was not so much in letting the cheap booze run into the gutters as terrorizing the guys who had their snouts in the beaker. There was a religiosity to it, a superiority, now enjoyed by the aerobic crowd who prance down the sidewalk in their skintight jogging spandex, glaring grimly at cars that refuse to give them the right-of-way.

We have long since abandoned the offer (years ago proffered on this here page) of $1,000 to the first witness who could remember ever seeing a smiling jogger. But we retain our puzzlement why they can't go about their joyless reclamation of their bodies in more private surroundings. It is the firm belief here that if there were a full Olympic-sized track available every other block in our cities, the joggers would still be dripping their sweat on you at every red light because of their need to punish you for going out to a disgusting lunch that might include 43 things that are either banned, polluted, blighted or injected with cyanide.

The New Puritans, blissful in their certainty because they know their hearts are pure, have found someone to punish—just as Carry Nation and the prim-faced pillars of the church meted out their form of justice to the boys at the bar. For New Puritans, their temple is the body—purified in the gym, preened on the sidewalk at lunch hour, cleansed of everything but organically raised broccoli. They have become the new bores, if you must know it.

I feel sorry for any persecuted minority. At one newspaper I know, the designated smoking room at the back—rather like a ward where you consign lepers—has spawned at least two romances between addicts who have commiserated (and obviously done other things) about their fate. It is rather like what springs up among people in a lifeboat after two weeks at sea.

The point is that we've got these pitiful addicts on the run. Though I've yet to ever see one empty his own ashtray (the visual blight as bad as the ingested one), we've taught them a few manners—not in the elevator thank you, not in my face when I'm eating, only between two consenting adults in bed. But do we have to kick them when they're down? They ought to be pitied, not hung by the thumbs. Enough. They deserve only so much.

This advice won't do much good, we realize, cognizant of the perversity of the human animal. There is the essential need to feel superior, to exult in being in on the new fad, the wave of the moment, the secret to one-upmanship. The wave is currently controlled by the aerobic icon, Jane Fonda, the god, Arnold Schwarzenegger—the Moses who will lead the flock into the land of pecs and deltoids.

I just don't like their smugness. I don't like their grim superiority, grinding their fitness into the face of the poor wretch sucking on his smoke in the parking lot, shame written on his face, a man shucked from the Right Place in society—in his office, in his building—because the Right People want to punish him. I had the distinct impression of the stocks in Puritan times, his head and his hands locked in the wooden device.

In truth, that's where the designer-jogger crowd has got him. There's just one problem. I don't like the cruel look of pleasure I see on their faces as they smile on him, freezing, as he sneaks a puff.

December 6, 1993

Done in by the PC Police

They are everywhere around us. They creep soft-footed, stealthy in their vigilance. They emerge from the woodwork. They hide behind the hedges. They now have us surrounded. They are the Political Correctness Police.

One cannot wake peacefully in the morning, or go to bed content at midnight. They are on 24-hour watch. These are the Political Correctness Police, guardians of our conscience, new arbiters of public welfare, sole judges of right and wrong. We should be grateful to them, since they make things go simple.

The other day, in this space, an editor didn't like the word "females." He replaced it with the word "women." "Females" to me is a more interesting word than "women." Can I take it that they actually refer to the same "persons?" Thank you.

We have already lost the word "sex." The Political Correctness Police have decreed that we must use "gender" instead. Can one consider the romance involved in asking a lady (very broadline PCP word) to "Come over and have gender tonight?"

One must first understand a little secret. All writers hate all editors, thinking them insensitive clots who think bowling on Thursday nights is interesting, couldn't find a nuance in a haystack and probably don't have any children or books in their houses. All editors think all writers are spoiled brats who have never grown up or met a payroll, unreasonable prima donnas who need a sharp smack across the chops with a shovel to bring them back to reality. Both opinions have more than a smidgeon of truth to them.

What has happened in newspapers and magazines is that they used to be edited from the top down. Meaning that senior editors would guide and instruct and inform the younger twerps who toiled beneath them. Newspapers and magazines, in the domain of the Political Correctness Police, are now edited from the bottom up.

Most editors, being of that dreadful species known as the mature white

male, are terrified of those beneath them, especially of the feminist variety, but also of the young males who are SNAGs, a SNAG being a Sensitive New Age Gentleman.

The endangered species, being the mature white male, now edits the newspaper or the magazine—not for the readers—but for the alert PCP who lurk at copy desks and cafeterias and next-door pubs, determined these dinosaurs at the top must be taught the PCP litany, the bible of literature having been cleansed and made philosophically pure.

The editor who changed my pristine word happens to be my favorite editor, the two of us drinking companions from Fleet Street in London 150 years ago. He is a superb trustee of the English language. I would go into the trenches with him, I would spend two weeks in a lifeboat with him, but "females" must become "women."

The PCP reign everywhere. The University of New Brunswick, to its utter disgrace, recently suspended a professor—who had long established a reputation for controversial views (what else are universities for?)—for writing a rather frank piece in the student newspaper on date rape.

The contemptible UNB administration—terrified to death of the Political Correctness Police—immediately toasted him. This is a university, an institution representing the philosophy of tenure, a practice that was established centuries ago to ensure that academics could speak out without threat of death or firing or censure.

When the craven UNB brass quickly lifted the suspension, the student body protested the professor's reinstatement. Which proves that not only are the UNB heads cowards and hypocritical, the students are ignorant and intolerant. Oh boy, 1993. Hello there, Mr. Orwell.

At the University of British Columbia, the Tiny Tories who populate campus politics have castrated the *Ubyssey*, the most celebrated university paper in the land, ruling that student counsel gauleiters will watch over the content, ever-threatening to shut the joint down again. No one seems to mind, the major Vancouver newspapers not seeming to realize that the freedom of speech they enjoy is not divisible: if it does not apply to all it applies to none.

The advent of the Political Correctness Police goes on apace. I work for a television program that is currently trying to turn me into a touchy-feely, warm-and-fuzzy social worker. It's not going to work, of course, because the raw material they have to mould is a reporter with strong views. What is wanted, apparently, is Oprah North.

If they want a touchy-feely, warm-and-fuzzy social worker masquerading as a reporter with strong views they should hire the authentic product, not the guy misfit in the role.

What I would suggest, as a solution to all this angst, is that the owners of newspapers and magazines take the shortcut. Sack all these old dolts with white skins and replace them with the PCP-approved candidates who can eradicate such disgraced terms as "females" from the public prints.

"Sex" will no longer befoul the public prints and children will be safe in their beds at night. Once Preston Manning is prime minister and those who would cleanse our language are in charge of all the major publications, all our lives will be better and the sun shall rise in the west.

April 29, 1991

A name! A name! Anything for a name!

In a year of unremitting dismal news, from the Gulf insanity to J. Clark's reluctant submission to B. Mulroney's suicide mission, the only cheer is the recent honorary award to Clyde Gilmour, the chap who delights all thinking Canadians with his droll introductions to his hour-long CBC radio selection of his musical favorites, ranging from Callas to Mel Tormé. If truth be told, however, his main claim to fame came eons ago, at the *Vancouver Sun*, when he invented SVEFNAP—the Society for the Verification and Enjoyment of Fascinating Names of Actual Persons.

For reasons hard to discern, Gilmour from his present retreat has designated this scribbler as the inheritor of the mother lode, the weary collector of submissions thrust through the mailbox by eager supplicants. Each mention, through the years, brings yet another mailman complaining of hernia. The gems follow.

It must be understood, first, that there are high standards involved here. None of this paltry stuff of an undertaker whose name is I.M. Digger. Or dentists unfortunate enough to be born under the imprimatur of Sam Driller. Gilmour set higher standards. And we maintain them, on pain of death, since the inventor emeritus watches still.

Could we, for a starter, submit the crime-busting sheriff of Selmer, Tenn., one Buford Pusser. In Washington, the Senate voted to confirm the nomination of Procter R. Hug Jr. of Nevada to be a judge of the U.S. 9th Circuit Court of Appeals. Polly Wanda Crocker lives at Shingle Springs, Calif., and we won't even get into the locale of Sexious Boonjug and Philander Philpott Pettibone.

In the SVEFNAP are such human beings as Zilpher Spittle, Petrus J.G. Prink, Burke Uzzle, Pansy Reamsbottom and Dunwoody Zook. I remain puzzled to this day why a mother would name a Toronto Blue Jays pinch hitter Rance Mulliniks.

We do not know if he is still there, but the Rockwell Space Division launch operations at the Kennedy Space Center had a vice-president of the space shuttle program named Bastion Hello. The Affiliated Fund Inc., 63 Wall St., N.Y., had a vice-president named Fang W. Wang. Judge Montague Tyrwhitt-Drake of Victoria, a former SVEFNAP regular, submitted one Nimrod Spong and, from court records, Dulcie Pillage and Jake Moak.

SVEFNAP fans will recall Sir Tufton Beamish, Sir Basil Smallpiece, Sir Malby Crofton, St. Bodfan Grufydd and Hon. Sir Reginald Aylmer Ranfurly Plunkett-Ernle-Erle-Drax—in their prime, in order, a Tory MP, the chairman of Cunard, the chairman of Kensington Borough Council, a writer of letters to *The Times*, and a much-decorated old sea dog. There apparently is, hard as it is to believe, someone called Sir Ranulph Twisleton-Wykeham-Fiennes.

How lucky it was that a hailstorm hit Viking, Alta., one year. How else would we know of Mayor Selmer Hafso? When SVEFNAP held a meeting in Toronto way back, the winner was the late and great Ralph Allen, once editor of this here magazine and who, journeying in the United States, stole the telephone book from a small Alabama town to verify the existence of his candidate, Miss Addylou Ebfisty Plunt.

You probably don't know, though SVEFNAP does, that the inventor of the auto lubrication gun was Oscar U. Zerk, father of Tosca Zerk. There is Titus Cranny, a priest in the Society of Atonement. How about the Chicago schools superintendent, Noble Puffer?

Vancouver's Chuck Davis has a 1955 issue of *Modern Screen*, featuring columnist Gay Head, admittedly a marginal entry. Washington's Tom Geohagen checks in with Wolfidether Fill, Chetwind Delminico Montague Piggott III, Mineral Phlegar and Rousas J. Rushdooney.

Sports fans will remember golfer Sewsunker Sogulum, who played cross-handed and almost won the Houston Open one year. The University of British Columbia faculty of medicine contributed F. Merlin Bumpus, Dr. Sibley Hooper and Sue Piper Duckles. The B.C. Workmen's Compensation Board yielded Burpee Wickham along with Onofly Steffuk and Wiggo Norwang.

A letter to the *New Statesman* revealed that a new publication, *The Book of the Sausage*, was written by Anthony and Araminta Hippsalty-Coxe. Shere Hite, the semifamous author, has colleagues P.V. Glob and Redding Sugg. George Robertson, on a trip to California, found the director of the San Diego Institute for Transactional Analysis, Hedges Capers, PhD.

Hymn No. 598 in the Anglican Church hymnal was written by Folliott Sandford Pierpoint. The chap in Colorado who wanted to marry his horse had to deal with a clerk in the district attorney's office, Clela Rorex.

Washington's Geohagen can be relied on, with such as J. Flipper Derricoate, Ovid Parody, J. Boxter Funderback, Middlebrook Polly, Lester Ouchmoody and Spencer Hum. Not to mention A. Smerling Lecher.

Some years ago, your faithful SVEFNAP owner was wandering the United States and came upon, in the masthead of the *Cincinnati Enquirer*, executive editor Luke Feck. Tears came to my eyes. Luke Feck was already in the SVEFNAP Hall of Fame. He was there because of the Clyde Gilmour dream of arranging a golf foursome involving three of his other favorites gathered over the years: Bosh Stack, Fice Mork and M. Tugrul Uke.

Gilmour imagined himself doing the introductions: "Feck, this is Stack. Stack ... Mork. Mork ... Uke. Uke ... Feck...."

November 23, 1981

Love letters, advice for Dr. Foth

What is most heartening, most touching in this job is the warm relationship with my readers, the easy familiarity we enjoy. Their affection and love is often expressed to me and to this magazine, and I think it would be selfish if I did not share some of it with you.

Canon Stanley E. Higgs of Vancouver writes: "It's too bad about Allan Fotheringham. I could be sorry for him, but little that he says or does could make legitimate claim for such concern. On the other hand I am really sorry for the many people he insults and maligns. Fotheringham is a blatherskite and an idiot, but it would seem that he doesn't know it. My profession and the conviction that goes with it prevent me from hating any person, but do not prevent me hating treason and treachery, which things I hate with a passion. I am, however, permitted to hold certain people and their devious causes in contempt...."

Donna L. Davis of Inverness, Cape Breton Island, writes: "What? Yet another article on the Liberal leadership! Consistently misinformed, Fotheringham certainly has a limited literary repertoire, and his tedious column is beginning to discredit your excellent magazine. It is time for this scurrilous scribe to shape up or shut up!"

B. Kennedy of Toronto writes: "Allan Fotheringham is the most convincing argument for euthanasia that I have ever come across."

Jeff Mackwood of Ottawa writes: "Allan Fotheringham has once again revealed his true colors. While his articles masquerade behind the pretense of political know-how and humor, they stem from the cynicism of a man who would debase an entire city based on his myopic view of said location from the local press club bar. You, Mr. Fotheringham, have only slept in one bed. Come back and sleep around a bit. Then, maybe you could base your columns on the whole truth."

Nancy Hemingway of Sault Ste. Marie writes: "I enjoyed your Aug. 10 issue, except for Fotheringham's diatribe. I once vowed never to read his column again, in the interests of my blood pressure. Enclosed is the result of one method of relieving the strain:

I know of a scribe called Fotheringham
Who says that ties British are botheringham
He so constantly toils
To be nasty to Royals
That I usually feel like clobberingham!
I despise all things English, says Fotheringham,
Yet a horrible thought may be latheringham
He must hate to admit
That a transplanted Brit
Was the earliest Canadian Fotheringham!

Donald R. Cunningham of Montreal writes: "Why is Fotheringham constantly allowed these full pages in *Maclean's* to vent his hatred of all things British? Less fortunate Canadians would have to pay expensive psychiatrists' fees for this kind of therapy."

Laura E. Lindsay of Moncton writes: "The 'nonsense of the royal wedding' and the excuse for 'church-dropping' mark Fotheringham as perhaps a lone 'wise' person among the thousands along the procession route of the wedding of the year. Finally, Fotheringham, after referring to certain wedding guests as men without chins, look at [your] fat face ... and notice that it might be improved with one chin less."

James C. Newell of Petrolia, Ont., writes: "Re Fotheringham's column titled *Goddam the CPR*. I wish to protest the use of profanity. Mr. Fotheringham to my mind is the wittiest political and social columnist this country has produced in 50 years. Unfortunately, other less skilful writers will decide to copy his style and his acceptable—for him—excesses. Surely Mr. Fotheringham or his editor can find alternate ways to create interest without taking in vain the name of the Creator."

Malcolm Lewis of Niagara Falls writes: "My enjoyment of the Aug. 10 issue was tempered when I read Fotheringham's column. Surely a columnist can create more than the unreasoned dribble that soiled the last page! (One might suggest it should have been relegated to a location outside the cover where it might have been at least partially hidden by the postal sticker.)"

D. Robert MacKay of Ottawa writes: "I find for once I agree with Fothering-ham. The government made a serious error in sending him that questionnaire because he is anything but Highly Qualified. Jokes about 'what my sex was, not how it was' got boring after public school. I suggest that the *Maclean's* readership would benefit from columnists that actually are Highly Qualified."

Hugh Campbell of Edmonton writes: "It is pleasing to have Fotheringham's column on the last page of your magazine. After 50 pages or so of writing, there is little left to say, and Allan is most successful on that line. My question: would it be possible to move his column further to the back?"

Andrew D. Irvine of London, Ont., writes: "How pleasant these last few weeks have been. Spring was in the air, and with it the chance for new begin-nings. But no, it wouldn't last. Fotheringham has returned. Cynicism is once more the norm."

Bob Metcalfe of Calgary writes: "I have read Fotheringham's column about being *Adrift With Al, Bill and Herb*, and I notice you forgot to put in that dis-claimer we've become used to at the bottom of his page. You know, the one that says, 'Allan Fotheringham is ill.'"

By early 1998 Anne Libby and I, after three years of friendship, were ready to get married. She, a Toronto art dealer, was 46 and had not yet been married and couldn't see herself walking down the aisle in a long white gown.

Mineself, after a 17-year marriage that produced three nice kids (now grown adults that Vancouver Sun *columnist Denny Boyd dubbed "the Fothlets") had been single for 18 years and agreed with her. A quiet, secluded wedding ceremony in some romantic spot was the solution.*

At first we thought the Amazon. South America was the only place in the world I had never travelled and my employer, the Financial Post, *had devised a tourist boat trip down the Amazon in September with me as tour leader. Doesn't every ship captain have the right to perform marriages?*

That goofy plan torched—she gets seasick easily—we moved to Plan B. That was a lovely English rural churchyard; the church and town were picked out. We would invite a few close London friends out for lunch—including "Blitz babies" Pamela and Patricia who had lived with Aunt Ruby and Uncle Lloyd Miller in Moose Jaw during the war—and then spring the surprise on them.

Alas, English residency rules for lovers were too strict. Ditto, the next choice: the Ritz in Paris. The Italians were ridiculous in red tape, as usual. The solution—lovely Bermuda, only a week's residency required.

In early February, the bride-to-be asked an obvious question: When was the last time I had had a physical? I couldn't, in my vast snobbery over my disgustingly good health throughout life, even remember.

I've never been sick (clean living, no doubt), never even had a doctor and couldn't remember even being in a hospital. I've been in jail, but not a hospital. I felt terrific, as well as being in love.

I went to a doctor, the lovely Dr. Lorraine Philp, raised in Thunder Bay, who went to Memorial University in Newfoundland and is a one-person tourist bureau for The Rock. Heart good. Blood pressure good. She did the usual rectal examination along with all the other probes. Nothing wrong, but why not—she suggested—a routine PSA test, which involves taking a drop of blood to detect any trouble.

Weeks seemed to go by. Why not a little biopsy test? We're focused on the secrecy of the Bermuda date. More weeks seemed to go by. A bone scan. We try to get the wedding announcements printed in New York to allay Toronto gossip.

We are married on Easter Saturday, April 11, at the Coral Beach and Tennis Club. Dick Currie, a close friend of Anne's and president of Loblaw's, by chance is in Bermuda with wife Beth and ends up the emergency best man. "I just beat out," he allowed later, "the tennis pro and the doorman." Beth becomes "matron of honor."

The bride and groom had first met at a birthday party for little Zoe Band, daughter of Anne's best friend, Sarah Band, a Toronto Tory provocateuse. Sarah, Zoe and Zoe's grandmother Mona Campbell stumbled upon the "secret" plot two days in the Coral Reef before the appointed date and now nine-year-old Zoe became the delighted flower girl, in a new frock.

In May, three weeks and three days after the marriage, the groom was informed he had prostate cancer. A great wedding gift for the bride. I blamed it all on the Mike Harris government with its health cuts—which were actually the blame of Paul Martin, who fed his Liberal leadership lust by slashing the federal deficit on the backs of the hospitals (and my prostate).

The operation was June 15 at Toronto Hospital, 3½ hours under a great doc, Mike Robinette—nephew of the famed legal beagle J.J. Robinette—and he chopped out the prostate and threw it away, apparently, into the garbage can. I should have had it bronzed.

I was off work for three months. Following is the first column, in September, which then appeared in Maclean's.

September 14, 1998

As I was saying, before I was so rudely interrupted ...

B y a surgeon, it was. Well, I suppose that's better than if it was a lawyer. Or a bailiff, bearing a shotgun. Or an undertaker. Everything in life is relative.

A bout with prostate cancer (a 15-rounder no less) can be educational, as well as painful, not to mention humiliating. The medical boys call it the "Silent Disease," since there are often no symptoms at all (we have one witness here) and it never gets much publicity. Mainly, one suspects, because the macho male instinct wants to hide it from disclosure.

This despite the fact—the witness has only learned this—that prostate cancer is the most frequently diagnosed cancer in Canadian men, accounting for almost 30 per cent of all cases. After lung cancer, it's the leading cause of cancer death in men. And it's the most rapidly increasing of all cancers.

It kills some 42,000 men in the United States and will do in some 4,300 Canadians in 1998. It's about time someone paid some attention to it.

One gets the impression that prostate cancer (down in that delicate area of the frame) is about in the same state today as breast cancer in women was a decade ago. Women then felt ashamed, if not guilty, about being afflicted and tended to remain quiet about it. Only when prominent women went public with it did the general population wake up to the threat.

Cancer of the prostate is coming out of the closet because, in the same way, well-known personalities are testifying that they survived the ordeal. General Norman Schwartzkopf of Gulf War fame has made a defiant and useful video explaining his experience with it.

Roger Moore, *à la* James Bond, is still with us. So are Sidney Poitier and Michael Milken, the former Wall Street junk-bond king. Arnold Palmer in August completed a seniors tournament and then checked back into hospital for some repair work on his operation.

One of the reasons why we haven't taken this malady seriously, one finds out, is because of the nature of its location. If I was found to have lung cancer, or a tumour of the brain, no one would think it funny. But anything below the belt—in what the *Monty Python* troupe called "the naughty bits"—is considered hilarious by even the best of friends. The jokes abound.

As someone who has enjoyed disgustingly good health and boasted (unwisely) throughout my life that I didn't even have—or need—a doctor, I not only didn't know exactly where the prostate was, I didn't know what it did.

It's not exactly, you will concede, a common garden-variety object like the appendix, the liver, the spleen or even the gall bladder. The prostate has remained The Mystery Organ of our time. (If you don't know where it is, how can you worry about it?)

In an attempt to get something going, September 21 to 27 has been declared Prostate Cancer Awareness Week. In the United States, the postal service, after issuing in July the first American stamp to fund research—fighting breast cancer—will issue one for prostate cancer next year.

In Canada, as recently as 1996 only $560,000 was spent on research on the disease. Very little is known about prostate cancer, according to molecular biologist Paul Rennie, director of the prostate laboratory at the Vancouver General Hospital. For some reason, as an example, the incidence is higher among black men. And anyone with a history—father or brother—of the disease should consider early detection by age 40 (a simple blood test).

There are other problems, all to do with public perception. This patient's summer under the knife coincided with the advent of Viagra. I was inflicted with so many Viagra jokes that I could have become a stand-up comedian—if I could stand up. As a matter of fact, due to the aftermath of the surgery, I couldn't sit down either.

I approached life in a half-crouch, leading bystanders to puzzle as to whether I was about to attack them or was preparing to set a world record in the standing broad jump.

Princess Margaret Hospital in Toronto has launched a $12-million drive to raise funds to study and treat the disease that men tend to ignore until it is too late. There is the complaint that Health Minister Allan Rock has yet to commit any major funding to specific research on prostate cancer.

In essence, the male species with a male-only disease—just as breast cancer is a female-owned disease—had best get over the mental disease endemic to men: pride. Such is the protective male tendency to go into denial when there is anything involved in the nether region below the belt, especially when involved with sexual function, there is a blanket of silence.

So far, that blanket has enveloped the public at large—just as breast cancer was once a verboten subject of discussion. Come out of the closet, prostate cancer. It's about time.

P.S. Thanks for the messages. It's nice to be back.

February 1, 1999

A sensitive poet meets the $4,000 raccoon

First, the disclaimer. The scribbler was born in Hearne. Hearne is in Saskatchewan. In Saskatchewan they have winter. Snow. Ice. All that. But this is Toronto.

Scribbler wakens with a headache. Scribbler never has headaches. Lady of House smells something funny. Scribbler agrees, something funny in the air. Lady of House phones brother. Brother knows about things. Sez sounds like gas leak. Find the vent outside house. Open all doors and windows, he sez, as safety measure.

Lady of House, as usual, does the heavy lifting. Goes outside with shovel. Starts shovelling in search of vent. Location of vent unknown. Scribbler, a sensitive poet, goes upstairs to computer. On deadline as usual. Possibly behind deadline. As usual.

Neighbourhood children, demon shovellers, join hunt for mystery vent. Four feet of snow. Brother thinks may be carbon monoxide leak from gas furnace. Sensitive poet keeps hammering away at computer. Carbon monoxide one thing. Editors are another.

Neighbour comes by. Wonders why Lady of House trying to dig to China. Lady of House explains sensitive poet upstairs. Can't be disturbed. On deadline. Neighbour is architect. Knows something about houses. Comes in. Sniffs. Orders Lady of House to call 911 immediately. Sensitive poet upstairs remains aloof from fray.

Three minutes go by. Sirens sound. Huge fire truck, size of Prince Edward Island, pulls up. Inhalator truck. Fire captain's truck. A fourth truck. Fifteen firemen emerge. Sensitive poet types on.

Fire captain tells Lady of House worst mistake was to open doors and windows. Must contain gas. Thinks dead raccoon in chimney to blame. Raccoon, like Toronto's mayor, probably seeking warm place to sleep. Or hide. Sensitive poet doesn't understand. Doesn't want to. Carbon monoxide? Carbon dioxide? Sensitive poet never did pass Grade 9 chemistry.

Very impressed with firemen. Polite. Disciplined. Try to tell fire captain a joke. Rookie firemen silent. Squad leader silent. Fire captain laughs. Squad leader laughs. Rookies laugh. Sensitive poet thinks paying taxes OK after all.

Next squad arrives, with Geiger counter to check gas. Geiger counter needle goes nuts. Fire captain orders everyone out of house immediately. Sensitive poet races upstairs. Fire captain yells. But got to get laptop. More scared of editors than gas.

House evacuated. Retreat to fire captain's truck. Sit there typing. Show must go on. Feel like ingenue backstage at Broadway on opening night, leading lady being sick. If only cruel editors knew what was going on.

Gas company arrives. Shuts down furnace. Chimney people on way. In search of alleged raccoon. Or Mel Lastman. Whichever comes first. House freezing. Must search for hotel. Firemen wipe up floor before they leave. Lady of House loves them, every single one. Sensitive poet jealous, considers changing professions. Concludes wouldn't work.

Neither sensitive poet nor Lady of House smoke. Fire captain sez if either had lit up, or started fireplace, four houses would have gone to moon. Wonder if neighbours appreciate us.

By now 3 p.m. Sensitive poet and Lady of House, starving, repair to neighbourhood pub for sandwich. Immediately become heroes to the locals since they greatly amused at traffic chaos caused by four fire trucks. Which is why they can't get home. Flee to pub. The alleged raccoon in chimney becomes instant icon. Some think he looks like Mel Lastman.

House now secure, but freezing. Power shut off. Lady of House returns to pick up shaving kit on way to hotel. Lady of House hears waterfall. In basement. Rush down. It's flooded. God damn raccoon strikes again.

Flood rising rapidly to adjoining room where sensitive poet, wisely, has stored his entire literary output since 1908 in scrapbooks in mouldy cardboard boxes. Did Hemingway do this? Poet and Lady of House risk hernias in mad marathon to lift everything to kitchen. Feel exactly like farmers in Red River flood rescuing their pigs from rising waters.

Basement alien territory to sensitive poet. Never been there before, as one recalls. Like never having been to Siberia. Lady of House, she of the heavy lifting, knows that. Talk to chimney/gas people. They, too, astounded. House is 100 years old. Furnace, they claim, must be 200 years old. Looks like designed by Rube Goldberg. And possibly retrieved from *Titanic*.

Gas furnace must be replaced. Chimney wrecked. Must be repaired at great cost. It now a $4,000 raccoon. The lads in the pub would love it.

Sensitive poet and Lady of House finally find hotel in a city where army and P.E.I. snowblowers have been recruited, after most interesting day of 1999. Stagger in. Fall into bed.

At 5 a.m. hotel fire alarm goes off. Triggered by the usual weekend drunk. Sirens sound. Fire trucks roar up. Lady of House phones the insurance company.

Afterword

Teddy Roosevelt, who charged up San Juan Hill in Cuba with his Roughriders, as 26th president of the United States at the turn of the century invented the "bully pulpit."

Meaning that the power of the White House was such that the incumbent should use its moral authority to lead the citizenry to a more honest life, a more worthwhile life, a more idealistic life.

Teddy used the bully pulpit to destroy the cartels and monopolies of the Gilded Age tycoons such as John D. Rockefeller, getting the courts to break up the abstemious Christian John D.'s grip on the nation's oil industry, railways and shipping companies.

(Bill Clinton, by contrast, with his selfish, reckless private conduct, has abandoned any claim to the bully pulpit, since no one respects him or believes him anymore. And so such as Tony Blair, from weak Britain—and even bankrupt Russia—are allowed to take the lead role in brokering a peaceful solution to the Kosovo mess. I digress.)

What advantage does a chap have in being the proprietor of the bully pulpit on the back page of Canada's national magazine—the best positioning in Canadian journalism? Aside from attention-getting, not much.

People don't take to preaching. Nobody ever changes a vote because of what a magazine columnist says. People—all the surveys prove it—don't read editorials. Perhaps 12 per cent glance at them, and one wonders how many get to the portentous end.

Aside from sensations such as the Woodward/Bernstein Deep Throat saga that brought down the Nixon government—and zoomed journalism school applications everywhere—scribblers don't destroy politicians. They destroy themselves.

The only real hope for a quarter-century columnist is the Chinese water-torture method, drip by drip. An arrogant $140,000 assistant deputy minister who loses her cool and curses out a scribbler at a high social occasion. A jerk of a cabinet minister who pretends (i.e., lies) that he can't even remember whether his seatmate on a plane was male or female.

One can peck away at the Neanderthal thugs who coach junior hockey teams, as in this collection, but it doesn't have much effect. Society changes very slowly. Government patronage—see the previous progression of Roméo LeBlanc, a modest man of modest talent, from press secretary to MP, to cabinet minister, to the Senate, to Governor General—is allowed because Canadians are too polite, or too lazy, to complain.

(Speaking of LeBlanc, Winston Churchill said in the House of Commons one day that Clement Attlee was "a sheep in sheep's clothing." I digress.)

It is always claimed by the detractors that the proprietor of Canadian journalism's bully pulpit is a cynic, a full-time detractor. That is not true. Beneath the heart of a bruised idealist lies an optimist.

Pessimist on the short run, optimist on the long run. I do not believe, as the editorial writers doom-and-gloom, that our children will have worse futures than we had—pollution, crime, bad food full of engineered additives, traffic jams, cloned dogs and babies.

My three kids will have better lives than their parents did. The human race is remarkably inventive. It is not to suggest, wildly, that letter-writing to friends might become fashionable again. But, over-all, life will be better, as more and more madmen—in the Pentagon as elsewhere—learn that war is the ultimate insanity.

Enough preaching, lecturing. Enjoy.